PATHWAYS TO AN INNER ISLAM

PATHWAYS
TO AN
INNER ISLAM

Massignon, Corbin, Guénon, and Schuon

PATRICK LAUDE

STATE UNIVERSITY OF NEW YORK PRESS

Cover photograph by Patrick Laude
Allahverdi Khan Bridge (Si-o-Seh Pol), Isfahan

Published by
STATE UNIVERSITY OF NEW YORK PRESS
ALBANY

For information, contact State University of New York Press, Albany, NY
www.sunypress.edu

Production by Laurie Searl
Marketing by Anne M. Valentine

Library of Congress Cataloging-in-Publication Data
Laude, Patrick, 1958-
    Pathways to an inner Islam : Massignon, Corbin, Guénon, and
Schuon / Patrick Laude.
        p. cm.
    Includes bibliographical references and index.
    ISBN 978-1-4384-2955-7 (hardcover : alk. paper)
    ISBN 978-1-4384-2956-4 (pbk : alk. paper)
    1. Sufism   2. Mysticism—Islam.   3. Shi'ah.   4. Islam—Study and
teaching—France.   I. Title.
    BP189.2.L38 2010
    297.4—dc22   2009015477

10 9 8 7 6 5 4 3 2 1

CONTENTS

ACKNOWLEDGMENTS

The author wishes to express his gratitude to the following individuals and institutions : Aun Ling Lim, Reza Shah-Kazemi, Henri Lauzière, Clinton Minaar, Patrick Meadows, André Gomez, Jean-Pierre Lafouge, Mahmoud Binah, Renaud Fabbri, Seyyed Hossein Nasr, Amira El-Zein, Aisha Al-Ghanim, Muhammad Agus Mulyana, His Excellency Rozy Munir, Mark Farha, Suzy Mirgani, Mehran Kamrava, and the Georgetown University School of Foreign Service in Qatar. Many thanks to *Sophia: The International Journal for Philosophy of Religion, Metaphysical Theology and Ethics* at the University of Melbourne, for authorizing the reproduction of the article "Reading the Quran: The Lessons of the Ambassadors of Mystical Islam" included in 46(2), 2007.

Chapter One

INTRODUCTION

The spiritual, mystical, and esoteric doctrines and practices of Islam, which may be conveniently, if not quite satisfactorily, labeled as Sufism, have been among the main avenues of the understanding of this religion in Western academic circles, and possibly among Western audiences in general. This stems from a number of reasons, not the least of which is a diffuse sense that Sufism has provided irreplaceable keys for reaching the core of Muslim identity over the centuries, while providing the most adequate responses to contemporary disfigurements of the Islamic tradition. It is in this context that we propose, in the current book, to show how the works of those whom Pierre Lory has called the "mystical ambassadors of Islam"[1] may shed light on the oft-neglected availability of a profound and integral apprehension of Islam, thereby helping to dispel some problematic assumptions feeding many misconceptions of it. The four authors whom we propose to study have introduced Islam to the West through the perspective of the spiritual dimension that they themselves unveiled in the Islamic tradition. These authors were mystical "ambassadors" of Islam in the sense that their scholarly work was intimately connected to an inner call for the spiritual depth of Islam, the latter enabling them to introduce that religion to Western audiences in a fresh and substantive way. It may be helpful to add, in order to dispel any possible oversimplifications, that these authors should not be considered as representatives of Islam in the literal sense of one who has converted to that religion and become one of its spokesmen.[2] None of these four "ambassadors" was in fact Muslim in the conventional, external, and exclusive sense of the word, even though two of them did attach themselves formally to the Islamic tradition in view of an affiliation to Sufism, in Arabic *tasawwuf*. The four of them experienced, at any rate, the spiritual influence of Islam in a very direct, profound, and powerful manner.

By contrast with some other areas of Western scholarly discourse on Islam, most of the greatest works of French Islamic Studies have been informed by an inquiry into the inner dimensions of Islam.[3] These terms cover a diverse range of phenomena, from popular *tasawwuf* to Shī'ite theosophy, but they all point to an understanding of Islam that breaks away from the reductionist view of that religion as a strictly legal, moral, and political reality. This may prima facie come as a surprise in light of the French and French-speaking intellectual and academic climate, one that has been most often character-ized by its rationalist and secular bent, but most of the seminal contributions to the field published in the French language have tended to take the road of an inquiry into the supra-legal and supra-rational aspects of Islam, whether this be as a reaction against the rationalist and positivist ambience of French academia, or as a result of a residual but enduring influence of the Christian spiritual heritage. In this context, the current study focuses on two intellec-tual lineages within the domain of Islamic studies: One ran from the seminal and "revolutionary" contribution of Louis Massignon (1883–1962) to Islamic Studies and was continued, along a significantly different line—more gnos-tic than mystical, more centered on Shī'ism than on Sunni Islam—by his student Henry Corbin (1903–1978); the second originated with the works of René Guénon (1886–1951) in metaphysics and the study of symbols, and was pursued in a distinct way by the religious philosopher Frithjof Schuon (1907–1998), whose notions of esoterism and tradition have played an influ-ential role in redefining the nature of religious intellectuality among a signifi-cant number of contemporary Islamic and non-Islamic scholars. One of the theses put forward in the present book is that these two intellectual lineages are complementary in more than one way: On the one hand, Massignon and Corbin were both deeply rooted in the Christian tradition (Catholic in the former, Protestant in the latter) while being intensely involved in a scholarly redefinition of the academic study of Islam; on the other hand, both Gué-non and Schuon developed their works outside of academic institutions and protocols, and were able to illuminate central facets of the Islamic tradition from the point of view of an actual participation in its spiritual economy. This book aims at introducing these four major figures to the English-speaking world by concentrating on their parallel and complementary contributions to a wider and deeper understanding of Islam as an intellectual and spiritual real-ity. Such a task is all the more important in that most of Massignon's work has not yet been translated, just as some important books by Corbin—such as his monumental *En islam iranien*, are not accessible in English. As for the books of Schuon, they are now widely available in English, but his correspondence and some of his unpublished writings are not, and his work has yet to give rise to a wide spectrum of in-depth studies. Finally, while most of Guénon's writings were recently or less recently translated, they remain poorly distributed in the English-speaking world.[4]

Our previous works have focused upon the role of Sufism, Shī'ite *'irfān,* gnosis or spiritual knowledge, and spiritual hermeneutics in the redefinition of Islam propounded by Massignon and Schuon.[5] This inquiry extends to the works of Corbin and Guénon to shed light on such central questions as the complex relationship between Sufism and Christianity, the spiritual dimension of Quranic hermeneutics, the role of the feminine in Islamic spirituality, the spiritual implications of the concept of *jihād*, or striving, and the universal horizon of Islam as most directly manifested in the Schuonian notion of the "transcendent unity of religions." What has been stated so far indicates clearly that the current study addresses pressing questions that are most relevant to our present-day international predicament since studies in Sufism and Islamic spirituality have been widely recognized as most conducive to bridging the gap between Islam and the West, opening the way to fruitful dialogue between Islam and the Christian traditions, reconnecting a section of the younger Islamic intelligentsia with its own spiritual heritage, and providing original answers to the challenges of modernization and fundamentalism by unveiling and explaining the inner and universal dimension of Islam.

Before we engage in a brief introduction to the life and works of these four figures whom we have deemed most directly representative of an "inner Islam," we would like to point out the main reasons for this choice, thereby outlining some of the guiding principles of our current inquiry. First, one must bear in mind that all the writers under consideration were Westerners born within the religious fold of Christianity. As a result, they envisaged Islam a priori from the outside, or rather independently from the social and cultural determinations that weigh upon most Muslim-born faithful and scholars. This situation, which could be prima facie envisaged as defective, or prejudicial to their understanding of the religion, has provided them, in fact, with a number of opportunities and advantages that we would like to analyze in the following lines.

Although the assimilation of the principles and practices of any given religion through familial and social conditioning has been universally a normative process, we would like to suggest that the particular conditions prevalent in the modern world in the last few centuries, and even more so in the last decades, have been far from facilitating an access to the spiritual fruits of the tradition. In fact, it would not be an exaggeration to argue that, in Islam, the inner realities of the religious universe have become considerably more difficult, if not impossible, to access through this normative channel. As we will see, this has been by and large a result of an increased "ideologization" of Islam. By contrast, in a traditional setting such as was prevalent at the time of classical Islam the entire society and the educational structures were set in such a way as to preserve and promote an organic hierarchy of knowledge and action that integrated the whole array of human endeavors and culminated in the spiritual sphere of inner realization. In fact, the civilizational structures of Islam lead to contemplation since, as Schuon has written, "one of the reasons for Islam is precisely the possibility of a 'monastery-society,' if one may express it so: That is, Islam aims to carry the contemplative isolation in the very midst of the activities of the world."[6] In underlining the spiritual

entelechy of the Islamic tradition, we do not intend to paint an idealized
picture of traditional Islamic societies, which, like any other society, entailed
flaws, disruptions, and disorders, but we merely wish to stress the principle
of a general cohesiveness of vision and purpose that was widely recognized
as finding its ultimate goal and achievement in *wilāyah* and *hikmah*, sanctity
and wisdom. This socioreligious order was therefore innervated by a sense
of transcendence, and each of its facets was, at least normatively, a stage on
the path of realization of the highest religious knowledge, or a component
thereof. Spiritual education was therefore gradual and integrative: Access to
the highest spiritual realms presupposed one had acquired a sure footing in the
preliminary stages of religious training. Sufi hagiography is replete with anec-
dotes that highlight the legal, moral, and social preconditions for the spiritual
path. Thus, for example, in the eighteenth century, a Sufi Shaykh like Mūlay
al-'Arabī ad-Darqāwī could set the outer knowledge of the *sharī'ah*, or Islamic
law, as a precondition for any further advancement, while at the same time
emphasizing a need to focus on the essentials of this external domain.[7] In the
same order of consideration, Michel Chodkiewicz has emphasized the extent
to which one of the greatest gnostics of Islam, Ibn 'Arabī, "establishes (. . .)
an exact correlation between spiritual realization (*tahaqquq*) and humble,
painstaking submission to the *sharī'ah*."[8] Let us mention, finally, that some of
greatest spiritual figures of Islam, the so-called *malāmatiyyah,* or people of the
"way of blame," cultivated the study of exoteric sciences, the *sharī'ah* and *adab*
(conformity to social and religious usages) as an inner discipline of perfection
and a way to dissimulate their inner station in order to preserve their spiritual
sincerity.[9] All of the preceding examples highlight the traditional connection
and organic cohesiveness between the more or less external dimensions of the
Islamic context and its innermost spiritual goal and content.

The contemporary situation is different on two counts at least. First, the
integrality of the hierarchy of knowledge is far from being guaranteed, if only
because spirituality, or Sufism as spiritual training, has tended to recede, in
most sectors, from religious pre-eminence, or because it has been forcefully
eradicated and expelled. Second, the irruption of Western modes of thinking,
and the introduction of heterogeneous educational structures, has upset the
balance of religious life and called into question some of the basic requirements of the traditional approach, beginning with the understanding of the
nature and status of religious and spiritual authority. In one sense, the field of
religious knowledge has been spiritually decapitated, in another it has been
corroded by epistemological premises that are foreign to it. This is epitomized
by the intellectual disorientation of many Muslim scholars, whose anchoring
in the traditional notion of *tawhīd*, or doctrine of Unity, has become more
and more superficial and tenuous, and certainly not central to their primary
philosophical concerns. Such a corrosion has been far from being limited to
modernist circles but has in fact characterized, in an even more direct manner, the so-called "fundamentalist" quarters that, as Seyyed Hossein Nasr

judiciously pointed out, "outwardly oppose things Western while at the same time allowing modern ideas to fill the vacuum created in their mind and soul as a result of the rejection of the Islamic intellectual tradition."[10] Such a state of affairs leaves most sociocultural structures and living representatives of Islam hardly able to provide nourishment to intellectual and spiritual seekers. The socioreligious and cultural apparatus of the religion is torn, as it were, between a literalist crispation on a mostly external comprehension of the Islamic path and an utter surrender to the ideological trends of modernity, the former attitude not being necessarily exclusive of the latter. This is what has been rightfully described as an "ideologization" of Islam, whether it proceeds from a desire to "adapt" Islam to the circumstantial norms and directions of the modern world and dilute it into a secular contemporary ethos of humanitarian and democratic values, or to extol its message as a rigid and proselytizing sociopolitical agenda that would withstand and ultimately overcome "globalization" perceived as a Trojan horse for Western politico-economic interests and secular goals. It has been revealingly noted that, in both camps, the emphasis of religious discourse and concern has shifted from God to Islam, if one may say so. In other words, the path has become the end, precisely because it is upon the path that worldly interests of power and counter-power converge, together with the collective passions that are their vehicle and their fuel. This paradoxical commonality of focus between "modernist" and "fundamentalist" forces manifests itself through an indifference to metaphysics, mysticism, the science of virtues, and the arts. These aspects of religious expression, which defined for centuries the very language of the tradition, have been abandoned or neglected as "irrelevant" to the interests of the modern world. Instead, wide segments of the Muslim liberal intelligentsia and leadership have busied themselves discussing how to dissolve Islam into modernity in order to allow Muslims to enjoy the worldly fruits of the latter, or, in "fundamentalist" circles, how to "submit" the modern world to "Islam" by expelling or annihilating any kind of alterity and diversity from the "perfect" restoration or realization of an "Islamic society." Such is by and large the situation of contemporary Islam. In a striking paradox, it must be suggested that those who have been exposed to a religious ambience may be the most incapacitated in their ability to recognize, and even envision, the inner, spiritual sap of their faith. The social, cultural, and familial circles that used to be potential ways of access to the core of the tradition have nearly, if not utterly, become an obstacle to spiritual fruition.

By contrast, the preliminary status of "outsider," which has characterized the Western seeker and scholar, guarantees a strong measure of independence vis-à-vis the limitations and deviations of the contemporary community of believers, or *Ummah*.[11] It fosters a fresh intellectual outlook that is unhindered by sociopsychological conventions. As Latifa Ben Mansour has cogently noted, an access to the spiritual treasures of Islam that would have remained buried under the rubble of conventional religion and narrow, or ideological, interpretations of the creed, is now most often opened through the works of Western intellectuals sympathetic to Islam such as Arberry, Nicholson, Massignon, Goldziher, Berque, and Corbin. [12] Their cultural and social exteriority vis-à-vis Muslim structures has provided the most spiritually inspired Western scholars with the freedom to encounter Islam on the highest reaches of its spiritual territory. As a result, whereas "fear" used to be the initial step leading to knowledge—in the sense that elementary notions and fundamental religious discipline and training would be the first steps on the way to spiritual realization, it is now spiritual knowledge, or at least knowledge concerning spirituality, that may give access, downstream as it were and by way of spiritual consequence, to the whole realm of religious "fear." In other words, a theoretical recognition, or intimations, of the spiritual goal of the religious tradition has become the primary key to an understanding of the need for the whole gamut of mental structures and practices that define Islam as an institutional set of prescriptions and proscriptions. This anomalous situation bears witness to the breakdown, or radical impoverishment, of traditional authorities and structures, while at the same time providing unprecedented opportunities in terms of access to the core metaphysical and mystical substance of Islam. This explains why and how a French Catholic scholar such as Massignon, nourished by the mystical trends of Christianity, found himself in a more advantageous position than most of his Muslim counterparts to rediscover the towering figure of Mansūr al-Hallāj, and Henry Corbin, hailing as he did from the study of German phenomenology, was more acutely prepared to understand the *kashf al-mahjūb*, a process of unveiling of meaning through spiritual intuition, of Ibn 'Arabī's Islam and Shī'ite gnosis (it is also the title of a major Sufi treatise by the eleventh-century mystic Hujwīrī) than the Muslim academics whom Daryush Shayegan has analyzed as victims of a tragic "cultural schizophrenia." Shayegan has made a forceful case against the "grafting" of Westernization and neo-Islamization on contemporary Muslim minds and societies. For him, these artificial graftings result from a "mutilated outlook," that is to say, an incomplete contextualization and integration of tradition and modernity on the part of individuals and societies that claim to pursue either, or both, of them. [13] This lack of intellectual integration is a major obstacle to a thorough and balanced understanding of the Islamic spiritual tradition, while at the same time obstructing a lucid understanding of the modern world. Such a dysfunctional ideological context allows one to better understand why it is not uncommon for Muslim intellectuals to rediscover their own spiritual heritage, or at least recognized why and how it should be taken seriously, through Western secondary sources and interpretations.

The case of Seyyed Hossein Nasr is quite eloquently representative in this respect. While Nasr was born in Iran and fed from his earliest age on the spiritual nourishment of the 'irfānī tradition through the twin channels of the Persian poetic tradition and his intellectual family heritage, his destiny was to move to the West, where he studied modern physics and lost for a time his spiritual bearings before gaining a new, deeper grounding in Islamic spirituality and world mysticism through the later discovery of the works of Western interpreters of the Islamic tradition such as Guénon, Schuon, and Corbin. As a student at MIT he was soon to realize that the study of modern physics "could not provide ultimate knowledge of the physical world" and the question then came to his mind, "if not modern physics, then what kind of science could provide such an answer?"[14] Focusing then on philosophy, Nasr was introduced to the works of René Guénon by the Italian philosopher Giorgio di Santillana, and turned to "traditional cosmologies from the Pythagoran and Platonic (. . .) to Aristotelian physics, to the *Sāmkhya* in Hinduism, to Chinese philosophies of nature found in Taoism and Neo-Confucianism."[15] It is through contact with the writings of Guénon, and later those of Ananda K. Coomaraswamy and Schuon, that Nasr was able to settle his intellectual and spiritual crisis. A number of Muslim intellectuals, mostly among those trained in the West, have experienced a similar itinerary through the mediation of interpretations issued from outside the cultural terrain of Islam. It may be that the often-quoted *hadīth*, or Prophetic tradition, "Islam began in exile and will return to exile"[16] is not without relevance in this context, by suggesting the need for a "spiritual exile" as a precondition to a deeper interiorization of the message of that religion.

With regard to the religious predispositions of our four "mystical ambassadors" to enter the world of spiritual Islam, it must even be suggested that an a priori familiarity with the Christian emphasis on an inner, extra-legal, definition of religion may have been for them a fertile ground to become attuned to the manifestations of an inner Islam. While this very aspect has been taken by some Muslim intellectuals as conducive to a distorting bias on the part of Christian-born Islamicists, it can be retorted that this arguments may be returned against its proponent. To wit, a measure of Christian "ex-centricity" may constitute a further qualification when it comes to an intuition of the diversity of degrees and modes of manifestation of Islam. A religion is neither absolutely unique in all respects, nor a "spiritual island" isolated from interactions and cross-fertilization with other faiths. While it is undeniable that Massignon's Catholic outlook may have sometimes amounted to a sort of "Christianization" of Islam, it also endowed him with a spiritual sensibility that facilitated his understanding of the Christic or *'isawī* aspects and traditions of this religion. Moreover, it thereby provided a bridge from Christianity to Islam by making use of some elements of the Christian outlook as particularly consonant ways of "entering" the world of Islam and sympathizing with it. By contrast, while Islam is prima facie a law, an exclusive, socially conditioned, consideration of this fact may obstruct one's perception of the deeper, more hidden, reaches of Muslim spirituality.

As a complement to the apprehension of Islam from outside the realm of an a priori cultural assimilation of its message, we would like to emphasize the

fact that all of the four figures that we propose to study have nourished their
meditations through the direct transmission of a knowledge imparted to them
by living and authoritative representatives of the intellectual and spiritual traditions of Islam. In fact the a priori outsider's perspective of these scholars
would have had less or little value and impact had it not been informed by
a living, authentic connection with some of the highest living authorities of
Islam. In all four cases, intellectual and mystical intuitions were either cata-
lyzed or sustained by direct contact with Sufi and '*irfanī* scholars and masters.
The case of Massignon was in that respect somewhat distinct in the sense
that his primary Islamic contact was with al-Hallāj, a tenth-century mystic
of Baghdad who was put to death for having voiced publicly a state of inner
union in ecstatic terms. If Massignon devoted a major part of his scholarly
career to the study of this figure, which lies at the center of his magnum opus
in four volumes, the *Passion of al-Hallāj*, it would be insufficient to categorize his relationship with the Muslim mystic as a mere scholarly rapport. In
point of fact, Massignon considered his discovery of Hallāj to be a spiritually
seminal, intimately personal and life-altering encounter that pertains more
to the realm of living relationships than to that of archival study. Besides,
Hallāj was not the only "living" source for Massignon's inquiry into Islam.
His familiarity with the world of spiritual Islam was primarily predicated
on personal contacts and tireless traveling, and meeting with Muslims of all
walks of life, through the lands of *dār al-islām*. One of the greatest spiritual
lessons that Massignon confessed having learnt harks back, in fact, to his personal bond of friendship with the Alusi family of Baghdad, in a context in
which his life was endangered and he was most needful of human guarantors
and protectors. [17] As for Henry Corbin, it must be noted that from 1954 till
his death in 1978, the French philosopher spent half of each year in Tehran.
He considered Iran to be his "elective homeland" ("*ma patrie d'élection*") and
was privy to the philosophical and theological conversation of traditional and
sapiential authorities among whom Allāma Tabātabā'ī, a master of theoretical
gnosis, Sayyid Muhammad Kāzim 'Assār, a great authority in the fields of law
and philosophy, and Jawād Nurbakhsh, Sufi Shaykh of the *Ni'matullāhī* order.
He was considered by these masters of gnosis and philosophy to be one of
them. In fact, it would be no exaggeration to say that by the time of his death
in 1978, Corbin had become one of the important intellectual figures of the
spiritual landscape of Iran, and he continues to be well-known in religious
circles devoted to esoteric religious knowledge.[18]

The same cannot quite be said of René Guénon in relation to Egypt in
the 1940s and 1950s. [19] Although at his death in 1954 a number of prominent
Cairene personalities bore witness to his intellectual fame, especially in the
Francophone milieu of Egypt, [20] it appears that the relationships between the
Shaykh 'Abd al-Wāhid Yahyā and the Islamic society that surrounded him
were in fact minimal, and confined to his family circle and some attendance at
Sufi gatherings. The somewhat retiring life of Guénon and his non-affiliation

with academic institutions or social organizations were no doubt the primary
reasons of this state of affairs. Actually one of the main concerns of Guénon
from the time he settled in Cairo in 1930 was to preserve his privacy and
tranquility against unwelcome visitors from the press and the world. His main
intellectual contact with the traditional Egyptian elite was through the major
figure of the Shaykh 'Abd al-Halīm Mahmūd, an authority in both the fields
of *fiqh*, or Islamic jurisprudence and *tasawwuf*. 'Abd al-Halīm Mahmūd was
actually to become the Shaykh al-Azhar between 1973 and 1978. He authored
a book on Guénon that was published in 1954 under the title *al-Faylasuf al-
Muslim: René Guénon 'Abd al-Wāhid Yahyā,* which was to be expanded in a
segment of a book devoted to the *Madrasa Shādhiliyyah* published in 1968 and
in which Guénon is referred to as *"al-'ārif bi-Llāh"* ("the knower by God.").
[21] Before settling in Cairo, Guénon had established contact with the Shaykh
'Ilaysh al-Kabīr through the intermediary of a *muqaddam* (representative) of
this Shaykh, the Swedish painter Ivan Agueli ('Abd al-Hādī). 'Ilaysh al-Kabīr
belonged to a Morroccan family settled in Egypt and occupied a position of
authority both in the exoteric field of the Mālikī juridical *madhdhab* and the
esoteric domain of his Sufi order, the *Tarīqah Shādhiliyyah*. Guénon had been
corresponding with him before World War I, and he entered the Islamic tradition in 1912 as a result of this contact. He dedicated his book *The Symbolism of the Cross*, published in 1931, to this *Shaykh* with the following words:
"To the venerated memory of al-Shaykh 'Abd al-Rahman 'Ilaysh al-Kabīr
al-'Ālim al-Māliki al-Maghribī, to whom I owe the first idea of this book."[22]
It is important to stress that Guénon wrote a book devoted to the central symbol of Christianity at the suggestion of a Sufi figure while envisaging his topic
from the point of view of universal, supra-confessional, metaphysics. Two
elements of the relationship between Guénon and the Shaykh 'Ilaysh deserve
to be emphasized, as they appear to have borne upon Guénon's understanding
of the relationship between tradition and esoterism. First, the Shaykh 'Ilaysh
was a continuator of the school of Ibn 'Arabī, which was to remain the main
source of metaphysical inspiration in Islam for Guénon, as well as for his main
continuators such as Michel Vâlsan and Michel Chodkiewicz. Second, the
double function of Guénon's traditional mentor as Shaykh Mālikī and Shaykh
al-Shādhilī, that is, an authority in both the exoteric and esoteric dimensions
of Islam, may have provided a model for the way in which Guénon envisaged the necessary connection between the *zāhir* and the *bātin*, the outward
and inward sciences of Islam. In other words, it is likely that the Shaykh
'Ilaysh provided a human exemplar for understanding this connection. As we
will see, one of the fundamental features of Guénon's concept of Islam is the
emphasis placed by him on the necessary complementarity between the legal,
religious domain, and the esoteric, spiritual dimension.

Schuon's contact with traditional authorities was initiated during his trip
to Algeria in late 1932 and early 1933.[23] His intention was to meet circles of
tasawwuf and particularly the widely venerated Sufi Shaykh Ahmad al-'Alāwī.

Prior to this travel, Schuon had learned Arabic at the Paris Mosque. Through various circumstances and encounters, Schuon was led toward Mostaghanem where he met the old Shaykh who was sixty-three at the time. Schuon was initiated in the *Tarīqah Shādhiliyyah 'Alāwiyyah* by the Shaykh himself in 1933, and was made *muqaddam* of the *Tarīqah Shādhiliyyah 'Alāwiyyah* for Europe by the successor of the Shaykh al-'Alāwī, Shaykh 'Adda Bin-Tūnis.[24] His relationship with the brotherhood, the *tarīqah* in Mostaghanem became somewhat more distant with time, as there appeared differences of views concerning the function of the *tarīqah* and Schuon's vocation. The Shaykh Mahdī, who succeeded the Shaykh 'Adda at the helm of the brotherhood, understood the function of the *tarīqah* in the West in a more outward, public, way than did Schuon, for whom the order was primarily to exercise an inner "action of presence" in Europe without associating with any outer *da'wah* or "invitation" to Islam. Notwithstanding, it is clear that the young 'Isa Nūr-ad-Dīn (as Schuon came to be known in Islam) had found in the Shaykh al-'Alāwī, not only a *murshid* or a spiritual guide of the highest rank but also a spiritual figure whose notion of Islam was predicated on a universalist leaning and a methodical emphasis upon the "remembrance of God" (*dhikrullāh*) as defining the essence of religion. This universalist and essentialist orientation, which was not without being misunderstood by some of his early disciples better disposed toward a more strictly confessional outlook, did not prevent Schuon from continuing to seek the benefits of the traditional *barakah* (blessing) of Islam, as illustrated by his frequent visits to Morocco almost every year between 1965 and 1975. On these occasions, he met with a number of Sufi authorities, such as Shaykh Hassan in Chaouen, who testified to his being rooted in the deepest layers of Islamic spirituality.

As it has been intimated in the previous paragraphs, what differentiates further our four authors from most other Islamicists is the fact that their writings, whether "inspired" scholarship or intellectual insights, cannot be disassociated from a spiritual assimilation or actualization of the content of their object of study, or from the substance of their metaphysical exposition. This is a most important characteristic of their life and work: In them, intellectuality and spirituality are intimately wedded. This feature has been sometimes criticized by proponents of a "scientific objectivity" who consider inner "distance" vis-à-vis the object of inquiry as a prerequisite for any adequate perception, presentation, and interpretation of religious objects. Such a critique presupposes, as a kind of epistemological axiom, a dualistic separation between a thinking subject and a reified object of study. The phenomenological approach has provided a potent epistemological antidote against such illusions of scientific extra-territoriality by stressing the intentionality of the object, whether religious or other. Corbin, in particular, has equated phenomenology both to the Sufi concept of *kashf al-mahjūb*, a process of unveiling of meaning through spiritual intuition, and a "saving of phenomena" (*sozein ta phenomena*) in the sense of giving the phenomenon a true ontological status by grounding it in its essence. The "phenomenon," and particularly the religious phenomenon, is "that which appears," thereby testifying to a depth of meaning, an essence that can be "unveiled" only through the intentionality of a spiritual insight. The religious object is, in that sense, revealed in and by the subject, and conversely. In such a perspective, which is no less than the traditional outlook on religious knowledge, the "scientific objectivity" boasted by some scholars is in actuality a major impediment to any real understanding of religious realities. In fact, it symbolically amounts to the epistemological illusion of being able to reach a better understanding of a given text by studying the shape of the letters that form its external appearance under a microscope.

While we have just suggested how the works of Massignon, Corbin, and Schuon have functioned as secondary sources in the rediscovery of a spiritual Islam, it could be argued that some of their texts have become authentic primary sources in their own right when it comes to understanding Sufism and Islamic theosophy. It is no exaggeration to write that some of Corbin's and Schuon's writings, for example, by participating in the very spirit of the tradition that they prolong, are to be placed among primary treasures of Islamic spirituality. Corbin was not merely a commentator of Islamic philosophy and mysticism, he was also himself a participant in the very creative life of the intellectual tradition of Persian Shī'ism. [25] Analogously, some of the work of Schuon, such as his classic *Understanding Islam*, are not simply secondary descriptions of Islam but texts in which he demonstrates his spiritual capacity to "explain why Muslims believe in Islam," thereby participating directly in the living spirit of the tradition.[26]

Louis Massignon (1883–1962) was born a Catholic and died a Catholic, following a complex inner itinerary that led him through an early period of agnosticism, a phase of "sympathizing" proximity to Islam, and a final "reconversion" to the Church that was ultimately crowned by his being ordained in the Melkite Church during his later years, thereby reconciling his utmost fidelity to Rome and his no less profound devotion to the Arabic language, in which he was able, till his last days, to say the Mass. [27] The intimacy of Massignon with Islam was such that, during his audience with Pope Pius XI in 1934, the Holy Pontiff playfully teased the French scholar by calling him a "Catholic Muslim."[28] As mentioned above, Massignon has been hailed as the first European Islamicist to have supported and evinced the specifically Quranic roots of Sufism. In doing so, he not only dispelled the early academic bias according to which Sufism should be considered as extraneous to Islam, that is, an accretion of borrowings from Hinduism and Christianity, but also, correlatively, provided scholarly evidence for the presence of an authentically spiritual dimension of Islam, contrary to the reductionist view of this religion that had been prevalent theretofore.

The first significant contact of Massignon with Islam dates back to his traveling to Iraq on an archeological mission in 1907, although he had previously visited Algeria and Morocco, the latter in the context of the preparation of an academic thesis on the geographer Leo Africanus. It was in Iraq that Massignon was to experience a mystical epiphany that led him to recover a deep faith in Christ and the teachings of the Catholic tradition, as well as to become aware of his vocation as a friend, scholar, and Christian apologist of the spiritual and human values of Islam. This experience came in the allusive form of the "visitation of a Stranger" that confronted him with the sinful miseries of his early life and revealed to him the debt of spiritual gratitude that he owed both to those he came to know as his intercessors, and to the hospitality of Muslims. [29] In the wake of this growing inner and outer familiarity with the Islamic world, Massignon was directly involved in the activities of the official organs of French intelligence and diplomacy in the Middle East, and was assigned to the 1917 Sykes-Picot Agreement mission—the Franco-British "sharing" of the Middle East in the expectation of the upcoming fall of the Ottoman empire—in his capacity as an expert in Arab and Islamic affairs. Following World War I, Massignon further asserted his academic authority as witnessed by the publication of his four volumes on Hallāj in 1922, and his appointment to the Chair of Muslim Sociology at the Collège de France less than four years later. The convergence of his spiritual, academic, and political engagements were further confirmed in the fifties and sixties when he became a faithful, and later a priest, of the Melkite Greek Catholic Church, reached the pinnacle of his career as an internationally acclaimed Arabist and Islamicist capable of broaching upon virtually any aspect of the Islamic civilization, and also became very actively involved in political fights for justice and peace in the context of the Palestinian question, the French colonial rule of Morocco, and the Algerian war.

In the wake of Massignon's renewal of Islamic studies in France, his student Henry Corbin (1903–1978) vocationally delved into the hitherto uncharted territories of Shī'ite theosophy and hermeneutics. His intellectual background as an expert in German phenomenology and the philosophy of Heidegger paved the way for his discovery of Shī'ite epistemology and ontology—a discovery of which Massignon was the initial catalyst. [30] Corbin's life was much more exclusively devoted to academic pursuits than Massignon's, and it is not nearly as rich in upheavals and adventures as the latter's. The early stages of his intellectual and spiritual development saw him meditate, assimilate, and translate some of the foundational works of Protestant theology and German philosophy, such as Luther, Karl Barth, and Martin Heidegger. His first contact with the Islamic world took place during the Second World War when he studied in Istanbul, before becoming a professor at Tehran University following the war. He was to succeed Massignon in 1954 at the Ecole Pratique des Hautes Études, and continued spending half a year in Paris, half a year in Iran, a country he considered to be his spiritual home. The latter part of his life saw him closely associated with the yearly academic meetings of Eranos, where gathered such experts in mysticism and symbolism as Mircea Eliade and Gershom Scholem. Four years before his death in 1978 he founded the Centre international de recherche spirituelle comparée de l'Université Saint-Jean de Jérusalem, an institution that he conceived of as an intellectual and initiatory ark for academic representatives of the three monotheistic religions engaged in "comparative spiritual research," to use his own terms.

The main thrust of Corbin's contribution pertains to a prophetology and an imamology that outreach the exclusive province of the Law by tracing the spiritual lineaments of an inner, esoteric reading of Islam that transcends the strictures of collective religion. For Corbin, the esoteric reading of the prophetic and spiritual lineage is intimately bound to the concept of a theophanic vision, that is, a perception of the Divine in the visible realm. This theophanic vision is parallel, moreover, to a knowledge of oneself in God and God in oneself. Beauty as theophany, as a formal manifestation of God in this world, becomes the mirror in which the self perceives both its own reality in God's intention, and God in the "most beautiful form" (*ahsana taqwīm*). The external theophany and internal autology, or the contemplation of God in the beauty of the world and in the depth of the soul, are the two faces of esoteric knowledge. Such a transmutation of the experience of beauty as self-knowledge cannot be actualized without the mediation of the inner guidance of the *verus propheta*, the true prophet who is immanent to the soul. For Corbin, Shī'ite imamology is none other than the most direct expression of this esoteric prophetology, in the sense that it corresponds to the most radical stage in its interiorization and the concomitant liberation of the prophetic mediation from its association with the domain of the Law.[31]

Notwithstanding their atypical and original intellectual personalities and scientific contributions, Massignon and Corbin belonged to the academic establishment of the French university, and it is in this institutional framework that they primarily received recognition. Guénon and Schuon belonged, by contrast, to a radically different intellectual realm, one that remained distant from official institutions of learning, even though their respective positions vis-à-vis academia happened to be, in fact, distinct and even divergent on more than one count.[32] Guénon (1886–1951) is known as one of the seminal figures of what has come to be known in North America as the "Perennialist School." He hailed from a Catholic, bourgeois family and received a classical education—his primary early academic focus was in mathematics and philosophy—before he immersed himself in the spiritualist milieu of the first years of the twentieth century in search of an authentic initiation. He was to verify the little spiritual weight of the various occult and initiatory organizations to which he affiliated himself while establishing contacts with some Eastern forms of spirituality, namely Hinduism, through unidentified Brahmin informants, Taoism, through Albert de Pouvourville (alias Matgioi), who was himself initiated into a Taoist secret society in Vietnam, and Sufism

through the figures of Albert Champrenaud ('Abd al-Haqq) and Ivan Agueli
('Abd al-Hādī), the latter having transmitted to him a *Shādhilī* initiation. His
first works, *Introduction to the Study of Hindu Doctrines, East and West, Man and
His Becoming according to the Vedānta*, and *The Crisis of the Modern World*, published in the 1920s, set the tone for his further works, which culminated, by
the mid-forties, with *The Reign of Quantity and the Signs of the Times* and *The
Great Triad*. These works are essentially composed of three elements, that is,
the exposition of universal metaphysics, the definition of esoterism in contradistinction to exoterism, and the analysis of a wealth of universal symbols.
To these three elements one must add, especially in his early years, a rigorous
critique of the modern world and the various forms of pseudo-spirituality that
it fosters, and particularly in the later part of his work, considerations on the
requirements and modalities of spiritual initiation. His penetrating critique of
the modern world and his emphasis on tradition led Guénon, in his early years,
to envisage the role of the Catholic Church as the only viable response to the
unprecedented spiritual crisis at work in the West. Soon enough, though, his
aborted contacts with neo-Thomist circles and the negative response of such
Catholic intellectuals as Jacques Maritain to some of his major themes led him
to seriously doubt the possibility of a restoration of sacred intellectuality and
spirituality in the context of the Roman Church.

   Even though he affiliated himself with Sufism as early as 1912, it is only
during the last twenty years of his life that Guénon formally adhered to the
outer and constitutive elements of Islamic practice. He moved to Cairo, first
with the mere intention of completing some research on editing a manu-
script there, before deciding to settle in Egypt. The remaining years of his
life were spent in Egypt, where he became known as Shaykh 'Abd al-Wāhid
Yahyā. He married a daughter of a Sufi *Shaykh* and had four children with
her. He resided in the suburban neighborhood of Duqqi [33] until his death in
1951. Even though, as we have indicated earlier, his contacts with the Muslim
milieu of Cairo were limited to some circles of *tasawwuf*, which hardly made
him a public figure of Islam—a role that he would have rejected out of hand as
incompatible with his purely esoteric function—he led the life of a traditional
Egyptian scholar, while continuing his work and keeping up a generous correspondence with numerous seekers and readers the world over.

   As for Frithjof Schuon (1907–1998), a metaphysician and a spiritual
teacher who, like Guénon, always remained distant from academic institutions and protocols, his perspective on Islam derived from gnosis, that is,
a spiritual and supra-rational "heart-knowledge" that finds its most direct
expression in the primordial and universal wisdom referred to as *sophia perennis*. Born a Lutheran, Schuon entered the Catholic Church in his youth. Intellectually confirmed by René Guénon's critique in his own early rejection of
the modern world and experiencing a profound affinity with the metaphysical
perspective of the *Bhagavad Gītā* and Shankara's *Advaita Vedānta,* he became
a disciple of the Algerian Shaykh Ahmad al-'Alāwī, as indicated earlier. He

was later invested as a Sufi Shaykh himself, [34] in the continuity of the spiritual lineage of the Shaykh al-'Alāwī, while expressing the esoteric dimension of this lineage in a decidedly more direct and supra-confessional way, remaining thereby faithful both to the traditional integrity of forms and to the primacy of their esoteric core and their universal horizon. His entering Islam was prompted by his quest for an authentic initiation and for a religious framework consonant with his innate sense of universality and his inner rejection of the modern West. For Schuon, the manifold manifestations of this "sacred science" point ultimately to a "transcendent unity of religions" and it is from this perspective that a profound understanding of Islam could not but flow from the foundational ground of a universal *scientia sacra*. Islam is no more and no less than the final manifestation of the "Ancient Religion" (*dīn al-qayyim*), [35] which quintessentially consists in a discernment between what is absolutely real and what is only relatively so, and a concomitant concentration, both spiritual and moral, on the former. Discernment corresponds to doctrinal exposition, whereas concentration, together with moral conformity, pertains to method. As expressed in the bedrock principle of discernment between the Real (*Atman*) and the illusory (*Māyā*)—this term not to be taken literally as meaning "nonexistent" but simply to point to the fact that *Māyā* has no reality independently from *Atman*—Schuon's intellectual background was firmly rooted in Shankaracharya's discriminative doctrine of *Advaita Vedānta* while the formal context of his traditional affiliation and spiritual function was Islam, for reasons that pertain primarily to the universal and esoteric horizon of that religion and to a variety of circumstantial factors, the first of which is the existence of an unbroken line of initiatory transmission in the world of *tasawwuf*. Schuon's attachment to Islam did not imply, in his view, an intrinsic preeminence of the religion of the Prophet over other integral faiths, although it certainly raises the question of the specificity of Islam with respect to its ability to serve as a vehicle of the *sophia perennis* understood as an underlying, universal wisdom common to all civilizations of the sacred. As such Islam can be considered as the "religion-synthesis" or the "religion-quintessence" that encompasses the doctrine of the one Absolute, the universal Law, the "essence of salvation" through the recognition of the Absolute, and the "link between the Absolute and the contingent" through the Messengers. [36]

Finally, the considerable influence that these four authors have already exercised upon the intellectual life of their time must be commented upon, as well as their spiritual impact both within the field of Islamic studies and beyond. It is undeniable that their works have inspired a number of intellectuals in the French-speaking world, in Islamic countries as well as in Europe and North America. Beginning with Louis Massignon, although he cannot be said to have left a school of thought *stricto sensu* behind him, he can be considered as having "fathered" a fresh way of approaching Islamic studies, while having also initiated a new manner of understanding Islam from a Catholic point of view. It must therefore be stressed that his influence has been ponderous not only, or primarily, because he trained some Christian and Muslim scholars of the first rank, but also, and more importantly, to the extent that he contributed to informing the vision of the Roman Catholic Church in relation to Islam. It must be granted that the forcefully original, independent, and heroic personnality of Massignon, as well as the idiosyncratic character of his mode of speaking and writing, did not lend themselves to leave him with a large following of disciples walking in his steps. However, a number of eminent and influential scholars were able to receive the imprint of his scholarly genius: Let us mention, among the most important, Louis Gardet, George Anawati, Roger Arnaldez, Jean-Marie Abd-al-Jalil, Vincent Monteil, Henry Corbin, Herbert Mason, 'Abd al-Halīm Mahmūd, and 'Abd ar-Rahmān Badawī. He has instilled in these scholars, in various degrees and modes, a new outlook on the study of religion and Islam: With him, religious and Islamic studies participate in an existential dynamics that is inseparable from the inspiration of faith. Spiritual empathy must be understood as an integral part of envisaging religious objects of study. Scholarship and existential engagement, whether of a spiritual, moral, or even political kind, are intimately intertwined, and this close association must be the ferment of penetrating and creative insights. The old scientific presuppositions of *Religionwissenschaft* have to be critically examined and the validity of the light of faith in academic pursuits must not be discarded. Besides this "revolutionary" way of envisioning religious studies, Massignon has marked the twentieth century by altering the ways in which Christians can approach, and often have since then approached, the realm of Islam. His sympathetic apprehension of Islam, based both on a personal experience of its *barakah*, and an extensive familiarity with its sources, was to bear most significant and lasting fruits in the Catholic Church, mostly due to his influence at the Roman Curia and his friendship with the future Pope Paul VI, Monsignor Montini. Although Massignon did not take part in the deliberations of the Council Vatican II, his influence was to be felt in the dogmatic constitution on the Church *Lumen Gentium*, [37] which includes Muslims in the economy of salvation by referring to their Abrahamic ancestry, a theme that is quite prevalent in Massignon's work. As for the segment of the "Declaration on the Relation of the Church to Non-Christian Religions, *Nostra Aetate*"[38] devoted to Islam, it clearly bears the imprint of Massignon's spirit in its full recognition of the spiritual and moral values of Islam. These texts manifest most directly the spiritual legacy of Massignon in the wake of his death in 1962. This extension of his life and work was also expressed in the further development of interfaith engagement in the West, of which he was a pioneer. In this respect, one of his most enduring and symbolically meaningful legacies is the yearly Islamo-Christian encounter of Vieux Marché in Brittany, which he attended in 1953, and which has combined, since then, the offering of the Mass and the psalmody of the *Sūrah Al-Kahf.*

Henry Corbin's intellectual legacy manifested mainly in two areas: the restoration of a supra-rational concept of philosophy that breaks away from

the philosophical mainstream of the post-Cartesian and post-Kantian Western thought, and, concurrently, the rehabilitation of imagination as an ontological and cognitive realm without which there could be no relation between
the realm of the intelligible and that of the sensory. In the first respect, Corbin
was to influence a small number of philosophers who have been intellectually
sustained by the inspiration they derived from his works. The generation of
the so-called *Nouveaux Philosophes* (New Philosophers), which emerged in the
seventies, although extremely diverse and contradictory in its characters and
aspirations, was partly shaped by Corbin's intellectual outlook. Mention must
be made, in particular, of Christian Jambet and Guy Lardreau, who, hailing
from Maoist philosophy in the sixties, rallied to a spiritualist philosophy that
they conceived as the only serious antidote against the totalitarianism of the
Gulag. Christian Jambet has been, since then, a major academic contributor
to the diffusion of Shī'ite theosophy through his most recent published works
and his editorial role at the *Editions Verdier*. As for the second dimension, it
manifested itself primarily through the channel of the Eranos annual meetings, in which Corbin participated with a number of prominent experts in
religious studies, philosophy, psychology, and social sciences, such as Mircea
Eliade, Gershom Scholem, Carl Gustav Jung, Jean Brun, Pierre Hadot, and
Kathleen Raine. His revivification of the concept of imagination by contact
with Shī'ite and Sufi visionary gnosis has been instrumental in the works of
two major theorists of imagination, namely the French anthropologist Gilbert
Durand and the American psychologist James Hillman. Durand is the author
of the magisterial *Les Structures anthropologiques de l'imaginaire,* which constitutes
an authentic *Summa* of the imaginal realm as manifested in religion, myth,
literature, and psychology. The *Centre de Recherches sur l'Imaginaire* (CRI) at
the University of Grenoble has been, under his leadership, a laboratory of
study of the imagination as a central means of knowledge and creation. As for
Hillman, his "acorn theory" of the development of the self and his "polythe-
istic" psychology may be deemed to have roots in Corbin's rehabilitation of
the imaginal. The latter counters both the dogmatic and rationalist constructs
of modernity by asserting the need for nonconceptual modes of knowledge
through a cultivation of the world of imagination and myth. As for Hillman's
"acorn theory," it contradicts the social determinism of many social scientists
by referring to a kind of personal "archetype," or inner soul, the development
of which is fundamentally independent from outer constraints such as parental
influence. It appears through these various examples that Corbin has opened
the way to reevaluations and reinterpretations of a host of intellectual premises inherited from the positivist presuppositions of modernity.

René Guénon's influence on the literary and intellectual life of his time
has been recently documented in an impressive 1,200-page book by Xavier
Accart, *Guénon ou le renversement des clartés*, which spans fifty years of French
history and demonstrates the pervasive, if sometimes subterranean and implicit,
impact of the works of the French metaphysician on personalities as diverse

as André Gide, Simone Weil, Pierre Drieu la Rochelle, and Henri Bosco. [39] Upon going through the pages of Accart's impressive volume, one is literally astounded by the breadth, and sometimes the depth, of Guénon's presence in the intellectual landscape of France between 1920 and 1970, a presence that a cursory, conventional consideration of the French intellectual history of the time would not betray. Who would suspect prima facie that Guénon's works have been known and appreciated by personalities as diverse as André Breton and Charles de Gaulle? It must be noted, however, that the influence of Guénon outside of France, including in the Arab and Islamic world, although not negligible by any means, has not been as pervasive, perhaps due in part to a mode of exposition that has been sometimes defined as akin to Descartes'. Notwithstanding, Guénon may be said to have exercised an important influence upon his contemporaries on two different levels. On the one hand, his works have had an impact on a large number of prominent academic and literary figures. In academia such an influence has been for the most part implicit or extremely discrete. The case of the foremost historian of religions, Mircea Eliade, whose central intellectual concerns have an unmistakably Guénonian flavor, such as in his classic *The Sacred and the Profane,* is quite representative of this mode of presence. In the social sciences, the impact of Guénon on Louis Dumont's sociological studies of the Indian caste system was seminal. [40] Aside from this subtle, and often unacknowledged, presence of Guénon in academia, we find that elements of Guénon's traditionalist perspective have sometimes been integrated into the intellectual and artistic search of figures whose works are far from being strictly congruent with its principles, like Raymond Queneau, the painter Albert Gleizes, and Antonin Artaud. This shows that Guénon's work may be read in a variety of ways that do not necessarily do justice, to say the least, to the integrality of his traditional perspective. [41]

There is, however, a more rigorous "Guénonian" influence exercised over a number of intellectuals, mostly French, who have followed in the footsteps of Guénon in entering Islam and affiliated themselves to *tasawwuf* in the strict continuity of his teachings. Michel Vâlsan is undoubtedly first among those scholars of Islam and Sufism who have been profoundly marked by Guénon's teachings. In addition to his meditations of Guénon's works, Vâlsan became known as a translator and commentator of Ibn 'Arabī. Besides Vâlsan, one can mention Michel Chodkiewicz, Roger Deladrière, Denis Gril, Maurice Gloton, Charles-André Gilis, and Bruno Guiderdoni, who have all contributed to studies in traditional Sufism. In that sense Guénon's most immediate function has been to inform the scholarly and spiritual search of contemporary scholars in the field of esoteric Islam, most often on the margins of the official institutions of learning, but nevertheless with a rigor of their own, thereby injecting into this field of study a spirit radically distinct from that of mainstream scholarly endeavors.

Frithjof Schuon is undoubtedly the least widely known figure among our four authors, at least in the French-speaking world, even though his work has reached a considerable audience in the English-speaking world, as testified to by the high regard in which his work was, and has been, held by prominent figures such as T.S. Eliot and Sir John Tavener. In the United States, the academic fame of two prominent scholars who had a close association with Schuon, namely Huston Smith and Seyyed Hossein Nasr, also contributed to widening his intellectual reputation in the English-speaking world. Nasr was actually the editor of the *Essential Writings of Frithjof Schuon*, first published in 1991. [42] As for the Islamic world, the works of Schuon have had an impact on a number of scholars and readers in countries such as Iran, Turkey, Pakistan, and Malaysia. It must be noted that this influence has often been indirect in the sense of being imparted through the mediation of public Muslim scholars close to Schuon, first among whom are Martin Lings (Abu Bakr Sirāj-ad-Dīn) and Seyyed Hossein Nasr. The decidedly universalist and supra-confessional thrust of Schuon's works makes it at times difficult to access for readers and seekers whose religious sensibility has been profoundly molded by an exclusive confessional outlook. It may therefore require a measure of "translation" in religious terms more immediately familiar to its audience. In the Arab world by contrast, the works of Schuon have remained particularly little known, in spite of his *Understanding Islam* being published in Arabic translation in Beirut in 1980 under the title *Hatta Nafhama al-Islam*.

But the most direct legacy of Schuon remains the existence of the *Tarīqah Maryamiyyah*, which he founded in the lineage of the *Shādhiliyyah 'Alāwiyyah* order, and which has continued after his death in 1998, following his wishes, through independent branches sharing in the same fundamental spiritual teachings. This Sufi order, the appearance of which was saluted by Guénon in the thirties as the most direct means of access to an authentic initiatic path in the West, has been receiving spiritual seekers in many parts of the globe, including the Muslim world. Although Schuon asserted that his spiritual perspective was primarily a response to the needs of Westerners and Westernized Easterners, the degree to which the Muslim world has been "Westernized," in terms of a loss of metaphysical and spiritual bearings, has made a number of educated Muslims receptive to the themes presented by Schuon. However, because Schuon's teachings can be defined as both traditional and esoteric, they necessarily give rise to interpretations that emphasize either the former or the latter dimension of his work. On the one hand, Schuon's work is a defense of the sacred prerogatives of traditional religions, on the other hand it points to a "transcendent unity" of traditional forms the metaphysical and spiritual content of which cannot but remain independent from confessional limitations. This means that, referring to Schuon's intellectual legacy, one can speak of a universalist and primordialist pole and an Islamic and Sufi pole, without attaching to this distinction the implication of an exclusiveness that would dispense with either aspect. In point of fact, Schuon's opus has continued and widened Guénon's work in a way that articulates more explicitly the central concept of the so-called Perennialist School, that is, the transcendent

unity of religions, while providing his readers with a most profound and comprehensive defense of religious orthodoxies, including Islam. The complexity of Schuon's perspective, as we will see, calls for an ability to distinguish
between different planes and aspects of reality as well as a willingness to take
heed of the multiplicity of human perspectives.

As we have indicated, the four intellectual figures who will be the focus
of our study have provided French-speaking and Western audiences with
intriguing, seminal, and challenging new ways of addressing the *res islamica*
or Islamic matters that may be instrumental in unveiling, questioning, and
correcting the stifling and dangerous assumptions and ready-made formulas
that have encumbered the chaotic market of ideas about Islam in the West.
As for the Islamic world itself, beyond the temptations of dismissing or belit-
tling as un-Islamic whatever might not be compatible with a sociological or
political reduction of the religious reality, these works may help some Muslims to reframe the definition of their own faith by unveiling the profound
connection that link our authors' inspiration to a long and deep tradition that
reaches back to the spiritual impetus of the Prophetic mission. This could
be the best antidote to the philosophical disarray, intellectual poverty, and
spiritual pathology that characterize too many sectors of Islamic thought and
practice. There are obviously many ways to approach such a rich and manifold
universe as that of Islamic spirituality: Historical and sociological methods
have had, among others, much to offer in terms of promoting a more accurate
understanding of the external motivations of inner Islam. However, it is our
conviction, hopefully communicated to the reader in the following pages and
chapters, that no integral understanding of Islam can be reached without a
clear and profound awareness of the spiritual intentionality and modes of interiorization that lie at the core of Islam as an inner and lived reality. At the risk
of attracting to themselves the routine academic rebuke of "essentializing"
what many can only perceive as historical constructs, the works of our four
"ambassadors" of mystical Islam remain an invitation to delve into a depth and
wealth of symbolic and conceptual representations that provide irreplaceable,
and in fact today nearly indispensable, keys to an integral approach to Islam.

Before engaging in an attempt to define with some degree of specificity
what we have in view when we refer to "inner Islam," let us from the outset
acknowledge that introducing this concept amounts to encountering likely
objections and resistances on the part of some, perhaps even many, potential readers. These a priori doubts, reservations, or even outright oppositions
would fall under distinct headings that provide, in a sense, an overall picture
of the ideological debates about Islam in the contemporary world. First of
all, some analysts and commentators would flatly deny the existence of such

a reality as "inner Islam." Their argument, which seems to be somewhat on the wane in academic circles, but still vocal in the popular media and general public, runs along the old Orientalist view that Islam is a law and nothing else, and that it thereby eschews any kind of interiority, the best symptom, from the diffuse Christian background that determines this kind of outlook, being its ignorance or denial of the divine and redemptive nature of Christ, and its reduction of religious life to abiding by a syllabus. Second, we also come across a line of reasoning according to which "inner Islam," or let us say "spiritual Islam," has indeed existed and continues to exist within the Islamic *ummah*, its existence drawing its origin and persistence, however, primarily from sources that are external to Islam. This was, by and large, the academic discourse prevalent at the time when Louis Massignon took up his seminal thesis on the Quranic origin of the themes and vocabulary of Muslim mystics. [43] In other words, this view tends to sever the spiritual bond between inner Islam and the Islamic religion as stemming from the *Qur'ān*. In some cases obviously, these two arguments can be two faces of the same kind of appraisal. A third objection consists in fully acknowledging the reality of inner Islam, which we will conveniently and provisionally equate with what is broadly referred to in the West as Sufism, or *tasawwuf* in the Islamic world, [44] while adding the proviso that the existence of this type of Islam has been marginal to the development of the community, and is not representative of its mainstream. Such a view is generally couched in such a way as to suggest that what we call "inner or spiritual Islam" has no real impact on the "realities" of Islam, being as it is infinitesimally diluted in "sociological Islam." [45] In some cases, a suspicion is even raised that a presentation of, or emphasis on "inner Islam," may be used as a Trojan horse to introduce Islam into the sociocultural precinct of Western values and democracy in order to engage in an indirect proselytization. Along these lines, some neo-Evangelical controversialists have been accusing academic circles of propagating, through liberal complacency, a mystical Islam that is, in their opinion, by and large mythical or irrelevant to today's world predicament.

On a more general theoretical level, the very notion of an "inner Islam" directly conflicts with the pervasive postmodern mood that questions, and dismisses, all references to inwardness and interiority as hermeneutic fallacies. Reduced to the status of a semiotic system of representations, Islam, like any theoretical construct, is deprived of ontological referentiality, and the very possibility of a spiritual self dissolves into what a postmodern author has referred to as the "zerological subject," that is, an ontological and epistemological void that constitutes the elusive background of syntagmatic combinations. The radical lack of inwardness that presides over the postmodern understanding of sense is connected to an approach to concepts and symbols that emphasizes their constant, inherent, *différance* (to use Derrida's term) or ever-moving distance vis-à-vis that which they signify. This characteristic of postmodern thinking has sometimes been placed in parallel with mystical discourses such as Sufism, which highlight the inability of human language to reach, fix, and exhaust divine and spiritual realities, thereby propounding the notion that mysticism converges with postmodern concepts in suggesting paradoxical theoretical and existential stances such as Ibn 'Arabī's "station of no-station".[46] Although the limits of our context do not allow us to address this critical question in detail, we would like to mention that mystical and spiritual concepts such as Ibn 'Arabī's presuppose two essential realities that have no place in postmodern discourse, that is, the infinite wealth of being of the Absolute, and the inner experience of its "Names" or aspects by an individual subject. The mystical concern with the inherent limitations of concepts, words, and even inner stations, far from stemming from the postulation of a radical lack of ontological substance and from a cancellation of inwardness, is in actuality predicated upon an inexhaustible fullness of being, which means that the subjective, individual, interiorization of it can only be partial, mobile, and alternating inasmuch as the "heart" of the mystic is constantly "turned up and down" or "right and left" by the impulse of the limitless act of being, the divine command to which the *Qur'ān* refers by the imperative "*kun!*"[47]

This very brief panorama of contemporary objections to a serious consideration of inner Islam would not be complete without mention of the definite reticences, or even violent oppositions, coming from the Islamic world itself. We will deal briefly with Salafi-inspired total rejections of *tasawwuf* on the basis of a literalist, legalist, and formally "orthodox" concept of Islam. [48] This interpretation—which claims quite ironically to stay clear of any "interpretation"—has grown in the last decades, and it has penetrated large segments of the Islamic world to the point of being equated, in many sectors, to Islam as such. Its power of propagation is primarily supported by the large revenues of some countries intent on disseminating it throughout the Islamic world and beyond, as well as by its compatibility with the increasing ideologization and politicization of Islam. Moreover, it has been observed that this reductive, literalistic, and "horizontal" vision of Islam tends to promote a flattened down and syllabus-like version of religion that may not be without fostering both worldly proclivities and righteous self-images; not to mention that such a vision can easily cohere with and be fed by emotional reactions to the caricature and polemical images of Islam that have pervaded the Western media. Finally, it can be suggested that the spread of Salafi-inspired Islam is also proportional to the challenges faced by Muslims who are still aware of, or living from, the authentic spiritual heritage of the Islamic tradition, in their attempts at conveying the message to a critical mass of their coreligionists, as well as to the most influential and still relatively unjaundiced representatives of the faithful of other religions. Besides the negative effects of this most serious betrayal of the spirit of Islam as epitomized in the principles of the *Qur'ān* and the virtues of the Prophet, more interestingly in our context, a number of Westernized Muslim intellectuals have expressed a strong animosity toward what they consider to be an irresponsible "mythologization" of Islam disconnected from the political and sociological dimensions of contemporary Islam. Daryush Shayegan, in his insightful book *Cultural Schizophrenia*, has argued against "Sufi" Western intellectuals who "mutter pious phrases in Arabic all day long, (. . .) condemning the monstrous materialism of the West (. . .) and still rather stay at home, snuggled into the warm comfort of satanic democracies."[49] His sarcastic remarks point to a perceived connection between the artificiality of the forms in which Western religious aspirations may at times manifest themselves and the self-contradictory psychological and social contexts upon which they thrive. In a similar vein, Mohammad Arkoun, a principal advocate of a modernization of Islamic discourse on the basis of the rational and analytical principles that he deems to have presided over its development, ponders the psycho-cultural phenomenon of "all these Western apologists of Islam whose common trait is that they do not share in any kind, or at any degree, the difficulties of daily life in contemporary Muslim societies while they think that they can compensate for the fundamental ignorance, on the part of all external observers, of the concrete, historical destiny of a group or community, by unconditional professions of faith or enthusiastic intellectual adhesions."[50] Here, it is the utter severance between the theoretical and social dimensions of Islam that poses problems for an analyst whose primary focus is clearly defined as a progressive sociological and political agenda. In a different ideological context, which is neither dismissive of Islamic spirituality nor glibly derisive of its Western proponents, Tariq Ramadan still cautions his readers against "a Sufism so interior that it has become disincarnated, almost invisible, or a façade with only blurred links to Islam."[51] For Ramadan, Sufism lays the foundations of an authentic Islamic spirituality based on an interiorization of the *Qur'ān*, but its inner bent can deflect the social and political aspects of Islam, thereby preventing an integration of Muslims into the societies, and particularly into the Western societies, in which they live. This type of integration, and the transformative virtues it may inject into both Western Muslims and non-Muslim societies, is evidently the centerpiece of Ramadan's propositions for a reformed, but authentically grounded, Islam. In such a context, any form of "inner Islam" may easily be deemed irrelevant to the external goals that define and limit the realities of Islam. In fact, it may even be received negatively as a "covering" of "real" political and social issues, and a potential way of "neutralizing" Islamic forces of self-assertion in the West.

The fundamental purpose of this book is not to provide an explicit response to the aforementioned objections and reservations on the level, as it were, of their presuppositions, claims, and objectives, but rather to propose a synthetic and comprehensive critical examination of the works of four major European authors, whose intellectual contributions have helped redefine the ways in which Islam can be approached and understood in the context of Islamic studies and, to some extent, in wider circles of public discourse. It is our conviction that, in and by itself, a thorough examination of the key concepts, methodological choices, and spiritual contributions of these authors can make a decisive dent in the presuppositions and defective conclusions of those who have denied the significance and genuinely Islamic character of inner Islam. As for those critics of Western presentations of Islamic spirituality, who claim that these authors are presumably ignorant of the sociopolitical realities of Islamic lands, or who lack interest in them, in order to dismiss the relevance of the spiritual treasures upon which they themselves are sitting as Muslim intellectuals, it bears stressing that a religion is not an ideology, nor even the cultural superstructure of a society. The philosophical study of Shankara's doctrine of Advaita Vedānta, or the enthusiastic rediscovery of John Scot Erigenus, or Meister Eckhart's metaphysical and spiritual treatises, are not to be invalidated on account of the fact that their contemporary authors and contributors do not share in the economic and social vicissitudes of present-day India, Ireland, or Germany. To think otherwise would amount to reducing religious consciousness and phenomena to the sociopolitical structures with which they coincide at a given time and in a given place, a coincidence that is far from always being directly traceable to the principles of the religion, the complexity of the interplays and tensions between traditional structures and modern orientations being what it is.[52] Irrespective of these complexities and their sociopsychological bearings, any serious understanding of what Islam treats as spiritual reality has to address, first and foremost, the *religious fact* of Islam, and, as Henry Corbin put it, "the authentic religious *fact* (. . .) is the *Qur'ān* as it has been read and understood by believers, and even more so, by those of high spirituality."[53] We would add that, more generally, the religious fact of Islam is Islam itself as it has been understood and practiced primarily by "those of high spirituality," and not a priori the circumstantial socioeconomic situation of any given contemporary Muslim country. In this respect, the objection that the case of Islam would somehow be different from that of other creeds, in the sense that it is not so much a religion as a "way of life" encompassing the totality of human existence, does not essentially affect our argument. Islam is, without doubt, a totality that ideally or principially integrates all spheres of human reality—a feature that it is far from possessing exclusively, as indicated by the ethical and sociopolitical dimensions of Hinduism and Judaism. However, this totality is not a homogeneous and, as it were, planimetric whole, since it implies a clear hierarchization of knowledge, human practices, and social values. *Tawhīd*, the doctrine of Divine Unity that informs the whole of Islam, is not a horizontal system of colorless unification and busy systematization; it is, first and foremost, a vertical axis of integration in which the spiritual consciousness of Divine Unity is essential, determining, and binding. This is beautifully suggested by a suggestive *hadīth*:

> Abu Sa'eed Al-Khudri narrated that God's Messenger said, "Moses said:
> 'O my Lord, teach me something by which I can remember You and

supplicate to You.' God answered: 'Say, O Musa, *Lā ilāha illa'llāh* (no god but God).' Musa said: 'O my Lord, all your servants say this.' God said: 'O Musa, if the seven heavens and all of their inhabitants besides Me, and the seven earths were in a pan of a scale, and *Lā ilāha illa'llāh* was in another pan, *Lā ilāha illa'llāh* would outweigh them.'"[54]

In other words, the *shahādah*, the Islamic profession of faith that states that there is no god but God—and which is, as we will see, given to several levels of understanding, through the discernment that it implies between what matters and what matters not, also implies a comprehensive recognition of what matters more and what matters less, or matters not at all. The crystalline discernment between the Divine and all relative realities is the direct expression of the unmitigated primacy of the consciousness of the Divine in Islam, and the essence of all further discriminations and prioritizations downstream. The spiritual consciousness of Unity that is—or should be—at the core of Muslim identity is not, for example, situated on the same level—to say the least—as such and such political and social aims, as legitimate as they may be. To think otherwise, or to act otherwise, as too many contemporary Muslims do, may be deemed to amount to *shirk*, an "association," a "superimposition," or a subjective "idolatry" that denies the very tenets of the *shahādah*, therefore of Islam. Terrestrial aims may, and must, be informed by *tawhīd*, but they can never be substituted for it, or confine it to the function of a kind of abstract background or ideological recipe. Islam is about God first, not about man as such, not even about man in society, as so many commentators would like us to believe.

The preceding considerations have already suggested that there are basically two approaches to Islam in the world today, both of them having a central impact on the ways Muslims can live and function in the West, as well as in the Muslim world, *mutatis mutandis*. The first approach, which is by far the most visible, starts from a concept of Islam as a set of external social forms that are intended to determine the moral life of individuals, or at least social morality as such. This approach has been particularly prevalent everywhere a sense of a decline of Islam as a civilization has converged with a perceived need to resist the West, or to compete with it. The first component of this attitude flows from a sense of decadence and weakness: It appeared as early as the late eighteenth century with the Wahhabi inspiration and impetus. It has been said that the French conquest of Egypt was in that sense a catalyst for many Muslim intellectuals. They needed to understand why Islam as a worldly power had become weaker, and why the West had become stronger. In a sense, the way in which the question was framed was already indicative of a certain one-sided apprehension of reality, with the scale of *al-dunyā*, this world, clearly outweighing the scale of *al-ākhirat*, the next world: many Muslims fell into the trap of a purely external, material definition of success and strength. The fact that Islam as a civilization was at a time outwardly strong and expansive, primarily thanks to its spiritual, moral, and intellectual vigour, does not mean that the inner vitality of Islam should be judged exclusively or primarily by external and terrestrial standards of outer realization, especially in a world that is almost entirely divorced from transcendent ends. But, leaving aside for a moment this important point, it must be emphasized that it is precisely at the moment when many leading Muslim intellectuals began to think in terms of civilizational and outer comparison and confrontation with Europe that Islam was almost imperceptibly reinterpreted as an ideology. By ideology is meant a totalizing philosophical and political system that provides an integral interpretation of reality and is geared toward promoting sociopolitical changes in the world. In fact, however, it should have been clear to Muslim intellectuals that a religion like Islam is not an ideology, first because it is not a set of human concepts, but a divine revelation (*tanzīl*, *wahy*), and second because its fundamental goal is not the creation or the promotion of a given type of sociopolitical order but the religious salvation of the largest possible number of individuals. In other words, the sociopolitical dimension of Islam, while real and important in its own sphere, is only at best instrumental. The fact that Islam went, very early on in its history, through stages of violent internal oppositions over its sociopolitical leadership and structure, while being able to survive and provide religious nourishment for millions of people the world over for fourteen centuries, is in itself evidence that the sociopolitical dimension of Islam does not in fact touch upon the essential meaning and function of its mission. By entering into a kind of ideological competition with the West, Islam, or rather important segments of the Islamic world, have subjected themselves to standards and definitions that more or less ignore or instrumentalize the essence of the Islamic message. As a consequence, moreover, such a misunderstanding has led too many Muslims to be drawn either into a competitive, antagonistic stance vis-à-vis the West that fuses artificially an attempt at a restoration of the external forms of the past and a faith in technological progress, or into a rallying to Western "rationality" that Eric Geoffroy has cogently characterized as a "rationalism induced by the inferiority complex of the ex-colonized." [55]

The impatience expressed by some Westernized Muslim scholars at the evidence of the spiritual power of attraction exercised by inner Islam over a growing number of Western intellectuals amounts in a sense to a dismay at seeing their own, very circumstantiated and reductionist, understanding of Islam being challenged and undermined by a metaphysical and spiritual dimension that they have a priori excluded or disdained as irrelevant to the human predicament *as they have chosen to define it*, that is, within the exclusive strictures of the sociopolitical horizon of *homo economicus*. As for the "invisibility" criticized by Tariq Ramadan, it must be fully recognized that inner Islam has not always been characterized—far from it—by public manifestation. Even though Islamic mysticism, in the form of *tasawwuf*, cannot be dissociated from Islamic life and civilization, and while its popular and devotional dimensions permeate the existence of most Muslim societies, it remains nonetheless true that Sufism, especially in its highest and most subtle intellectual and spiritual manifestations, shares in the more or less exclusive withdrawal from social agitation and worldly goals that have characterized spiritual and mystical disciplines in all religions. This withdrawal is in no way incompatible with outer engagement, since its principle is "inward detachment" more than outward severance, and it has in fact often been the engine of political and social action, as circumstances and vocations dictated. The case of the nineteenth-century Algerian figure of 'Abd al-Qādir, commentator of Ibn 'Arabī, contemplative ascetic, and inspiring leader of an army fighting the colonial rule of France in the name of justice *and* respect for human life and dignity for all, Muslim or not, is one of the best examples of such an effective integration. Notwithstanding, although Sufism has been an important force in the dissemination of Islam, and a powerful instrument of social, and even political, action in Islamic history, the "disincarnated" aspect of *tasawwuf* that Ramadan deplores, at least among Western Muslims, is far from being a novelty, as testified by the "implicit," not to say secretive, presence of most Sufis in Muslim societies. If Ramadan bemoans the "discretion" of many of those affiliated with Sufism it is because he wishes to foster a presence of Muslims on the public square *as Muslims*. What he might ignore here, is the fact that *presence* comes in many forms and in many degrees. On the one hand, it can be argued, following Ramadan, that the identifiable presence and contribution of Muslims in Western society can be a positive factor in bridging the gap between Islam and the West, presupposing as it does that Muslims make themselves publicly recognized as speaking and acting *from* Islam, or from the point of view of Islamic principles, of which they are representative and exemplary embodiments, as it were. This would be parallel to the recognition of a "universal commonality" between Muslims and the non-Muslim societies in which they live. However, it is also conceivable that such contributions might be most often acknowledged by non-Muslims, *independently* from Islam, or as stemming from individual ethics and talents, irrespective of religion. In other words, the positive contribution of such and such an individual to society is not necessarily likely to be considered a priori as an expression of his or her religion, especially in societies in which the individual is conceived as the primary autonomous unit of civil and ethical identity. Moreover, while a public visibility of Muslims may foster, in some contexts, a greater sense of familiarity with Islam among Western societies, it may also be received, in others, as an object of fear or an agent of subtle or outright proselytization, on the part of not a few non-Muslims; and this is especially the case when Muslim participation manifests itself in an activist mode, rather than as a moral and spiritual presence. Needless to say, all these arguments, and counter-arguments, are open to debate and do not constitute, in our view, a decisive case. The fundamental question has to do, once again, with a prioritization of modes of consciousness, being, and acting, and, consequently, a full recognition of the diversity of ways and vocations. The presupposition of many critiques of "inner Islam"—of it being irrelevant to contemporary predicaments—lies precisely in the assumption that outer action, or even outer speech, constitutes a necessary component of spiritual presence, a presupposition that amounts ultimately to a lack of awareness of the multi-layered structure of being and consciousness. True *tawhīd* is in and of itself, as an inner and lived reality, the most powerful instrument of improvement, both individually and collectively, inasmuch as it is the very principle of genuine being, speaking, and acting. But *tawhīd* cannot be defined a priori externally, because it is, first and foremost, a mode of consciousness, and this mode of consciousness is, in and of itself, if fully grasped, a way of being. This way of being is not to be "visible" in the sense of a "label" that would primarily foster such and such an external integration, with such and such an ideological purpose in mind; it is rather traceable in the spiritual and moral fruits that it produces as a result of an inner integration, the consequences of which are literally incommensurable by external, including social, standards.

At the end of history, as in the beginning of Islam, Muslims will be "in exile," or "foreigners," (*gharīban*) as stated in a *hadīth*. This exile can be understood on several levels. One of them is external and geographical. It may mean that Muslims, or the best of them, will be found outside of the regions that have been historically associated to Islam, the *dār al-islām*. This first interpretation may have very direct implications for the meaning of the status of Muslims in the non-Muslim world, and particularly in the West. But this *hadīth* may also mean that Muslims will be, or are, in exile in relation to the sociopolitical framework that should normatively define their religious home. It means that there will not be, or there is already no, authentic actualization of an external social structure for Islam. The first Muslims, obliged to leave Mecca, had to exile themselves in the sense of not being able to be at home, yet, in a terrestrial structure of their own: They could do so only in Medina, in an ideal of external realization upon which Islamist utopians have been gazing back with nostalgia. Similarly the later times may be characterized as a time when structures are corroded and collapse, or else are distorted and subverted from within. The responsibility of Islam weighs, therefore, on the shoulders of each and every individual believer; hence the need for *ihsān*, or inner excellence and beauty, and concrete, spiritual knowledge of *tawhīd* as the foundation of the Muslim identity. Muslims are foreigners (*ghurabā*) in the world because they must live their faith in the absence of satisfactory external traditional supports. As such they are more and more in exile in this world because the world of *al-dunyā* is increasingly bereft and ignorant of the vertical dimension of Islam. This is the paradox of Islam at the end of times. At the same time, this exile, and all the sufferings and sense of disequilibrium that it entails, is also a source of inner grace because it fosters a more profound sense of *islām*. This is why the same *hadīth* concludes on a rewarding note: "Blessed will be those who are in exile."

All the considerations that precede here have, in a sense, already suggested an implicit approach towards a definition of "inner Islam," if such a term may be fully delimited. It stems from these considerations that "inner Islam" can be identified, albeit not exclusively, [56] with what has been commonly referred to as Sufism, spiritual or mystical Islam. Moreover, when refering to "inner Islam" we allude to a set of interpretations of Islamic spirituality that, while not exhausting the entire range of Muslim faith and practices, provides an access to the heart of Islam. Our sense is that the interpretive spectrum under consideration encompasses the most central and most spiritually fruitful dimensions of Islam at large. This "inner" dimension refers first and foremost to a metaphysical content that underlies Islam and constitutes its most consistent affirmation of Unity ("there is no reality but *the* Reality"); it also refers to a spiritual method of interiorization of this affirmation that can be, and has been, equated to *ihsān,* or perfection of sincerity and beauty of soul. What precedes amounts to a synthetic definition of Sufism. Obviously, a more analytic delimitation of Sufism itself is no easy task in practice, first because the term *tasawwuf* appears only at a given stage in the history of Islam, in fact not earlier than the end of the second century of the hegira; second, because of its extreme historical diversity in terms of institutional development, as expressed by the multiplicity of *turuq* (brotherhoods) and subbranches of these *turuq;* and third, because this "horizontal" diversity is complicated by the plurality of "vertical" understandings of what Sufism *is,* not to mention the ineffable character of what constitutes its "spiritual flavor." We cannot provide our reader with a sufficient definition of Sufism within the limited focus of our current study; however, we cannot avoid an attempt to synthesize some of its features, especially those that are most prominently relevant to the object of the following chapters.

One of the most frequently trodden and most plausible paths in attempting to define Sufism has led scholars to refer their readers back to the putative etymology of the terms *Sufi* and *tasawwuf.* We have chosen this approach in so far as it allows one to emphasize a few important features of Sufism in a pedagogical manner. According to the first, and most widely accepted, etymology for the term, it derives from the Arabic substantive *sūf,* which means wool, thereby alluding to the material from which the garb of some early practitioners of Islamic asceticism was made, by contrast with the cotton that was widely used in Islamic lands. The connotations of this term are at least two: First, those clothed with wool "distinguish" themselves from the rest of the community, and thereby become an identifiable category of faithful within Islam—which has obvious implications with respect to the question of the legitimacy of their spiritual enterprise; second, *sūf* is understood as a marker of outer poverty, which is itself considered symbolic of an intended state of inner poverty, or psycho-moral "emptiness" for God. The latter connotation is confirmed by the terms that have traditionally been used to refer to Sufi practitioners, such as *fuqara,* or dervishes, two Arabic words denoting poverty.

The second etymology assigned to *tasawwuf* makes it akin to *sāfā,* thereby referring to purity. The purity of Sufis refers to their cultivation of right intention and sincerity, *sidq* or *ikhlās,* in their practice of Islam. Bundār Ibn al-Husayn, fourth-century companion of al-Shibli, writes that "the *sūfī* is the man that God has chosen for Himself, giving him a sincere affection (*sāfā*) (. . .) thus he is made friend (*sūfī*)."[57] In that sense, Sufism clearly manifests an affinity with the inner, spiritual aspect of Islam that extols intentions and inward recollection, as well as a search for an intimacy (*uns*) with God beyond, but not against, the prescribed regimen of the Law.

A third origin is related to the expression *Ahl al-Suffa*, the People of the Bench, a characterization of a privileged group of the Prophet's companions who, having no home of their own, were regularly invited by the Prophet to his meals. They were engaged in unceasing devotion and spiritual recollection, [58] and used to sit on a specific bench at the Mosque of Medina. Some historians say they were forty in number, including Bilāl, the first muezzin, and Abū Hurayra, who is at the origin of the *isnād*, or chain of transmission, of a large number of *ahādīth*, or traditions attributed to the Prophet. This association evokes the fact that Sufis do not consider themselves as a *madhdhab*, a juridical school, or a sect that appeared at some point in history: Sufism was already a living reality at the time of the Prophet, even though this reality did not bear any name. This is expressed by way of the tenth-century Sufi Abū'l-Hasan Fushanji's statement: "Today, *tasawwuf* is a name without a reality, but formerly, it was a reality without a name." The need to designate specifically a category of believers considered as "pure" or "perfect" obviously stems from the spiritual degeneracy of the religious collectivity at large. In a similar vein, Massignon has mentioned another explanation for the term Sufi, more rarely referred to, according to which it derives from the expression *saff awwal*, first rank before God. [59]

Finally one must mention al-Birūni's derivation from the Greek *Sophos*, an unlikely phonetic relation, which has nevertheless the merit of emphasizing the fact that Sufism has constituted a "wisdom tradition," and that its relationship with Neoplatonic philosophy has sometimes been instrumental in shaping its concepts. Henry Corbin was particularly receptive to the philosophical implications of this linguistic connection in which he perceived the philosophical dimension of Islamic mysticism.

The picture of *tasawwuf* that these various derivations suggest is one of continuity and discontinuity with the mainstream concept of Islam. From the first point of view, the association of Sufis with a group of perfected Muslims (*saff awwal*) evokes the concept of *tasawwuf* as a spiritual culmination of Islam: The spiritual elite of the religion can be distinguished from the rest only insofar as it takes the spirit of the religious message more seriously, as it were—or "impatiently" to use Huston Smith's expression referring to their urgent need of God and the hereafter, giving privilege to the otherworldly aims of Islam over its balancing, social, stabilizing dimension. The *Ahl al-Saffa* are part and parcel of the community, but they do not share as much in its aspect of stability along the horizontal axis of social transmission as they embody the spiritual demands of Muhammad's predication. Their living without a roof and being subject to the hospitality of the Prophet expresses outwardly the essence of their inner *tawakkul* (reliance) on God. There appears in this double identity of members and guests of the community a suggestive anticipation of the status of Sufism in Islam, *tasawwuf* being paradoxically both aboriginal and somewhat "foreign" to the outer fold of the *Ummah*. As for the aspect of sincerity and purity, it clearly points to the primacy of methodical, spiritual, and moral concerns in the Sufi path. William Chittick defines one of the central tenets of Islamic mysticism as polishing "'the mirror of the heart' by overcoming one's own desires and making way for God's desires."[60] This, in a sense, is the central symbol of Sufi asceticism since it conveys both the moral and spiritual requirements of the path, that is, self-purification, and the epistemological, gnostic dimension of *tasawwuf* as reflection of the Divine Light. The two dimensions, which may seem to be disconnected when considering the historical development of Sufism—stemming from an ascetic tradition that later flowered into a metaphysical theosophy—are in fact two faces of the same coin when considered within the integral context of the tradition.

"Pathways to an inner Islam": The title of our study is already suggestive of our main intent. The pathways that we have in mind are to lead us to hidden layers of meaning and consciousness. This is the essence of Sufi knowledge and practice: *kashf al-mahjūb*, the unveiling of the hidden. This implies that Islam is a two-leveled tradition characterized by the coexistence of a *zāhir* and a *bātin*, an outer form and an inner essence. These two levels are the keys to what Martin Lings has refered to as the three-dimensionality of Sufism.[61] Those who limit Islam to a two-dimensional understanding and practice of its forms do not err in affirming the *zāhir* but are misled in denying the *bātin*. Doing so they deprive religion of what constitutes its raison d'être, the divine dimension of height and depth, of transcendence and immanence: transcendence because the meaning of religion lies above the letter of human understanding, immanence because the substance of Islam, like that of the *Qur'ān*, is an inexhaustible wealth of reality.

By referring to "pathways" in the plural, we do not only allude, moreover, to the fact that all of the works that we propose to study are, out of necessity, interpretations of Islam. We also suggest that Islam includes a variety of perspectives and aspects. Our point is not to deny the diversity of Islam but to point to the centrality and essentiality, in fact the necessity, of the *bātin*. We also contend thereby that the four authors who are the subject of our inquiry, despite the important differences that separate them, or make each of their contributions unique, do share in a same vision of Islam as a spiritual reality. Islam is one and diverse at the same time. It is one in the basic concepts and practices of its creed, but diverse in the modes and levels of understanding it. As the Shaykh 'Abd al-Qādir al-Jazāirī puts it in his *Mawāqif*, "God manifested himself to the Muhammadan community itself through multiple and diverse theophanies, which explains that this community in its turn includes up to seventy-three different sects, within each of which one should further distinguish other sects, which are themselves varied and different, as anybody familiar with theology can observe it."[62] By virtue of its unity, Islam is profoundly egalitarian, but but virtue of its diversity it asserts distinctions of ranks, as well as degrees in understanding and actualization of its meaning. Contrary to what many contemporary advocates of Islam have claimed, the metaphysical leveling down of Islam, as expressed in the creed of "no reality but God's Reality," is not exclusive of a spiritual hierarchy among men, and among Muslims. Some *ahadīth* make explicit references to spiritual distinctions such as that between *ahl al-jam'* and *ahl al-karam,* the people of common rank and the people of noble rank, the latter being identified by the *hadīth* with the "people of the sessions of invocation" (*ahl al-majālis al-dhikr*).[63] It must be emphasized that if these people are "superior" in some way, it is only because, and to the extent that, they have consented to be poorer, and ultimately nothing, before God's Unity. As we hope it will be clear to the readers of this study, the works of Massignon, Corbin, Guénon, and Schuon have provided illuminating insights into the content, goal, and meaning of these "sessions of remembrance" in which the quintessence of Islam is distilled in the pure affirmation of the One.

Chapter Two

SUFISM, SHĪʿISM, AND THE
DEFINITION OF INNER ISLAM

The very mention of an inner dimension of Islam brings to the fore the question of the definition of Sufism and the related assessment of its relationship with Islam at large. These matters were central to European Islamology in the twentieth century, and they continue to be vital to any integral understanding of Islam in our times. It is no exaggeration to say that the four figures upon whom we have chosen to focus were literally molded by their personal relationship with Sufism, and that their understanding of Islam cannot begin to be envisaged outside of a consideration of the doctrines and disciplines of what has been called "Islamic mysticism." It may not be without importance to specify that a definition of Sufism within the category of mysticism is far from being agreed upon among the very participants of this intellectual and spiritual tradition. Such foremost contemporary experts in Sufism as William Chittick[1] have, for example, been reticent to make use of this term, primarily because of the connotations of vagueness, sentimentality, and irrationality that the word too often carries in its wake. In his own time, René Guénon was adamant in rejecting the term "mysticism" and refusing to apply it to metaphysical doctrines and initiatory paths of the East on account of the fundamentally "passive" character that he assigned to mystics, by contrast with practitioners of initiatory disciplines, such as *tasawwuf* precisely, whom he described as being devoted to an exclusively "active" and methodical spiritual way. While one can understand how the circumstances in which Guénon had to introduce his ideas to European twentieth-century audiences could lead him to systematize such distinctions, it remains nevertheless true that not all mystics, including Christian ones, are exempt from making use of specific methodical supports, as the history of medieval Christianity amply demonstrates. It is no less undeniable that not a few paths that are technically akin to the kind of initiations Guénon has in mind do involve an element of "passivity" in their methods, if only because no such methods could be effective without a measure of "receptivity" on the part of the initiate, and above all because the human side of the spiritual equation is necessarily passive in relation to the Divine. As Massignon suggestively put it, "before God every soul is feminine." It must be added that other students and authorities of Sufism or *tasawwuf*, such as Arberry or Martin Lings,[2] had no qualms in using the term mysticism to refer to their object of study. Based on its Greek etymology indicative of "silence" (*muô*: to remain silent), and thereby suggesting a transcending of verbal, external means of apprehension and transmission, the term mysticism may refer to a set of doctrines and practices postulating a supra-rational mode of knowledge—not irrational and denying the validity of reason on its own plane, but simply pointing to its epistemological limits— leading to a type of spiritual knowledge through identification, whether in the mode of a nondualistic unity or a dualistic union through love. In parallel, mysticism is most often understood as additionally involving a set of ritual and methodical practices, and a conformation of the soul through a spiritual and moral discipline of action and being. Provided one agrees on the essentials of this definition, there is no decisive reason to refrain from characterizing Sufism as a form of Islamic mysticism. Whether in the form of an ascetic discipline centered on the fear of God and punishment—characteristic of early developments of "Sufism without a name," or in the mode of an ecstatic station of love for the One Beloved—as epitomized by Mansūr al-Hallāj and Jalāl-ad-Din Rūmī's poetic utterances, or else in the metaphysical concepts of a doctrine of nonduality or unicity—as developed in the treatises of Muhyi-d-Dīn Ibn Arabī or 'Abd-al-Karīm al-Jīlī, *tasawwuf* undoubtedly fulfills the mystical requirements and norms that have been set out. Moreover, it has been, and continues to be, a concrete spiritual reference and principle of spiritual action for a vast number of Muslims who strive to come closer to God through practices that intensify or deepen their conformity to the *sharī' iah* under the spiritual direction of a *shaykh* and in the context of initiatory brotherhoods, or *turuq*.

Louis Massignon has often been credited with being the first "Orientalist" to acknowledge and establish the fundamentally Quranic and Islamic roots of Sufism. Before his time, it was not uncommon for Islamicists to postulate a non-Islamic influence, or even origination, in order to account for the spiritual content of *tasawwuf*. Such a position was predicated on a perceived disproportion between the fundamental teachings of Islam in the literality of the *Qur'ān* and the Sunnah and the concepts and practices of Sufis throughout the history of Islam. It is thus, for example, that Western analysts of Islam could conclude that the feats of asceticism characteristic of early mystics such as 'Uways al-Qarnī and Rābi'a 'Adawiyah could not be reconciled with the "middle way" characteristic of Islamic realism, starting with the example of moderation and equilibrium set by the Prophet. Massignon took a different road: He considered the matter "phenomenologically," as it were—that is, from the standpoint of the spiritual, intentional horizon of the mystic—and to this end he first delved into the relationship between mystical experience and language.

This methodical approach to Sufism was not coincidental, nor haphazard. It actually stemmed from Massignon's own encounter with mysticism. It is impossible to reach any intimation of Massignon's thought on the subject without taking into consideration the impact of his own religious biography in shaping his very particular understanding of *tasawwuf*. With Massignon, scholarship is literally informed by inner experience, and it is in point of fact initiated by it. Without entering into the details of a biographical analysis that would take us too far from our focus, it is essential to understand that Massignon's whole vocation as an Islamicist flows from his own rediscovery of the Divine within the ambience of Islam. In 1908, while doing archeological work in Iraq, Massignon was captured by Turkish forces under suspicion of being a spy involved in an assassination plot against an Ottoman authority.[3] Here is the way he recounted the context, episodes, and spiritual impact of this destinal moment in his life some fifty years later:

(. . .) (In Baghdad, I was) chief of an official archeological mission, but (led) an ascetic, camouflaged life under the protection,*"amān"*, of an Arab family of Muslim noblemen; (. . .) trapped (in the context of preparation of the Turkish revolution, 1908), arrested as a spy, beaten, threatened of an execution, suicide attempt by sacred horror of myself, sudden recollection, the eyes closed before an inner fire, which judges and burns my heart, certitude of a pure, ineffable, creative Presence (. . .) . Disguised, treated as a spy (indiscrete observer), saved by my hosts, but not only by the living (a word, Hallāj, the mystical martyr of Islam, crucified for the inaccessible pure love of God; I would later write my doctoral thesis on this; intimated as early as Cairo). My first and shivering prayer, in Arabic, in jail, given as a vow to the salvation of a Muslim friend, a desperate renegade, and through Hallāj and him, to all my Muslim friends. "He who loves enters into the dependency of the one who is loved."[4]

We have quoted this long passage because it contains all the fundamentals of Massignon's spirituality while suggesting the secret of his relationship with Islamic mysticism. There is, first of all, the debt owed to those who protected him, the Alusi family from Baghdad, and by extension all Muslims. This inner debt was the seed of Massignon's commitment to Islam, and it colors his rapport with Muslims in the sense of a spiritual reciprocity under the sign of hospitality. The latter word could actually encapsulate Massignon's entire concept of mysticism. Mystical consciousness is envisaged by him as a "decentering" of one's ordinary perception, an opening to the "stranger" or "foreigner" who is ultimately identifiable to the Divine Host. This reciprocity is also placed under the aegis of a substitution that "absorbs" the sufferings and fault of others and sacrificially "transmutes" them into the fire of love. The mystical dependence that ensues weaves a divine fabric of compassion and gift of self in which the various persons reveal and find their most intimate identity in the qualitative interpenetration of their respective vows. These are, so to speak, supernatural societies of mystical reciprocity.

It is in this context that the figure of Hallāj acquires its deepest significance. The tenth-century mystic of Baghdad was Massignon's lifelong focus. In him the French Islamicist discovered the secret of the testimony of love, a testimony that finds its perfection in martyrdom—as the Greek root of this term implies. This martyrdom, "the supreme holy war of Arab Islam," distinguishes Hallāj not only from those whose *islam* does not yet intimate the existence of a realm beyond the horizon of the Law, but also from those Sufis who have not dared bear witness to the secret of Love in their outer terrestrial vocation. The opposition between the latter's point of view and the "theopathic" witnessing of Hallāj is beautifully expressed in the related exchange between Husayn and his Shaykh:

—Husayn: why cannot you remain silent on the secret of Islam?[5]
—Master: how could I? It is the Lord who decides, hallowed and exalted be He.[6]

Massignon's Sufism is almost entirely centered on this public confession of unity, which is also a consummation of the Love of God through a rapturous death under the blow of the Law. The Christic connotations of this vision of Hallāj could not be overstated. The reference to the statement signed by eighty-eight *'ulama* from Baghdad, Damascus, and Cairo, reading "kill him, from his death depends the salvation of Muslims," expresses the redemptive function of Hallāj's crucifixion by superposing to the literal words of the defenders of the Law—for whom Hallāj is but an ecstatic fool whose mystical statements represent a danger for the integrity of collective, conventional faith—the mystical meaning of a sacrificial "substitution" for the common faithful's infidelity to the real law of Love. In this context, mystical love is a paradox characterized by an unending alternation between the affirmation of a loving I addressing a Thou, and the extinction of the former into a single Divine I extinguishing the lover in his union. This mystery of mystical "hide and seek" is expressed throughout Hallāj's poetry, as in this famous quatrain:

He am I whom I love, He whom I love is I, (*Anā man ahwā wa man ahwā anā*)
Two Spirits in one single body dwelling.
So seest thou me, then seest thou Him,
And seest thou Him, then seest thou Us.[7]

In the *Qissa Husayn al-Hallāj*, a popular compilation[8] of narratives translated into French by Massignon, this alternation is expressed by the reoccurring and miraculous changes in size that accompany the last months and days of Hallāj. Such transformations and fluctuations are the fundamental life of the mystical heart, *qalb*, the etymology of which is akin to *taqallub* or "alternations". The alternations of the heart, as already expressed in the beating of the

physical organ, express the perfect submission to God's will, as epitomized by
the episode of the *Sūrah al-Kahf* (the Cave), central in the spiritual imagination
of Massignon, in which the bodies of the Seven Sleepers are "turned over"
by God in their sleep: "And thou wouldst have deemed them waking though
they were asleep, and We caused them to turn over (*nuqallibuhum*) to the right
and the left." (Pickthall, 18, 18).   *Mass → mystic experience = sudden*

Mysticism is decentering, a change of center, a withdrawal of the "old
man," and a new consciousness emanating from a "foreign" zone. This decentering results from, or rather coincides with, a "commotion" that reorients
the religious destiny of the person who undergoes it. Massignon likes to make
use of expressions that suggest a shock, or a sudden motion, an upheaval of
self. There is nothing methodical in this mystical occurrence, and nothing
active either, so that one would be tempted to say that Massignon's mysticism
is precisely the kind that Guénon refuses to equate with initiatory paths as
he conceives of them. The relationship between the two men was, for profound reasons of spiritual sensibility that have important implications, one of
mutual misunderstanding. Guénon seems to have considered Massignon as an
abstruse Catholic *littérateur*, while Massignon would classify Guénon under
the category of abstract "theosophists." Far from such presumed abstractions,
the *tasawwuf* favored by Massignon is thereby akin to an unexpected encounter, a sudden unveiling, *kashf.* Once the psychic ground has shaken under
the pressure of the divine quake, the landscape of the soul is forever altered,
marked; it *bears witness* to the divine event, not unlike the face of Massignon,
the ascetic and consumed expression of which can hardly leave any doubt as
to the presence that it has witnessed.   *betrays in*

Massignon's experiential apprehension of Islamic mysticism must more-   *that it doesn't capture*
over be understood in terms of the language that "betrays" the encounter   *its true*
with the Divine. The young Massignon had cherished and cultivated the   *essence?*
subtleties and stylistic indirections of the seventeenth-century *précieux*. His
essay of *licence*, written in 1902 at the age of nineteen, delves into the literary
characteristics of *L'Astrée*, a pastoral novel of more than five thousand pages
considered in its time as a foremost masterpiece of narrative literature, and an
epitome of the *goût précieux*. This background, and his personal affinities with
matters of literary expression, led him to focus on the ways in which Muslim
mystics have been able to translate the inner event they experienced through
language, and particularly poetic language. If one accepts Massignon's premise concerning the "de-centering" character of mystical insight, it will come
as no surprise that the language of mystics should itself be characterized by a
transformation of the linguistic substance bearing witness to the extraordinary
and supernatural nature of what transpires through it. Massignon approaches
this quasi-ineffable "modification" of language through mystical consciousness by highlighting the phenomenon of what he calls a *gauchissement* of the
usual syntax. Now the substantive *gauchissement* is akin to the French verb
gauchir, the connotations of which are usually negative,[9] implying the sense of

A mystical experience cannot be put into words.

warping, but also sometimes of veiling. The use of this unusual term is not without intention on the part of Massignon: It suggests that the usual nature of language is "warped," or modified, as if a different direction were taken, and it also evokes a lack of formal elegance or stylistic *préciosité* on the part of the mystic and poet. At a closer glance, however, this way of working on language may reveal a different type of *préciosité*, but one in which the indirection is less the result of a worldly conceit than the effect of a sudden change of level. In this connection, it is interesting to note that Massignon does not reserve the use of the verb *gauchir* for the poetic expression of mystics; he also makes use of the self-same term in the context of a study of the nature of Quranic language, another indication of his emphasis on the principle of the Quranic roots of mystical life in Islam.

The *gauchissement* of ordinary language that Massignon attributes to mystical poetry is also the criterion of a discrimination between two kinds of Sufism, as it were, one deemed by him to be consonant with his Christian outlook, the second falling short of a genuine insight into the life of the spirit as experiential "shock." Such a distinction cannot be better illustrated than by the respective treatments of two luminaries of *tasawwuf*, Mansūr al-Hallāj and Muhyi-d-Din Ibn 'Arabī. The contrasted examination of these two Sufis in the works of Massignon might actually be the best way to delineate the contours of his own understanding and vision of Sufism. While Hallāj represents, for Massignon, the epitome of an authentically Quranic and sacrificial witnessing that perfects Islam as a law while revealing its limits, Ibn 'Arabī is consistently envisaged by Massignon as an abstract theosopher whose doctrine denies the very life and tension lying at the core of mystical desire. We have already sketched a spiritual profile of Hallāj, but it may be helpful to underline that Hallājian Sufism is defined by Massignon as characteristic of the school of *wahdat ash-shuhūd*. This vision refers to a unity—or rather union—that occurs only in him or her who witnesses (*shahīd*), or in the subjective consciousness, without postulating a fundamental ontological unity.[10] It is therefore specifically "mystical" if the term is to be taken, as it often is, as suggesting a subjective experience of the Divine. Conversely, the school of *wahdat al-wujūd* is founded on the insight into an essential unity of being (*wujūd*).[11] It is predicated on the distinction between *wujūd*, or the act of Being as God's Essence, and *mawjūd*, this term referring to existents at any level of reality, including God considered as an existent Being. Even though Ibn 'Arabī himself never uses this term, the doctrine has traditionally been associated with his name because of the centrality of the concept of *wujūd* in his metaphysics. The unity of all things, or universal reality, in God's essential fold is thus expressed by Ibn 'Arabī:

> It is impossible for the things other than God to come out of the grasp of the Real, for He brings them into existence, or rather, He is their existence and from Him they acquire (*istifāda*) existence. And existence/Being

What is that relation?

is nothing other than the Real, nor is it something outside of Him from which He gives to them. (. . .) On the contrary He is Being, and through Him the entities become manifest.[12]

What, in such lines, was all too often considered by early Orientalists as "pantheism" is in fact much more accurately described as "panentheism" since it clearly indicates that "all things are in God" (pan en theo) while He is also beyond them. Irrespective of these distinctions, which he does not take into account in any of his works, Massignon is adamant in recusing what he characterizes as a "monistic" doctrine incompatible with the inner "dynamics" of mysticism. Such "monism" is most often associated by him with "neo-Platonic infiltrations" that fail to convey the spiritual call of the Living God. This is symptomatic, for Massignon, of a preference for "syncretistic vocabulary" and "theoretical concerns" over "experimental analysis and the introspection of ritual practice."[13] Ibn ʿArabī's doctrine is perceived by the Catholic Islamicist as a subtle betrayal of the Abrahamic message of faith, substituting a static, theoretical, and monistic metaphysics for a living relationship with God. Massignon sees in this impact of Ibn ʿArabī's doctrine on the development of Sufism a regrettable "divorce between ascetic discipline and mystical theology".[14] Thus, commenting upon Abū Yazīd al-Bistāmī and his doctrine of tajrīd al-tawḥīd (isolation in unity), which is akin to Hallāj's, Massignon spells doubt upon the inspiration by, and convergence with, Abū Yazīd, which Ibn ʿArabī claimed for his work. This is the clearest way to highlight the chasm between the practical and ascetic emphasis of early tasawwuf and later theoretical development. Massignon's Sufism is intimately bound to the "materiality" of Quranic meditation and devotional and moral practices to the point of excluding, quite abusively, the doctrinal elaborations of the thirteenth century and beyond. It is also important to note that Massignon's Sufism firmly rejects the so-called "syncretistic" dimension of Sufi esoteric doctrines such as Ibn ʿArabī's. It is, for him, once again a matter of Abrahamic integrity. The Sufism for which Massignon searched all his life ("On earth we find in people only that which we are looking for," to use one of his key statements[15]) is a mysticism akin to the early Desert Fathers and the pilgrims of Love belonging to Saint Francis' spiritual family. His Sufism is a matter of testimony, unveiling (kashf), states (ḥāl), and inspired utterances (shatahāt). Foremost among such "testimonial commotions," Hallāj's "Anā al-Haqq" ("I am the Truth") can only be measured by different yardsticks, depending upon one's vocation and spiritual perspective. For Massignon, it was the springing forth of naked sincerity. For others, it was indeed an indiscretion, and a confusion between the demands of the language of the "nuptial chamber" and the requirements of the "public square," to use Simone Weil's phrases. The opposition of metaphysical perspectives that Massignon outlined and solidified in his study of tasawwuf, unfolds in the distinct spiritual sensibilities that Ibn ʿArabī's concept of spiritual adab suggests, since, as noted by Michel

*So Massignon is concerned of exoteric...?
more so than esoteric?*

Chodkiewicz: "if the Shaykh al-Akbar does insist on a rule when he addresses
a disciple, it is the rule of sobriety (*sahw*) (. . .) (which) explains why, for him,
shatahāt ('theopathic locutions', to use Massignon's translation) are, in a saint,
always a sign of imperfection."[16]

Although Corbin acknowledged a profound affinity of method with Massignon, who was his professor at the *Ecole Pratique des Hautes Etudes*, he could
not but mention, on occasions, the measure of bewilderment that some of the
philosophical positions of his mentor arose in him.[17] First among those stands
was Massignon's partial and insistent misunderstanding of *wahdāt al-wujūd*.
It was to Corbin's merit that he pursued Massignon's search in the spiritual
depths of Islam while being able to envisage the reality of a profound, indeed
indissociable, connection between intellectuality, nay philosophy, and spirituality in Sufism. This position stands in sharp contrast to Guénon's dismissal
of philosophy, which he reduced to the status of a "profane" ratiocination.
On the contrary, Corbin established the connection between philosophy and
prophecy mostly through the study of the long Shī'ite tradition of theosophy;
and there is no doubt that for him, inner Islam had to be identified with
Shī'ism. We must, therefore, first delve into Corbin's argument for this assertion before we turn to the main components of his understanding of inner
Islam. Before we do so, however, we would like to specify the nature of
the relationship between Corbin and the *Shī'a*, thereby gaining some surer
footing concerning the question of Corbin's personal contribution to Islamic
studies. It has sometimes been said that Massignon's thought was an original,
indeed personal, crystallization that constitutes a cohesive whole expressive
of a cogent "spiritual philosophy," as it were. By these standards, which have
in fact been very diversely appraised by those who claimed for Massignon a
kind of genial mastery, and those who could hardly bear his "idiosyncratic"
approach, Corbin's work may appear more flatly academic, perhaps even lacking originality, in the sense at least in which it is substantially dependent
upon the translation of, and commentaries upon, spiritual and philosophical
luminaries of Islam. There is no doubt that Corbin's work was that of a pioneer, and in many ways that of a dis-coverer since he introduced to Western
readerships immense segments of philosophical and mystical discourse that
had been theretofore virtually unknown. It would, however, be unfair to
reduce his function to having merit merely for unburying spiritual treasur-
ies and offering them to a wider audience. This is so because his formidable
academic work was situated, from the outset, in the context of a spiritual
quest, without an awareness of which it is impossible to make sense of its
far-ranging implications, its inner unity, what he would have called its "har-
monics." In fact, Corbin insisted that the whole development of his work on
Islamic and Iranian studies was actually initiated in the context of his study of
German phenomenology. This is illustrated by his comment that Shī'ite gnosis is in fact an Islamic phenomenology, inasmuch as it unveils (*kashf*) realities
according to their divine intentionality. It is by this selfsame principle that the

Corbin's work based primarily on

contemporary student of religion must abide, through "an examination of the acts of consciousness which lead to (orders of spiritual reality), acts in which the region of being towards which they reach is *manifested*."[18]

There is probably no better way to approach Corbin's understanding of the relationship between Shī'ism and Sufism than through an analysis of his commentaries on the fourteenth-century Shī'ite theologian Haydar Āmulī. Corbin follows Haydar Āmulī in stating that Shī'ite imamology is the very foundation of Sufism, and that the latter proceeds from the former as its development and perfection. This is encapsulated in a quotation from Āmulī's treatise *Jāmi' al-asrār* (*The Summa of Secrets*): "The Sufis are those who deserve the name of Shī'ite's in truth (*al-shī'a al-haqīqīya*) and that of faithful whose heart has been tested."[19]   Corbin → Sufism = Shī'ism

This proposition, which cannot but be welcomed by Shī'ite Sufis but is at the very least ill-sounding to the ears of Sunni practitioners of *tasawwuf*, is founded on the principle that Twelver Shī'ism is indeed inner Islam. It would be inaccurate—however tempting it may be when reading some of Corbin's texts—to consider that *Shī'a* Islam is the esoteric dimension of the Islamic tradition, the exoteric side of which would be found in Sunnism. Haydar Āmulī's views do buttress the vision of an esoteric Shī'ism, but they go in fact further, in a direction that identifies Shī'a Islam as the totality of the tradition, by contrast with the incompleteness of Sunni Islam, confined to the province of the Law. However, this principle does not go without a paradoxical complement: While Shī'ism can be "exotericized" by those, within the Shī'a, who do not perceive, or even deny, the esoteric essence of their tradition, Sunni Islam, for its part, can be practiced as a de facto esoterism, or to use Corbin's term, as an "*incognito* representative" of Shī'ism within Sunnism. This situation allows the Shī'ite theosopher to enunciate a statement that Corbin will make part and parcel of his own gnostic philosophy. According to this view, an authentic gnosis must integrate both the exoteric and the esoteric sides of the religion. It therefore involves a middle ground between two opposite excesses. The first excess, curiously attributed to some of the Sunni Sufis, consists in severing the esoteric from the exoteric by claiming that inner Islam (or the truth of Islam, its *haqīqah*) exempts its faithful from the legal prescriptions of the *sharī'ah*. The second excess is characteristic of "metaphorical Shī'ites", that is, those who within the *Shī'a* do not recognize that inner Islam (*bātin*) is the true meaning of outer Islam (*zāhir*). However, what may not appear as clearly from Corbin's introduction and commentary as in his translation of Āmulī's text itself, is the fact that "the table has been turned," in the sense that it is now, in Haydar Āmulī's words, the Shī'ite side that is associated with the exoteric side of the tradition, that is, "the literal religion such as it is practiced by Imāmite Shī'ites among the various branches of Islam," whereas it is the Sunni side—in the person of the Sufis—that represents esoteric Islam, that is, "the esoteric which is the spiritual truth to which is attached the Sufi group."[20] So the truth is that, when he claims to "totalize within himself the literal religion and the gnostic

this person refers to esoteric as Sunni; exoteric as Sufi

truth," Haydar Āmulī understands these two sides as referring, respectively, to Shī'ism and Sunni Sufism, a situation that illustrates the complexities of the confessional layout within Islam, and the paradoxes of the interplay between collective religious structures and institutions, and spiritual understanding.

Corbin goes back to this question in the context of his study of the Isma'ili hermeneutics of the story of Noah. In this interpretation of the narrative, the flood is understood as referring to the "suffocation" of souls that results from a separation between the exoteric and esoteric sides of religion. It seems that this "suffocation" can be understood in two ways: either as a result of the "weight" of legalistic religion that does not allow for "spiritual breathing," as it were, or as a sort of "drowning" induced by the pressure of a spiritual content that cannot be integrated within the forms and limitations of human existence for lack of a *sharī'ah*. In response to these two perils, Noah's function was, as a *rasūl*, to remind humans of the need for a law, a *sharī'ah*, while preserving an access to its esoteric interpretation. The result of this integral predication is that it unites against it the two opposite groups intent on breaking the balance between the outer and the inner: " (. . .) those who consider that they can and must have immediate access to the esoteric, to the *bātin*; and those who are the prey of the exoteric left to itself (. . .) and who reject any esoteric implication."[21]

Shī'ite imamology is, analogically, a response to this twofold danger by its emphasis on the complementarity between *zāhir* and *bātin*, the Prophet and the Imām. Sunni Sufism derives from a perception of this same complementarity, but it substitutes, erroneously for Corbin and his Shī'ite sources, the figure of the visible *Shaykh* for the inner guidance of the *Imām*. Such a substitution runs the risk of replacing an inner, living source of inspiration, with an outer, institutionalized order. According to Corbin, this is what is primarily aimed at by Shī'ite critics of Sufism: The inner dimension of Islam becomes far too much externalized in outer signs of participation into mystical life, initiatory structures and brotherhoods, external hierarchies, and communal representations.[22] Corbin refers, in this respect, to what he calls a "materialization" of spiritual life. This thesis of a Shī'ite foundation of Sufism, and a gradual moving away from these esoteric roots, is supported, in Corbin's argument by the fact that all Sufi brotherhoods include holy men who are also Imāms in Shī'ism[23] among the original members of their *silsilah*—the initiatory chain that links all the historical *shuyūkh*, or spiritual guides of a given *tarīqah* (path, order) to the Prophet Muhammad, and through him to God. Corbin's conversion to the Shī'ite point of view on this matter most likely proceeded from his profound distrust vis-à-vis the mediating function of external institutions. His extreme emphasis on the purely inner dimension of spirituality in Islam led him to ignore that the association of esoterism with the invisibility of the guide has nothing absolute about it, since it is only the last and twelfth Imām Muhammad Al-Mahdi Al-Muntadar who has been in hiding, and since the need for an outer presence and guidance of the Shaykh is not unconditional in Sufism either. The type of the *'Uwaysi Sufi*, a disciple who has no living master,[24] although rare, is acknowledged as a reality in Sunni Sufi circles. Ultimately the distinction between an outer and inner guidance is relative, as indicated by the fact that the relationship between a disciple and his *Shaykh* cannot be severed by death. Moreover, the conclusion drawn from the attribution—following Haydar Āmulī—to some Sunni Sufis of a tendency to dispense with the requirements of the *sharī'ah* is unconvincing when one considers that the vast majority of the latter have in fact historically been remarkably intent on preserving a close connection between the *sharī'ah* and the *tarīqah*, this line of reasoning is all the more paradoxical in that an actual collective severance from the *sharī'ah* has never occurred in a Sunni context, but only in the Shī'ite ambience of the Reformation of Alamūt.[25]

Consistent with the Shī'ite inspiration of his scholarship, Corbin's "inner Islam" is almost entirely defined within the triadic structure of a relationship between the Book, the Guide, and the soul. The Book is the external support of Islam, without which there cannot be any real access to the *arcana islamica*. The Guide, in the form of the Imām, is the inner revealer of the real message of the Book. As for the soul, it is the object of the inner guidance and, concomitantly, the subjective locus of the unveiling of the Book's message, which is also, concurrently, the actualization of the true selfhood. Corbin's spiritual world is a world of mediations, but the spiritual media that it involves remain effective in a purely hidden and invisible way. One could say that, for him, there are two obstacles or pitfalls to a genuine unfolding of inner Islam, or inner religion in general, one being the historicization and institutionalization of spirituality, and the other being the disappearance of self in a pseudomystical absorption in the Divine. Corbin's responses to these two perils are intimately bound inasmuch as they delineate the contours of a fundamentally personal religion. The general narrative of this spiritual odyssey has been summarized by Corbin in his *Avicenna and the Visionary Recital*:

> At the moment when the soul discovers itself to be a stranger and alone in a world formerly familiar, a *personal* figure appears on its horizon, a figure that announces itself to the soul *personally* because it symbolizes *with* the soul's most intimate depths.[26]

This *symbolization with* is a spiritual consonance that reminds us that the symbol has etymologically two faces, the two forming a bi-unity. Such a personal understanding of the spiritual path is, in itself, nothing unusual in the world of mystical Islam, as expressed in the principle, and the *hadīth*, that says "the paths toward God are as many as the breaths of creatures" (*at-turuq ila'Llāhi ka-nufūsi bani Adam*). However, it takes a particularly significant meaning in Corbin's concept of inner Islam inasmuch as it coincides with a strongly emphasized angelology that conceives of the angel as a celestial "twin" of the soul, a sort of animic archetype that mediates the relationship between the human and the Divine. *Duo sunt in homine*, as Ananda Coomaraswamy would often quote: The inner event of the soul amounts to the spiritual fact that "human consciousness discovers *in* itself, *in front of* itself, and *behind* itself, a presence which is at once *oneself* and *other* than oneself."[27] In that sense the *hadīth*, "He who knows himself knows his Lord," often quoted by Corbin, could be paraphrased by the more explicit statement, "He who knows his angel knows himself, he who knows his angel knows his Lord." It is helpful to consider that this angelic presence, which is the personal revelation par excellence, is sometimes envisaged, as in Suhrawardī and the Hermetists, as the soul's "Perfect Nature."[28] In other words, there is a sense in which the encounter with the angel is a discovery of oneself in God's intention. The angel is the appearance of oneself on the horizon of the Divine, and the appearance of the Divine on the horizon of one's self. The angel is the mediator, as is *mutatis mutandis* the Imām, both of them manifesting themselves in this realm of imagination, the intermediary realm, that is their domain of predilection.

No discussion of inner Islam, Shī'ite gnosis, or Sufism in Corbin's opus can bypass an examination of the role of the *mundus imaginalis*, the imaginal world, in defining the situs and the form of spiritual experiences. To put it in Corbin's own suggestive pun, in the absence or neglect of this domain, spiritual events "have no place" (*n'ont pas de lieu*) of their own, and therefore do not "take place" (*n'ont pas lieu*). As an intermediary level between the realm of pure archetypes, or intelligible realities, and the world of physical manifestation, the *mundus imaginalis* is characterized by its capacity to lend form to the invisible, informal realities of the intelligible heavens. Metaphysically, the existence of this domain is demanded by the unity of being, which requires that the plurality of the levels of existence, which entails perforce an ontological discontinuity, be also related along a continuous chain of being. The structure of reality is thereby characterized by discontinuity in continuity, and continuity in discontinuity. The nature of the *imaginal world*[29] is to be endowed with the formal qualities of the physical world without being encumbered by its quantitative substance. As a symbol of this intermediary ontological status, Corbin refers to it—in the wake of Shī'ite theosophy—as a mirror in which the purely intellective realities come to be reflected in a formal, visionary mode that can give access to the above: "The material substance of the mirror, metal or mineral, is not the substance of the image, a substance whose image would be an accident. It is simply the 'place of its appearance.'"[30]

Corbin's spirituality is visionary: it is a Sufism of places and travels. However, it is important to bear in mind that these places and travels are, in fact, purely inward. As Tom Cheetham reminds us in his suggestive and comprehensive study of Corbin's thought, "the (imaginal) world (is) inside out." This is the "inversion of the relation of interiority expressed by the preposition *in* or *within*", and speaking of spiritual entities, it must be said that "it is their world that is *in* them".[31] "Inner Islam" is intrinsically connected to a landscape of the soul, hence its powerfully imaginal character in the spiritual world introduced by Corbin. This apprehension colors the presentation of even such Sufi luminaries as Ibn ʿArabī, whom Massignon tended to portray, by contrast, as a "monistic," "abstract" theosopher. The "creative imagination" that Corbin poses at the center of the Shaykh al-Akbar's spiritual universe—while losing no opportunity to underline his relationship with Shīʿism, especially through Haydar Āmulī [32]—confers on his metaphysical doctrine of the *tajallī*, the theophanic unfolding of existence, a decidedly more visionary character than do other scholarly approaches—we think particularly of Toshihiko Izutsu's and Michel Chodkiewicz' contributions—that have tended to situate it in a more strictly metaphysical framework. This even holds true of Corbin's presentation of such methodical supports of the mystical life as *dhikr*—the discipline of perpetual invocation of the Names of God, which is at the core of living Sufism. The inner modalities of this discipline are envisaged by him in the context of visionary photisms, a dimension hardly emphasized in mainstream *tasawwuf*. While Corbin's thought is intimately bound to an ontology of the image as "iconic" epiphany, it is not only for him an "archeological" heritage, so to speak. Flowing from a tradition that has run through centuries of Islamic philosophy and mysticism, it is also, and above all, an *actual* need on the part of the contemporary Western world, and indeed the entire contemporary world inasmuch as it is in fact determined by the latter. In this visionary doctrine of theophany, Corbin finds a response to the deficiencies and tragedies resulting from the Cartesian dichotomy between matter and mind:

> What is perhaps most deplorable in our Western philosophy since Descartes is that we have remained as if struck by powerlessness before the dilemma of the *res extensa* and *res cogitans*, and that we have therefore lost the sense of what is metaphysically concrete, the world in which are written the secrets of worlds and interworlds that are perpetually present. [33]

It is highly paradoxical, but hardly surprising when one considers the thrust of Corbin's "inner Islam," that Islam would provide for him the framework of a rehabilitation of images whereas it is envisaged by most from the vantage point of its "an-iconic," or even iconoclastic, dimension. There is perhaps no better evidence of the originality and usefulness of Corbin's work than the outlining of such a sharp contrast between an outer and inner Islam, a contrast that provides the tools for a critical reexamination of many assumptions East and West. The wide success, in the Western world, of Jalāl-ad-Dīn Rūmī's imaginal poetry may bear witness to some external aspects of this reexamination.

The contrast between an inner and an outer Islam that proceeds from Corbin's focus on the visionary, epiphanic layers of Islamic mysticism can be qualified on two grounds in the context of an examination of René Guénon's "inner Islam." First, in the sense that Guénon traces the presence and effectiveness of spiritual symbolism in the very texture of formal Islam. Symbolism is not primarily a matter of visionary privilege, as it were, it is also, and above all, the very language of tradition at large. Second, and conversely, the spiritual climate of inner Islam is characterized, with Guénon, by a sober, purely metaphysical "ambience" that shuns exteriorizations, including internal exteriorizations. There is actually a suggestive contrast to draw between the purely interiorized Islam of Corbin, who remained outwardly a Christian, and its imaginal and visionary wealth of manifestation on the horizon of the soul on the one hand, and the exteriorized Islam of Guénon, Shaykh 'Abd al-Wāhid Yahya, whose Muslim and Egyptian persona breathed in the daily forms and manifestations of outer Islam, while his metaphysical focus remained on the most universal, quintessential, and informal core of the doctrine. Now this contrast can be pursued in the ways in which each of the two writers approached the phenomena of symbolic imagination. For Corbin, the symbol, the image, the vision, is a presence that bears witness in the soul: It is, as he often wrote, an "animic event." This experiential and "presential" character is the very mode of operation of Islamic spirituality. Guénon's understanding of forms is quite different—even though not incompatible, in fact, being a matter of emphasis more than one of exclusiveness. For him, the image is primarily a symbol, as collected in the treasury of universal symbolism, through which are expressed ineffable principles common to the whole of mankind. Guénon's approach to symbols consists in a kind of metaphysical deciphering of their secret "number." Symbolism is more a matter of language than one of presence, even though the one evidently does not exclude the other.

It has been noted by some analysts that the paradox of Guénon's Islam lies in the disproportion between the high visibility of this religion in his destiny and his spiritual heritage,[34] and the relative paucity of Islamic references in his works. This may be attributed in part to the fact that his outer participation in the Islamic tradition took place only in the later part of his life. It can also no doubt be connected to the fact that his early intellectual focus, and traditional documentation, seem to have emanated from Hindu sources. Whatever might be the external reasons for this disproportion, it cannot but lead us to further examine the definition and nature of Guénon's esoteric Islam. Here, the data of biographical studies and those garnered from his writings converge to suggest the centrality of the notion of initiation in his understanding of inner Islam. If one defines the three thrusts of Guénon's contribution as being an exposition of universal metaphysics, an elucidation of universal symbolism, and a description of the nature and modalities of spiritual initiation, there is little doubt that the third element is the most closely and pervasively related to his incursus into the Islamic tradition. For Guénon, the initiation is a sine qua non of spiritual development, and the starting point of the inner path that leads to "spiritual realization." The fundamental reason for this state of affairs lies in the fact that the spiritual path can best be described as a passage from the individual to the universal:[35] Such a passage presupposes that the individual be in a position to benefit from the means of grace that transcend the realm of individuality, proceeding as they do from divine universality. From a biographical point of view as well, one must note that Guénon is considered by most of his biographers as having been initiated into Sufism many years before his departure for Egypt in 1930.[36] Thierry Zarcone indicated that "Guénon became a Muslim, or rather a Sufi, in Paris in 1911."[37] Zarcone's qualification " . . . or rather a Sufi" is made explicit in the interesting observation that "until his arrival in Cairo, Guénon did not adopt a lifestyle in conformity with the prescriptions of the religion of the Prophet."[38] The fact that the twenty-one years of his life in Cairo were, by contrast, characterized by a strict conformity to those prescriptions and, further, a participation into the psycho-cultural ambience of Islam through his marriage, family life, and attested—albeit mysterious—contacts with the world of tasawwuf in Egypt, raises interesting questions as to Guénon's views on the relationship between what he designated as the "exoteric" and "esoteric" dimensions of Islam.[39] As a matter of principle, it must be stressed that, in Guénon's own words, "the esoteric and initiatory point of view (. . .) to which refers, properly speaking, the consciousness of the essential unity of all traditions under the apparent diversity of external forms, is quite distinct from the exoteric and religious point of view, which is not my purview." This clear-cut distinction could account for the disconnection between "inner" and "outer" Islam in Guénon's life between 1911 and 1930. As for the connection between the two during the second half of Guénon's life in Sufism, it has been variously interpreted as referring to external circumstances or to doctrinal principles. The second interpretation finds some justification in the chapter "The Necessity of Traditional Exoterism," in which Guénon emphasizes that exoterism and esoterism are the two "faces" of "one and the same thing": this chapter defines exoterism as a foundation and an ambience. The first aspect refers to a "base" that has to be gradually "transformed" by the esoteric perspective. In other words, exoterism, or the sharī'ah, is an objective support of meditation, a formal starting point, but the distinctness of the esoteric, or inner, perspective consists in transmuting it to the point of making it refer to realities of a totally different order than that which a purely "exoteric" point of view would allow for. It is significant that Guénon refers to the sharī'ah both as a principle of veiling and unveiling, akin to "the exterior forms (which) hide profound truth from the eyes of the common man, whereas on the contrary they may be seen by the elite, for whom what seems an obstacle or a limitation to others becomes instead a support and a means of realization."[40] As for the second aspect of the need for the sharī'ah, it points in essence to a need for integrating one's life within the encompassing fold of the tradition, especially as a protection against the "profane outlook," thereby preventing areas of one's life or psyche from being affected by that outlook. This is also the reason why Guénon does not even exempt those who have penetrated the haqīqah, to one extent or another, from the discipline of the Law. If initiation, the cornerstone of Guénon's presentation, defines the preconditions and spiritual modalities of inner Islam, outer Islam delimits the formal framework conducive to the development of these modalities. This emphasis on initiation accounts, in a large measure, for the role that Islam has played in providing Guénon with a specific traditional structure defined by the contradistinction, and complementarity, between an inner, esoteric part of the tradition, and one that is outer or exoteric. In fact, it can be argued that no other tradition, with the possible exception of Judaism, could provide Guénon with such a recognizable partition between the exoteric and esoteric provinces. Hinduism, which had been his focus throughout most of his work, includes modes and levels of spirituality of such diversity as to defy any attempt at binary categorization. Christianity, for its part, was deemed to be an originally esoteric religion which had early on lost its esoteric character, remaining thereafter limited to the exoteric domain. Even Taoism, which Guénon tended to conceive in many ways as parallel to Sufism, could only be considered as an esoteric religion, the exoteric complement of which had to be found outside of its own confines, in the form of Confucianism. By contrast, Islam was clearly identifiable as distinguishing between a *sharī'ah* and a *tarīqah*, a law and a way:

> "Of all traditional doctrines, perhaps Islamic doctrine most clearly distinguishes the two complementary parts, which can be labeled exoterism and esoterism."[41]

In his article devoted to "Islamic Esoterism," Guénon further develops the implications of this duality by adding a third element to it. This third element, the *haqīqah*, is in fact the "inward truth" of the tradition. Through a graphic analogy, Guénon compares the *sharī'ah* to the circumference of a circle, that is, the most external and analytically expanded curve. This refers not only to the fact that the *sharī'ah* encompasses the greatest diversity of elements, such as the multiplicity of prescriptions and proscriptions, but also to the principle that the law addresses the generality of individuals, the identity of which might be symbolized by the indefinite number of points situated on the circumference of the circle. Moreover, as Guénon explains, the circumference implies both a distance from the center and a permanence in this distance. In other words, the Law is not only separated from the Essence in the sense that it does not fathom its reality, but it is also concentric with respect to it, thereby preventing the faithful "from going astray or from losing themselves."[42] As for the *haqīqah*, it is symbolically analogous to the center of the circumference. As such, it is both the very essence, or the very principle, of the whole, while remaining "imperceptible" or unmanifested as the hidden core of the totality. Finally, the *tarīqah* "is represented by the radius that runs from the circumference to the center," which accounts for the multiplicity of paths, as reflected not only by the plurality of *turuq* but also by the particularities of each individual path of access to the center, as exemplified, for example, by the Prophet's recommendation to speak to each according to his level of understanding: "Speak to people according to what they know (*Haddithū an-nās bimā ya'rifūn*)."

As an intermediary, or a path, between the *sharī'ah*, that pertains to the external needs of the individual as well as society qua collection of individuals, and the *haqīqah* in its purely universal and supraformal reality, the *tarīqah* pertains to a plurality of levels and functions that help integrate the individual within the universal, thereby prolonging and deepening the *sharī'ah*, but also, and above all, opening the way to a transcending of the individuality (*al-fanā'*), which results in a realization of the universal (*al-baqā'*). The intermediary status of the *tarīqah*, mediating between the individual and the universal, is manifested, extrinsically, by the plurality of modalities of affiliation, ranging from the *sālikun*, those traveling on the spiritual path toward the realization of the *haqīqah*, to those who are content with receiving the *barakah*, or blessing, of a Sufi *shaykh* without engaging themselves totally in the spiritual path. This is one of the fundamental reasons why Sufism has been characterized at one and the same time by its paradoxically dual identity as an elitist movement and a popular phenomenon. The "meeting of extremes" that Guénon has highlighted as one of the paradoxical characteristics of initiatory organizations such as Sufi *turuq* is in fact a manifestation of the intermediary status of the *tarīqah* between the outermost and innermost dimensions of the tradition. Guénon introduces this paradoxical mediation in terms of the law of reverse analogy that associates the highest and the lowest. The relatively frequent reference, in Guénon's texts about *tasawwuf*, to the spiritual type of the *Malāmatiyyah* way is directly connected to this analogical association. Without being able to enter, within the limits of our focus, into the complex question of the definition and modalities of the *Malāmatiyyah* way in Islam, it will suffice to say that the fundamental principle of this path consists in a dissimulation of inner states under the appearance of external ordinariness or, conversely, antisocial oddity. The *Malamatī* are known to emulate the example of the Prophet by combining the highest degrees of spiritual consciousness with the most disconcertingly unassuming external appearance and behaviour. In Guénon's terms:

> (. . .) The state of the *Malāmatiyah* is said to "resemble that of the Prophet, who was elevated to the highest degrees of the divine Proximity," but who, "when he returned to the people, spoke with them of external things only", so that, "from his intimate conversation with God, no trace appeared on his person."[43]

In a sense, this could be interpreted as emblematic of Islam's totality as encompassing all the realms of human existence, from the highest spiritual stations to the most minute practical aspects of daily life. From another point of view, the same spiritual situation can be referred to the specifically "inner" characteristic of esoterism in Islam, the *bātin*, which is such "by (. . .) (its) very nature and not owing to any conventions or to precautions taken artificially, if not arbitrarily, by those who preserve traditional doctrine".[44] It bears stressing, finally, that the duality between an outer and an inner dimension of Islam, or a *haqīqah* and a *sharī'ah*, is ultimately relative to the dualistic point of view upon which it is contingent. What is "inner" from the point of view of the initial "outer" standing of the individual transcends in fact this very distinction from the point of view of the center. Most paradoxical statements such as "the *sharī'ah* is the *haqīqah*" are actually allusions (*ishārāt*) to this perspective "from within," as it were.[45]

Guénon's "inner Islam" can ultimately be considered from two angles: first, as an expression of the doctrine of the "unity of Being," and second, as referring to the initiatory path as defined in his two treatises *Perspectives on Initiation* and *Initiation and Spiritual Realization*. From the first point of view, inner Islam is none other than the realization of Unity, objectively speaking, and the Supreme Identity, subjectively speaking. These two realizations, or perfections, are in fact the two faces of one and the same reality. The former is addressed in Guénon's article entitled "*at-Tawhīd*": It envisages the doctrine of unity as "everywhere and always the same (*at-tawhīdu wāhidun*), invariable like the Principle, independent from multiplicity and change, which can only affect applications of a contingent order,"[46] while the latter is considered, in the chapter "*Al-Faqr,*" as an identification with "the 'divine station' (*al-maqāmu-l-ilahi*), which is the central point where all distinctions inherent in outward points of view are surpassed."[47] According to the first point of view, which corresponds to the metaphysical dimension of Guénon's work, inner Islam is the essence of Monotheism, the solar character of which is expressed by the extinction of appearances under the sun of divine Unity:

> In the intense light of countries of the East, it is enough to see things to understand them, to grasp their profound truth immediately; and it seems especially impossible not to understand these things in the desert, where the sun traces the divine Names in letters of fire in the sky.[48]

To this objective and metaphysical "disappearance" of phenomena[49] corresponds a subjective and initiatory disappearance of the ego fed by these phenomena, which is the essence of *al-faqr*, the inner poverty that characterizes the *tasawwuf* of *fuqara*, the "poor in God." This second point of view opens onto the initiatory domain, which could be defined as the specific technical concern of Guénon. His articulation of the *sharī'ah* and the *tarīqah* and his specification of the functions of each is indeed predicated upon technical and initiatory considerations. The *tarīqah* consists primarily in the reception of an initiation that confers upon the aspirant the "spiritual influence" (*barakah*) of a *silsilah* (the initiatory chain) that goes back to the Prophet of Islam through a spiritual line of *shuyukh*. Guénon conceives of this initiation as a sine qua non of *tasawwuf*; and herein lies his primary focus.[50] Moreover, the *sharī'ah* itself is envisaged by Guénon from the standpoint of its technical necessity, since it is exclusively taken into account as an instrumental precondition for the *tarīqah*.

While Frithjof Schuon has rightfully been considered as following in the general *Weltanschauung* as René Guénon,[51] it is no exaggeration to add that the premises and modalities of his presentation of the inward dimension of Islam are considerably distinct. Schuon's understanding of the spirituality of Islam does not proceed from a consideration of initiatory realities and modes as such, nor from a focus on the esoteric hermeneutics of the *Qur'ān*, nor even from a study of the virtues, states, and mystical experiences of the *mutasawwif*, or Sufi practitioner, but simply from a meditation on the metaphysical and spiritual implications of the Muslim profession of faith, the *shahādah*, or rather the *shahādatain*, to refer to both segments of the creed: "(. . .) All wisdom (. . .) is contained for Islam within the *Shahādah* alone, the twofold Testimony of faith."[52]

In this sense, "inner Islam" is not to be found elsewhere than in what is most central and essential to Islam itself. This is a view that clashes with the ordinary concept of the *bātin* as a reality hidden from sight, reserved for an arcane domain, or associated with unverifiable speculations. It converges (although from a different point of view) with recent interpretations of Sufism that stress the continuity between Islam and Sufism.[53] Far from occultist and Orientalist understandings of Islamic esoterism as disconnected from Muslim tenets, Schuon considers the *shahādah* as the key to an interiorization of Islam, an interiorization that is in essence none other than Sufism, predicated as it is on the science of purification of the heart and intentions (*faqr*) and the invocation of God's Name (*dhikr*). Since the *shahādah* contains two parts, *lā ilāha ill'Allāh* and *Muhammadun rasūl Allāh*, the relationship between these two essential aspects of the Islamic creed gives rise to a plurality of points of view. According to a first point of view, the first part of the *shahādah*, concerning God, constitutes an integral statement concerning the nature of reality: In this capacity, "no god but God" can be metaphysically translated as "there is no reality but the Reality." This approach is characterized by Schuon as a properly metaphysical understanding of the *shahādah*, as opposed to a merely theological one. The metaphysical point of view refers to the Supreme Reality as Beyond-Being, beyond all determinations and oppositions, whereas the theological point of view stops short at the level of Being, thereby conceiving of God exclusively in terms of a Supreme Being. Therefore, the theological, or ordinary, understanding of the first *shahādah* means that only one being is the Supreme Being. Such a comprehension of the *shahādah* does not in the least invalidate, or even relativize, the "being" of other realities on the level of existence that is theirs. A metaphysical understanding of the first *shahādah* goes much further in its affirmation of *tawhīd* in the sense that the affirmation of one God is ipso facto the exclusive affirmation of only one Reality. Only one reality, God's reality, is really real, if one may say so. This means that all other realities are real only in a "metaphorical" sense, or as "symbols" of the one and only Reality. The *shahādah* thereby contains an inclusiveness within its very exclusiveness as a mercy hidden within the bosom of rigor. This is so because any negation of other than God through the *nafy* (or negation: *lā*) is *eo ipso* an affirmation of God, *Allāh*, while the latter intrinsically implies that all that is real is so inasmuch and insofar as it participates in the one and only Reality. In other words, the affirmation of everything in God is contained in the very negation of everything other than God. In and of itself an integral understanding of this metaphysical interpretation of the first *shahādah* would summarize the reality of inner Islam.

It must be added that the second *shahādah* does, in this context, correspond to the cosmogonic complement of the first, since Muhammad is thereby understood in an ontological sense as the prototype of Creation, the Messenger of the divine perfection in existence. Islam in its inner signification means entering into the mold of that perfection.

From another point of view the *shahādatain* may refer to the exclusive and inclusive faces of the divine Reality. The *lā* of the first *shahādah* has been compared, in this respect, to a pair of scissors (*lam-alif*) that cut into the nonexistence of manifestation. By contrast the second *shahādah* affirms that existence, in the perfect form of the Logos, manifests the Divine, since it is so to speak the external dimension of its Reality. Spiritually speaking, these two sides of the *shahādah* evoke the double vocation of mankind as *'abd*, servant, and *khalifah*, or representative. The *'ubudiyah* refers to the inexistence of "other than God," whereas the aspect of *khalifah* pertains to its "existence in God." Schuon expresses the spiritual meaning of this twofold metaphysical message by referring to what he considers to be the two essential components of Sufism, *faqr* and *dhikr*. Spiritual poverty is the direct manifestation of the first *shahādah* in the soul, whereas the remembrance of God is the very expression of the second, as indicated by the Prophet's name, *Dhikrullāh*. In other words, *faqr* is equivalent to the fundamental spiritual virtues that flow from a concrete awareness of one's utter dependence upon God, while *dhikr* refers generally to prayer, and specifically to that mode of inner, methodical, systematic prayer that manifests itself as "mention" of the Name of God. The *Qur'ān* clearly establishes the pre-eminence of this mode of prayer when stating: "recite that which hath been revealed to thee of the Scripture and observe the prayer, truly prayer preserveth from lewdness and iniquity, but the remembrance of God is greater." (29, 45)[54] Together, *faqr* and *dhikr* constitute the essence of Islam, and the essence of Sufism as the inner dimension of this religion. In other words, *faqr* and *dhikr* are the constitutive components of *ihsān*, which the *hadīth* of Gabriel defines as "worshipping God as if you were seeing Him, and if you see Him not He sees you."

Schuon's emphasis on *ihsān* as the operative truth of Islam informs his understanding and description of all the essential elements of Islamic practice. This is a manifestation of the fact that inner Islam, or *tasawwuf*, is not something external or superimposed on Islam, but strictly follows from the principles and essentials of the religion, both in terms of doctrine and method.

Ihsān is, in this sense, an "interiorization" of the external pillars of Islam. So there is an objective sense in which the pillars (*shahādah, salāt, siyām, zakāt, hajj*) are "symbols" of the inner truth of Islam, and another sense in which it is the way we consider them "subjectively" that unveils their intrinsic spiritual meaning.[55] Whether considered symbolically or operatively, the second pillar, *salāt*, "marks the submission of Manifestation to the Principle." This ontological submission is particularly expressed in the spiritual apex of the cycle of canonical postures that is the prostration, *sujūd*. In a sense, it could be said that the entire reality of inner Islam is contained, from a human standpoint, in this prostration. Whereas *salāt* is affirmative and akin to *dhikr*, fasting, *siyām*, is negative and pertains to *faqr*. It is a mode of emptiness for God that expresssees the metaphysical "vacuity" of manifestation considered in its subjective, or internal, dimension (i.e., the ego), and the spiritual poverty, hence dependence, of the human agent. As a complementary dimension of detachment, alms, *zakāt*, expresses the latter in regard to the external realm of manifestation, things and goods. Finally, the inner significance of *hajj* is one of "return to the Center, the Heart, the Self." It therefore expresses the affirmation of the deepest level of subjective reality. *Jihād*, as a sixth pillar which is sometimes added to the five already mentioned, is the complement of the latter in being a negation of the illusory self, or ego, as manifested in the *jihād al-akbar*, the "greater *jihād*." The fact that *jihād* is not always included among the *arkān* testifies to its extrinsic aspect. This extrinsic dimension is also expressed in the fact that the *hajj* is sometimes characterized as the *jihād* of women, which is all the more meaningful for alluding to the association between the feminine and the inward. Thus, throughout this inner explication of Islam in its most fundamental sense, the spiritual meaning of Sufism is unveiled at its source, as it were.

Schuon's emphasis on Islam as such as the starting point for his definition of Sufism has an intrinsic and an extrinsic raison d'être.[56] While the former has been discussed in the preceding pages, the latter must be examined as well, in order to approach the full specificity of Schuon's view of *tasawwuf*. Let us consider, from the outset, that there is something prima facie paradoxical in the way in which a presentation of inner Islam centered on fundamental Islamic tenets, as opposed, let us say, to historical or philosophical manifestations of Sufism, can reveal, in Schuon's perspective, a more universal dimension of Islam than would a focus on Sufism as ordinarily envisaged. We speak of a paradox because Sufism tends to be considered by most scholars, and most analysts of Islam, as the segment of Islam most conducive and sensitive to a universal paradigm. However, while Schuon would certainly not disagree with this view, he might add that the multifaceted phenomenon of Sufism presents us with a complex spiritual picture that is not always transparent to the universal principles of the *sophia perennis* that he is keen to expound. One of the most striking specificities and thrusts of Schuon's work with respect to Sufism lies, unexpectedly for many, in his overall agreement with those scholars and Muslim observers who have argued that Sufism, considered in its historical development, represents, in some of its most prominent aspects, a distinct move away from the general religious climate of Islam. These tendencies manifest primarily in the methodical or spiritual arena. From an altogether different—and in fact opposite—point of view, too many metaphysical expressions associated with Sufism have, in Schuon's view, obstructed the direct manifestation of pure gnosis, or esoterism, by reason of being in too close a solidarity with some questionable theological premises representative of the limitations of exoteric Islam. We will now examine some of the main implications of these two predicaments.

As regards the "un-Islamic" character of some spiritual tendencies and practices of historical Sufism—which have prompted Orientalists to deem *tasawwuf* to be the result of religious borrowings from other traditions, Schuon highlights the sharp contrast between the sense of equilibrium characteristic of normative Islam, as flowing from the *Sunnah*, and the ascetic feats of early Sufis such as Rābi'ah and 'Ataba bin Gulām. Without rejecting the idea that the Prophet's life provides examples of asceticism that have served as exemplars for early Islamic spirituality, he points out the fact that not a few of the hagiographic narratives of early saints stage all manner of mystical behaviors that are more representative of the re-equilibrating and compensatory function of extreme mystical scruples and feats than they are expressive of the spiritual archetype of Islam. In the increasingly worldly and ambiguous context of the centuries following the time of the Prophet and his immediate companions, *tasawwuf* seems to derive its sense of legitimacy and the ascetic and mystical modalities of its expressions from its counteracting influence on a gradual dilution and corruption of the original sap of Islam. It is as if Islamic spirituality were extracting from the Prophet's message and exemplary way those exclusive elements which could act as a challenge to, or a guardrail against, the tepid or cynical compromises justified in the name of Islam as a "middle way." For Schuon, it is therefore important not to confuse "pious excess" with the spiritual norm, hence the need to derive Islamic spirituality from an integral, balanced consideration of the founding message.

As for the theological "crutches" and voluntaristic biases that Schuon identifies as obstructing the way to an authentic esoteric vision, they crop up from the unsteady soil of an exclusively anthropomorphic and moral comprehension of the Divine. This type of theological understanding is predicated on fathoming the mysteries of Divine infinitude by means of the confessional sublimity of its concept of God's omnipotence. Schuon does not hesitate to show that Sufi theosophy does not always avoid the pitfalls of such a confusion of levels, attributing to the Divine Essence what pertains to the personal God, or confusing the will of the latter with the infinity of the former. Such confusions illustrate the encounter, within the fold of Sufism, of inspirations and ideas pertaining to different strata of religious consciousness, an encounter which is in itself unavoidable in a spiritual context that, in Schuon's words, joins the world of the Psalms of David with that of the Upanisads.[57]

In the same order of ideas, Schuon rejects Corbin's thesis concerning the specifically Shīʿite roots of Islamic esoterism. This divergence stems from the fact that Schuon does not strictly, or exclusively, associate Sufism with any theological, confessional, or genealogical phenomenon, his concept of esoterism involving the principle of an intrinsic independence of the Spirit visà-vis any of its historical or dynastic supports and vehicles.[58] This is also the reason why Schuon cannot follow Corbin when the latter exclusively derives the reality of esoterism from a hermeneutics of the *Qurʾān*. For Schuon, to say that the *Qurʾān* necessarily contains the principles of esoterism, if only elliptically or symbolically, does not imply that gnosis must necessarily be dependent on scripture for its unfolding and realization. The Intellect is the immanent *Qurʾān* and the immanent Imām, and both the formal *Qurʾān* and Imām constitute providential crystallizations of these inner realities that provide the faithful and the mystic with the means to reconnect with their intellective heart.

Be it in the realm of spiritual life or on the level of mystical speculations, Sufism presents Schuon with a kind of "enigma" that can only be solved through the distinction between two esoterisms: "possible Sufism" and "necessary Sufism," or "average Sufism" and "quintessential Sufism." The "necessity" of Sufism stems from the very nature of Islam, and is therefore a mere unfolding, as it were, of the *shahādah* on all levels of human reality. Schuon summarizes this "necessary Sufism" as comprising discernment, concentration, and conformity. Discernment refers to the discrimination primarily entailed by the first *shahādah,* whereas concentration and conformity correspond, respectively, to the aspects of *dhikr* and *faqr* ensuing from the second *shahādah*–while being also obviously spiritual consequences of the first *shahādah*. By contrast with this "necessary Sufism" there has existed a Sufism—or rather a whole set of forms of Sufism, which is only "possible" in the sense that it responds to the needs of particular vocations, circumstances, or mentalities and, although not incompatible with Islam, is not intrinsically resultant from its archetype and *Weltanschauung*. Because "possible Sufism" has manifested the multiplicity of its forms in the most peripheral, and therefore visible, circles in the world of *tasawwuf*, it has become more or less identified as the "average" or common form of Sufism. This de facto confusion between the norm as necessity and the norm as fact makes it necessary, acccording to Schuon, to distill the quintessence of Sufism on the basis of the principles that we have sketched in the previous pages, that is to say within the perspective of an integral and consequential understanding of the *shahādatain*. This distinction between "quintessential" and "average" Sufism may raise, in the eyes of not a few readers, the question of the historical reality of the former: Is not "quintessential Sufism" a merely "abstract" synthesis of principles, the concrete manifestations of which cannot easily be found in the actual history

of Sufism. Schuon's response to this objection is twofold: first, there have in
fact been representatives of Sufism who expressed in their works the quintessence of *tasawwuf* showing no, or minimal, compromises with the detours that
we have outlined earlier—Abdul Jabbār al-Niffārī being the epitome of this
kind of purely gnostic *tasawwuf*;[59] and second, the relative paucity of these representatives is to be explained by the primarily oral mode of transmission of
the most subtle and profound doctrines, not to mention the fact that the proponents of such a form of Sufism could not but be very reserved in the outer
manifestation of its tenets, considering the inherent limitations of the exclusive and limited confessional outlook with which they were surrounded.

The portraits of Sufism, and more generally of "inner Islam," that have
emerged from the preceding pages display certain constant and reoccurring
traits throughout the various contributions, while betraying some important
differences in outlook. The most obvious lesson to be drawn from reading all
four authors pertains to the authentically Islamic roots of *tasawwuf* and Islamic
gnosis, whether in the context of Sunni spirituality or Shī'ite theosophy as
approached by Corbin. Without denying the peripheral influence on Islamic
spirituality of such philosophical currents as Neoplatonism or such methodical practices as found in Hindu, or even Taoist, contemplative disciplines, our
authors affirm and substantiate the specifically Quranic and Muhammadan
nature of Sufism. They also concur in introducing the latter as the culmination or the path to the *haqīqah* of Islam as such. The ways they reach and
unfold these conclusions reveal, however, important differences that have
implications on their respective definitions of inner Islam. Massignon and
Corbin articulate their vision of Islamic spirituality within the framework
of a study of the foundational function of the *Qur'ān*. This commonality of
framework does not preclude some very important divergences with regard
to the ways in which inner Islam has gained access to the mystical meaning of
the Book. Massignon's perspective is primarily, albeit not exclusively, akin to
an understanding of the *Qur'ān* as a compendium of the ascetic virtues upon
which is based the development of a "rule of perfection" in early Sufism. For
him it is clear that this rule, which he envisaged as parallel but not similar
to the discipline of the Christian Fathers, reveals, from within the Muslim
consciousness, a desire for union that cannot be satisfied within the confines
of the Law. Sufism reproduces the patterns of the Prophet's contemplative
vocation, and the ascending journey of his *Mi'rāj*, while laying open the intimate shortcomings of Muslim devotion. By contrast, Corbin's emphasis on
the intrinsic bond between Islamic mysticism and scripture postulates the
need for an entrance into the esoteric or "real" meaning of the *Qur'ān*, and
hence the imperative co-presence of an initiator into that meaning, namely
the Imām. Inner Islam can be defined, in this context, as a coincidencial
event conjoining the unveiling of the interior meaning of the Book and the

revelation of the inner angel of the soul.] Such an understanding of Islamic spirituality is very closely linked to the principles of *Shī'a* Islam, and actually interprets the whole of *tasawwuf* as stemming from the latter. A critical appraisal of both Massignon's and Corbin's contributions would have to take account of the underlying Christian current that flows into their work. This is not to say, as too many Muslims have argued, that the two French Islamicists have provided their readers with Christianized versions of Islam. Such opinions do not do justice to the roots of their scholarship in the soil of Islamic texts and concrete spiritual expressions informed by the *Qur'ān*. It remains that their spiritual sensibilities and heritage may have predisposed them to highlight, and sometimes overemphasize, aspects of Islamic spirituality that should have been envisaged within the balancing context of the entire tradition. As Michel Chodkiewicz has argued:

> Massignon, up to the vocabulary of his translations (and the choice of the word "Passion") had not resisted the temptation of 'Christianizing' Hallāj, even raising thereby a fairly suspicious interest in some Christian circles and leading to a concomitant devalorization of other faces of Islamic spirituality.[60]

Corbin's sources and affinities led him to restrict artificially the world of inner Islam to a very specific imamology, an orientation that situates the largest segments of Sufism in an oddly displaced context that hardly makes sense of the richness, diversity, and self-productive energy of Sunni Sufism. It is as if the importance of Corbin's discovery of the uncharted territories of Shī'ite imamology had led him to artificially downplay the spiritual depth and strength of Sunni Islam. Not unconnected with this overemphasis, one must mention the stress on the imaginal world of visions and auditions, the importance of which, in Corbin's view of Sufism, may be deemed disproportionate, considering that the ultimate goal of classical *tasawwuf* has consistently been envisaged as a state of extinction and permanence in God, irrespective of occasional visionary mediations. As for Massignon, his virtual reduction of Sufism to the Quranic foundations of *mujāhadah* (fight against the soul) and the mystical interferences of Christic archetypes in Islam, cannot but be considered as highly selective and even idiosyncratic in its treatment of the material. On the other hand, the respective genius of the two Islamicists has unveiled and elucidated immense areas of mystical Islam, while their often very personal focus and treatment of Sufism has contributed to an approach to the spiritual arcana of Islam in a fresh, regenerating, and seminal fashion. The intimate conjunction of personal engagement, spiritual vocation, and scholarly work to which their life bears witness has introduced a new methodology in matters of mystical studies, dispelling the narrowness and sterility of alleged scientific objectivity and scholarly detachment, to propounding a phenomenological, faith-centered apprehension of the religious fact. Beyond the differences that separate their scholarly procedures from more exclusively spiritual and gnostic modes of exposition, it is actually this spirit of spiritual participation in inner Islam that relates Massignon's and Corbin's works to those of Schuon and Guénon.

The most striking aspect of Guénon's treatment of Sufism is the manner in which it is virtually independent from a consideration of the essentials of the Islamic faith, or the particular religious perspective propounded by Islam. If Massignon's and Corbin's readings of inner Islam are based on a prime consideration of the very basis of the faith, that is, the *Qur'ān,* as well as upon the spiritual sources of the tradition, Guénon's esoteric Islam appears in his work as one of the manifestations of an initiatory esoterism that is everywhere and always the same. As one among several spiritual idioms in the domain of esoteric science, Sufism merely reveals its specificity in some of the fundamental symbols in which its doctrines and methods are couched. One could not be at a further distance from Massignon's painstaking cross-examination of the ascetic implications of Sufi terminology and the immanent, concrete, historical components of the early development of *tasawwuf* than with Guénon's survey of universal metaphysics through Sufi concepts and symbols. The living fire of ascetic and ecstatic Sufism that is the focus of Massignon sharply contrasts with the theoretical crystal of Guénon's exposition of metaphysics, a contrast that is suggested to us by the title of Xavier Accart's article devoted to a comparative study of the two figures, and by Najmoudine Bammate's description of the two men: "(. . .) with Massignon, there was such a violence! . . . He was a man of fire, whereas Guénon was a diaphanous, translucid being, he was a crystal, a diamond. They moved in dimensions of being that were unlike."[61] Whereas Massignon devoted himself to unburying the principles of Sufism in the most immediate supports of spiritual life in Islam, Guénon shed light on some of the most central notions of *tasawwuf* from the standpoint of pure universal principles, the discovery of which had very little, if anything, to do with an engaged and systematic study of the historical development of Sufism. While the two men could not meet on the levels of their apprehension of Sufism, we would like to argue that their works find a point of articulation, to the extent that it is possible, in Schuon's presentation of Sufism. What Schuon's presentation may be deemed to have in common with Massignon's is the sense of the human that it involves in the spiritual life. Although the sources of Schuon's pages on the spiritual and moral dimensions of Sufism are significantly different from Massignon's—pertaining as they do to a direct participation in the life and spiritual economy of the tradition, rather than resulting from a scholarly study of its original sources—they nevertheless share in a spiritual sensitivity to the specificity and emphasis of Muslim virtues and devotion. Schuon's description of *tasawwuf* is far from being merely experimental; it is also grounded in a meditation on the Prophetic exemplar, which is itself envisaged as a manifestation of universal principles. While essentially sharing in Guénon's concept of a universal wisdom tradition, the multiple forms of which are circumstantial adaptations to the particular needs of such and such a historical or cultural context, Schuon is much more attentive than Guénon to characterizing the nature of inner Islam from the starting point of the central symbols and concepts of the Islamic creed itself. This allows for an integral and circumstantiated view of Islamic mysticism, one that does not blur the originality of its spiritual language while nevertheless relating it most explicitly to other esoteric expressions of the doctrine of Unity. Schuon's approach leads him thereby to establish distinctions, within the world of *tasawwuf*, between essential and contingent spiritual manifestations. While some may fault Schuon for a tendency to "abstract" and systematize such essentials in a way that amounts to a debatable choice of elements, and perhaps to a reconstruction of the tradition itself, Schuon's work in a sense preempts these objections by focusing on the most defining element of Islam from the very standpoint of its fundamental creed, that is, the *shahādah* and its unfolding in and through the fundamental religious practices of Islam. Such a focus results in bringing out the interior substance of the religion from the formal clothing of its message, thereby highlighting the paradox of the "discontinuous continuity" between outer and inner Islam.

esoteric dependent on exoteric but there is a clear division btwn. the two...

Chapter Three

THE *QUR'ĀN*

The contemporary renewal of religions bears witness to a quest for criteria of certainty in a world that is bereft of absolute benchmarks and appears increasingly inclined to accommodate a wide relativistic consensus as a guardrail against tyrannies and brutal exploitation. This need for certainty has primarily been focused on sacred Scriptures conceived as repositories of ultimate truth. The fact is that contemporary religious discourse can hardly rely on anything other than the bedrock objectivity of the revealed word since all other sources of religious knowledge have been made unavailable by the decline or collapse of what could be called the great civilizations of the sacred. Theological dogmas have been discarded by most in the name of individual critical inquiry. The religious *magisterium* has lost much of its authority and power on account of democratic concepts. Tradition has virtually collapsed under the onslaught of a pervasive spirit of reformation and adaptation to contemporary and circumstantial norms and practices. As for sanctity, or the summit of human realization of the religious ideals that used to inspire and nurture the communities of the faithful, it has become a purely moral ideal, while the old figure of the "man of God" has receded from the sphere of reality to enter that of nostalgic legend. Neither the saint nor the holy sage remains as a familiar reference in a world that is more intent on emphasizing the realm of action and worldly endeavors than the inner domain of self-transformation and self-transcendence. In fact, the perception of saintly sages has been obscured by the appearance of the self-styled guru on the contemporary stage; at best, sanctity is equated with admirable heights of selfless humanitarian service to mankind or tireless work for world peace and cross-cultural understanding, sometimes informed by religious faith.

By contrast with those receding principles and phenomena, the sacred text remains at the center of the religious stage, both because of its linguistic and literal objectivity and because its accessibility makes it an immediate reference and support for all those who want to buttress their faith or find a firm foundation upon which their quest for meaning may grow. Let us add that Scripture is almost as central to the arguments of secular malcontents of religious revival and opponents of its social influence as it is to the faith of religious movements and individuals themselves. Most intellectual and social critiques of religion are based upon historical or linguistic deconstructions of Scripture, while most inter-religious debates and polemics center on the "word of God" and its interpretations.

The irruption of militant and political Islam on the contemporary stage has illustrated in a most direct fashion this power of the Book. Political and social objectives of various kinds have been supported by Quranic references and quotations. Scriptural arguments and counterarguments have been pro-pounded by jurists, polemicists, and analysts to justify or condemn acts of political and religious violence. In Christianity as well the renewal of Evange-lism and the spread of so-called fundamentalist movements have been predi-cated on a culture of the Book. Much of the inspiration that animates the Evangelical upsurge in North America is associated with personal reading, meditation, and commentary on Scripture and public preaching of it.

While drawing the attention of our readers to the contributions of these four masters of French Islamology,[1] we willingly acknowledge that the con-temporary situation of Islam is, by and large, far removed from the metaphysi-cal heights and mystical dimensions that characterize their works. However, it is not unreasonable to think that a meditation on these "ambassadors of mystical Islam" may help reframe the perception of the Islamic tradition as a whole, at least among those perplexed but unjaundiced observers whose understanding has primarily been informed by the most outward and adver-tised aspects of the contemporary avatars of this religion. We will argue that such is especially the case with respect to the role of Scripture in religious consciousness and practice.

Massignon's Islamology, and his thought in general, lies at the junction of the eternal and the historical, the personal and the collective. This accounts for the extraordinary scope of his works on Islam, which touch upon virtually all the aspects of the Islamic civilization, from economic practices and popular folklore to ritual practices and the heights of mysticism. Massignon could write about the use of constellations for orientation in Medieval Arab seafar-ing as well as refer to the theological debates of Baghdad under the Abbasids; he could also relate those two topics to the spiritual development of a mystical figure like Mansūr al-Hallāj. Such ability to relate seemingly disparate reali-ties is not only the expression of an intellectual virtuosity on the part of the scholar, it is also, and above all, a manifestation of the intellectual and spiritual outlook of a profound and complex thinker.

Any discussion of Massignon's meditation on sacred Scripture must begin, it seems, with his profound conviction that the inner faith and commitment of a person—and particularly that of a spiritually exceptional person—is bound to the collective destinies of a whole group, nay of the whole of mankind. However, such a relationship is neither static nor horizontal, neither purely "economic" nor strictly human and terrestrial. In fact, Massignon asserts that the person and the social collectivity to which he or she belongs intersect at the point of resolution of social aporias or crises, which can only be resolved by a supernatural consciousness of "divine grace in us." A true person is therefore much more than an individual, a true person is a guest—the guest of a "foreign" presence accepted as messenger of the One who alone "can say truly 'I', in us."[2] If one were to propose a definition of Scripture in Massignon's outlook one could suggest that it is like the sacred trace of this visitation. Bearing testimony to this irruption of the transcendent crystallized in the sacred text, but in itself free to blow where it lists, the true person is a witness of grace and a sacrificial intercessor whose "isolated heroic act . . . possesses a trans-social axial value."[3] In other words, the receptivity to the Spirit that translates into heroic witnessing frees the spiritual person from historical conditioning while contributing to untie the knots of collective history. This heroic testimony is understood by Massignon as the *fiat*—let it be!—of the soul that consents to the divine visitation, in the image of the perfect submission of the Virgin to the Word. This consenting is therefore the very ground of the most authentic forms of action since it delivers the soul's doing from the intricacies and oppositions that imprison mankind by inspiring it with a pure, surging, and uncompromising quality.

The parallel between the scriptural text and human history manifests itself most clearly in the context of transcendence. Disconnected from the latter, both fail to teach their ultimate and truly real lesson. For Massignon, it is as true to say that history cannot be thought to be independent from a "finalist structural continuity" as it is evident that "linguistic facts" can be explained only "phonologically" and not merely "phonetically."[4] Historical finality must become "inwardly" intelligible in and through the spiritual continuum that it projects, which means that it requires true persons—such as defined above—to extract the meaning of the common trial staged by history. An individual is no more than "a differentiated element that is dependant upon a social group that remains its natural end,"[5] whereas a true person is like a supernatural flowering out of the collective destiny, the meaning of which it delivers, in both senses of revealing and setting free.

Analogically, linguistic facts must be understood in the context of the whole function and finality of language. But this finality is ordinarily obscured by the adscititious aspects of words, such as their communicative and rhetorical character. What sets scriptural language—and exceptional occurrences of mystical language—apart from other linguistic phenomena is that, like the Qur'ān, it "opens a perspective on the ultimate ends of language."[6] The paradox of this linguistic opening of a trans-linguistic perspective is intimately connected, in Massignon's thought, with a privilege of Semitic languages, and particularly Arabic, as fostering a specific "mode of recollection." This

spiritual eminence of the Semitic languages flows from some of their mor-
phological and syntactic characters, beginning with the importance of the
tri-consonantal root. Massignon refers to the Sufi notion of *tadmīn*, which
conveys a semantic implicitness, insertion, and involution—what the French
Islamologist translates as "germinative burying"—to allude to this self-en-
closed seed of meaning that is productive of spiritual understanding by implication, though being less akin to hermeneutic exteriorization than to a kind
of secret conception, like in the archetypical instance of Mary conceiving the
Word.[7] Therefore, when relating this to Scripture, the matter is not to decipher analytically, nor even to apply verses as moral formulae, but to bury a
mystical seed within the soil of the soul. This seed is an image of the "foreign
host" that the soul must welcome in inner hospitality.

   What are the characteristics of the Arabic and Quranic language that
invite such a meaningful receptivity and recollection? Massignon defines
Arabic as being "hard," "coagulated," "condensed," "metallic," "crystalline,"
"silex-like," and "dense." Arabic "coagulates and condenses . . . the idea it
wants to express . . . without bending under the grip of the individual speaking it".[8] It is characterized by an intensely expressive power of resistance and
irreducible objectivity. It resists the need for explicitness and explications.
This resistance is expressed, in the *Qur'ān*, by the fixity of a consonantal body
that is immovable, while only a small measure of leeway is consented, in some
rare instances, to vocalization. By observing the linguistic phenomenon of an
objective resistance to human instrumentalization on the part of the *Qur'ān*,
Massignon can emphasize that the Book is not merely an object of communi-
cation and "commerce," nor a poetical work, nor an intellectual treatise. Far
and high above these reductions of its literality to immediate ends, the *Qur'ān*
"can have a grasp on Reality;"[9] it can "allow us to access Reality, for it contains an anagogic meaning, a harpoon designed to draw the soul to God."[10]
Massignon oddly makes use of the French verb *gauchir*, to twist, to suggest
the way in which the language of the *Qur'ān* works on the Arabic syntax to
prompt its reader to "take off" from earth. In other words, the *Qur'ān* does
not leave the ordinary syntax unaffected: It uses it in order to operate a change
of perspective. Its language is not a confirmation or a justification of terrestrial, literal, formal existence. It takes us beyond words by "twisting" the
customary order of language. Massignon's recognition of an "anagogic meaning" in the *Qur'ān* makes it plain that, for him, this Book cannot be classified
among human works or mere personal inspiration.[11]

   The "transcending" and "liberating" function of Quranic language is
also evident in the two forms of "originality" that Massignon highlights as
being representative of the Book's mode of expression. First, there is a freedom from the magic rhythm of poetry, the latter pertaining to a technique
that is still plainly akin to the realm of nature. The "liberty" of the *Qur'ān*
vis-à-vis prosody is in that sense the symptom of an irruption of grace that
breaks the mold of human techniques, notwithstanding the fact that meters

and harmonies are reflections of an ontological order that transcends mankind's terrestrial condition. Second, the *Qur'ān* is *maknūn*, "well-guarded" (Yusuf Ali) or "kept hidden" (Marmaduke Pickthall), and therefore can be touched only by *al-mutahharūn*, the "purified ones" (LVI, 77–78). For Massignon, then, the *Qur'ān* is not a means of union with God: The Book keeps man at a distance from God, as it were, while obviously dispensing its teachings, or divine signs, to him:

> Single bearing upheld between the Creator and the creature, the *Qur'ān* does not trace a sign of union, but one of separation, the seal of forbiddance, a formal and permanent intellectual miracle perceived by a direct illumination of reason, each single verse being an integral proof of God.[12]

In this, Massignon undoubtedly reveals the spiritual preferences stemming from his own confessional outlook, by reserving the divine and sacramental privilege of union to the redemptive mediation of Christ. While acknowledging the analogy that associates the relationship between the Prophet and the *Qur'ān* with the bond relating the Virgin Mary and Christ, Massignon downplays the immanent "divinity" of the Book. In doing so, Massignon is in no way unfaithful to the Islamic overemphasis upon God's transcendence—as expressed most emphatically by the *Mu'tazilite* rejection of the notion of an uncreated *Qur'ān*—but he may tend to omit or underestimate, at least in this particular context, the theurgic and transformative dimension of the *Qur'ān* in Islamic life and practice and its immanent divinity within the soul. Massignon is keen on introducing the *Qur'ān* in terms of its exalted transcendence and supreme incomparability—*i'jāz al-Qur'ān*, not only because of the Islamic insistence upon these aspects of the Book, but also because he preserves thereby the exclusiveness of the sacramental economy of Christ's Redemption. The paradox is that Massignon's reading of the *Qur'ān* may burke any sense of sacramental union by highlighting its emphasis on the transcendence of the Divine, while elevating the Book to the selfsame forbidding realm as God himself. In this view, the *Qur'ān* draws its transcendent divinity from its function as an inspiring but prohibitive gateway to Divinity.

If Henry Corbin departs from his teacher Massignon, it is precisely—among other important aspects of his work—inasmuch as he emphasizes the participative and unitive dimension of the *Qur'ān* and its hermeneutics. The starting point of Corbin's meditation on the hermeneutics of the *Qur'ān* is undoubtedly encapsulated in his remark that "the mode of understanding (of the Book) is conditioned by the mode of being of him who understands."[13] In other words, one cannot understand the Book unless one already *knows* what it means. There is a profound correlation between the semantic latency of scriptural meaning and the spiritual virtuality of the soul for "the believer's whole inner ethos derives from his mode of understanding."[14] Spiritual hermeneutics is a reciprocal and gradual actualization of the unfathomable depth of scriptural meaning and the spiritual consciousness of the reader. More specifically, a meditative contact with the *Qur'ān* discloses her own true nature to the soul, by actualizing her relationship with her Lord, that is, the aspect of the Divine that "faces" the soul and constitutes her deepest ontological and spiritual ground. In reverse, the believer, through *lectio divina*, actualizes layers and aspects of the sacred text that lie within its inexhaustible wealth of meaning. Reading Scripture means to reconduct inward what is outward, that is, to operate a kind of inner "re-conversion" of the linguistic form of the Scripture. Such an inward reversion is precisely possible because the letter of the *Qur'ān* is none other than the analytic and external manifestation of the *haqīqah*, the true meaning of the text.[15] Therefore, while being exoterically a guarded book, the *Qur'ān* is esoterically an open book in the sense that each of its verses corresponds to a state of being or a state of consciousness. The literal meaning of the Book is not discarded, since its negation would amount to depriving the esoteric from a symbolic foundation—that is, the exoteric letter, from which to gain access, through *ta'wīl*, to its arcanum. The literal meaning of the text is like a body to a soul, or a protective container to a content.[16] It is by virtue of this correspondence between the two that *ta'wīl* may occur: *ta'wīl* consists in reconducting what has been received, that is the scriptural *sacratum*, to the very source from which its descent, *tanzīl*, originated. Spiritual hermeneutics pertains to levels of meaning that are also levels of being.

In his commentary of an anonymous treatise from seventeenth-century Persia on the seven esoteric meanings of the *Qur'ān*, Corbin refers to the letter of the Book as a mirror that reflects the Divine Reality itself.[17] More precisely, this Reality is, at it were, modulated along a plurality of spiritual levels in a gradation that ranges from the ascetic and dualistic meaning of *mujāhada*, or spiritual warfare, to the ultimate and plenary station of *wāsil*, "the one who has gained access to God." To deny this stratified polysemy of the Book amounts to denying both the "divine" depth of Scripture by flattening its meaning and the infinity of its facets, which are as many "revelations" within the myriad of human mirrors. It therefore amounts to denying the metaphysical infinitude of the Divine since each soulish crystallization is like a projection in the play of the innumerable divine aspects that lie in the inexhaustible Divine Treasure. On the highest spiritual level, the human soul is a perfect mirror of "the modalities in which is realized the epiphany of Divine Attributes."[18] This supreme degree of both autology and theosophy corresponds to the inner reality to which Henry Corbin likes to refer by quoting the *hadīth*: "He who knows himself knows his Lord." On that level the soul understands itself as being both created and, in its essence, uncreated.

Conversely, this prophetic *logion* could also be paraphrased as, "he who knows himself knows his *Qur'ān*," thereby bringing to the fore the coincidence between the created appearance of the *Qur'ān* in the consciousness of the faithful and its supreme identity with the Word. Such an understanding transcends the terms of the theological debate over the created versus uncreated nature of the Book. It is the best antidote against an abstract, literalist, and totalitarian perception of the Book as "absolute otherness" by means of a strong affirmation of its dimension of immanence, while undercutting, at the same time, the facile relativism of contemporary religious discourses that reduce the Book to matters of private opinion or feeling. In fact, there is perhaps no better way to suggest this mysterious paradox than by referring to Corbin's commentary on Ibn 'Arabī's statement, "No one will understand what we have just said except for him who is himself, in his person (*fī nafsihi*) a 'Koran.'"[19]

The meaning of "being a *Qur'ān*" is profoundly connected to the fundamental function of sacred Scripture in Islamic mysticism, that of *dhikr*, or remembrance of God, and to the highest stages of spiritual realization, that is, *fanā'*, extinction or disappearance, and *baqā'*, subsistence or permanence. The former is often described in terms of a "dissolution of self," an "annihilation," which one would be mistaken to understand literally. Sometimes *fanā'* is related to *baqā'* in the way the disappearance of the servant's qualities are related to the establishment of God's attributes. Corbin's commentary on Ibn 'Arabī is primarily focused on highlighting the crucial fact that *fanā'* amounts to a kind of metaphysical indistinction—since the self has "disappeared," whereas *baqā'* is characterized by a restoration of the servant in his metaphysical relationship to his Lord. This restoration is not equivalent to the stage preceding *fanā'* but it takes place, on the contrary, on the very basis and the very context of this extinction.

The respective terms used by Ibn 'Arabī to refer to these two states of being are *Qur'ān* and *furqān*, the latter being one of the names of the *Qur'ān* forged on the Arabic root FRQ, which implies the idea of splitting, separating, and dividing, whereas the roots attributed to *Qur'ān*—indicating reading aloud, that is, QRN and QR'—refer, respectively, to the idea of tying and bringing together and that of collecting. By contrast with Massignon's perspective, Corbin demonstrates that the *Qur'ān* is indeed unifying, but that it is also discriminative—as *furqān*—on the basis of this "unification," *tawhīd*, and therefore "instorative" of the true self as it relates to its Lord. The analogy woven by Ibn 'Arabī allows one to understand what could be called the two natures of the Book, first as a source of human disappearance in its "sea of wisdom," that is, union with God, and second as a means of true permanence, since the *Qur'ān* as *furqān* allows one to recover oneself in one's relationship with God as he "speaks" to us.

One of Henry Corbin's main contributions to the comparative study of Western and Islamic philosophy hinged upon a critique of the obstructions to spiritual hermeneutics in Christian Europe and their potential—and by now actual—spread within the Islamic world. The two main points of contention lie in the role of the *magisterium*, on the one hand, and the historicist perspective that has dominated Biblical exegesis, on the other. The first obstacle is perceived by Corbin as an institutional interference that tends to freeze the fluid relationship between the faithful and their God. For Corbin, whose Reformed religious background is seminal in this regard, the light of the relationship between the soul and her Lord has been obfuscated, in the West, by the darkness of an inquisitorial *magisterium*, since as early a period as the second century of Church history.[20] By contrast, Islam is perceived by Corbin as free from the limitations and pressures of an external hermeneutic authority. This situation has been a boon for spiritual hermeneutics, which has manifested itself through a "prophetic" lineage without being unduly obscured by the thick sediment of dogmatic fixation. For Corbin, Shī'ite prophetology and imamology offer avenues of access to a "hiero-history" that is out of reach of institutional reductionism. Quoting Semnānī's distinction between *zamān āfāqī*, objective and quantitative time, and *zamān anfosī*, subjective and qualitative time, Corbin objects to the historicist bent of most Western exegesis by affirming that "there are events which are perfectly *real* without having the reality of events of empirical history".[21] In the Christian West, however, dogmatic exegesis has tended to espouse the historic dimension to the gradual exclusion of the symbolic and theophanic meaning of Scripture. The traditional association of *litera*—the letter of Scripture—with *sensus historicus* already points to an impoverishment of exegetic potentialities on the part of mainstream Christianity.

Now this is precisely what has become a pressing danger in Islam, given the exclusive consideration of neo-puritanical and modernist Islam for the historical "letter" of the Quranic text. In this context, a confusion between "symbol" and "allegory" has tended to deplete the esoteric wealth of meaning in the *Qur'ān*. Allegorical readings dispense with the ontological and spiritual strata of Scripture by flattening our understanding of symbolic expression into a merely conventional and artificial exercise. Only a clear apprehension of religion as symbol can give access to the esoteric layer of meaning and reality that is "symbolized." In the *Qur'ān* as in other similar Scriptures, the religious textuality that is literally spelled out is the symbol of the hidden reality or archetype that is symbolized and that stands as the true and re-integrating meaning. The latter frees one from the strictures of historical consciousness whereas the former imprisons one in it; in the words of Nāsir-e Khosraw, "the exoteric is in perpetual flux along cycles and periods of the world; the esoteric is a divine Energy that is not subjected to becoming."[22] So, far from being the solid and unmoving ground that neo-literalists and fundamentalists desperately strive to protect, the external and literal meaning of Scripture is constantly subjected to transformation. This is the paradox weighing upon those who try to fix the exoteric irrespective of its essential relationship to the esoteric: unable to reach the bedrock of the sacratum, they offer its surface to the historical and ideological whims of the moment.

While Corbin's understanding of esoterism is a priori hermeneutical in nature, while also being finalized by an emphatic affirmation of the primacy of the relationship of the soul with her Lord, Schuon's esoteric perspective is akin to the Advaitin principle that "only *Atman* is real" and "everything is *Atman*," thereby highlighting the function of sacred forms as *upāyā* or "saving mirages," a Buddhist concept that has key implications in Schuon's metaphysical and spiritual lexicon. Such a conception is, in a sense, akin to the notion of symbol as it was developed and illustrated by René Guénon in most of his writings; the symbol being a form in which the ineffable realities of the intelligible and divine realms come to manifest themselves and become "legible," as it were, on the level of formal and terrestrial existence. The symbol is therefore a direct appearance of the realities it symbolizes. Whether manifested in a graphic, auditive, or gestural mode, it provides the means of a direct assimilation of realities situated beyond the epistemological horizon of reason. One of the primary reasons why Guénon's work is practically silent on the question of the *Qur'ān* and, more generally, the function of Scripture lies probably in the fact that the latter are exclusively considered by him as specific modes of the universal lexicon and syntax of symbols. While sharing in this fundamentally symbolist understanding of Scripture, Schuon is more interested in situating the specificity of the *Qur'ān* both in its metaphysical "grounding," as it were, and in its epistemological and spiritual implications.

In so far as they are *upāyā*, Scriptures are absolute with regard to the essence of their message but relative in their form, their essence being none other than the very immanence of the Self, the language of which is diversified and crystallized in and through them. Scriptures are binding in that they are the vehicles of the Absolute, but their relativity appears in the obscurities, even contradictions, that result from the contact between two incommensurable realities, that is, the Divine Reality and the language of men. Accordingly, Schuon refers to the revelation of Islam, the *Qur'ān*, as the outer and formal manifestation of the Divine Intellect, which is none other than the "Uncreated *Qur'ān* " posited by Ash'arī and most of the Sunni *Kalām* but rejected by *Mu'tazilite* theology.[23] For Schuon, the linguistic *Qur'ān* is the formal objectivation of Divine Intelligence, while the human reflection of the latter is like the subjective revelation of the Book.[24] This means that the Book is an instrument of discernment—whence its name of *furqān*, distinction or separation,[25] between absolute Reality and relative reality on the one hand, and a means of union with Reality on the other. The content, or the message, of the *Qur'ān* is a relentless reminder of the absolute primacy of God, with all its eschatological consequences, while its linguistic form, both visual and phonetic, is the vehicle of a saving and transformative grace actualized, primarily within the framework of canonical prayer, by the daily reciting and psalmody of its verses.

To use two terms that are recurrent in Schuon's vocabulary, it could be said that the *Qur'ān* is both Truth and Presence, the capital letters being used here to indicate that these two aspects are to be understood as divine modes, and not merely as human concepts. The element of Truth (*al-Haqq*, the Truth, is a divine Name in Islam) is akin to doctrine as a crystallization of the teachings included in the Book. This doctrinal dimension of the *Qur'ān* as Truth is foundational with respect to the whole tradition, but it must be irrigated, as it were, by the element of Presence, without which it would fossilize into formalism, or even harden into fanatic literalism. Presence is akin to sanctity and the sense of the sacred; it is in a sense the very ambience of tradition as a whole. When this perfume of Presence is lost or forgotten, scriptural words tend to dry up, and they can even become the vehicles of political passions that coalesce with the residue of formal religion, particularly in the modern world when ideologies have become substitutes for a genuine sense of the absolute.

As for Presence, it must be envisaged within the framework of Truth in order to radiate in all aspects of traditional life as well as dispense its blessings over the course of time. Moreover, Presence does not guarantee in and of itself the impossibility of misinterpretations and wanderings, nor is it immune to the dangers of degeneracy in superstition. This explains why the *Qur'ān* is much more than a doctrinal book—being a theurgic and transformative sacred text—but also why its content needs to be unfolded through the diversity of authoritative and explicit commentaries. With respect to the question of Scripture, the esoteric and traditionalist sides of Schuon's metaphysical position cannot be separated.

The *Qur'ān* contains all that needs to be known and all that saves, at least virtually. This does not mean, however, that its content is immediately and obviously available to all of its readers. First of all, there is undoubtedly an immense gap between the divine Scripture and human understanding. In his chapter "Keys to the Bible," included in *Light on the Ancient Worlds*, Schuon specifies that the literal meaning of a sacred text like the Bible or the *Qur'ān* is almost never sufficient in itself to make sense. There is in this remark, when it is really understood, a solid protection against the well-intentioned illusions of contemporary individualism in scriptural matters. In this connection, Schuon is particularly sensitive to the paradoxes, obscurities, and allusiveness of the *Qur'ān*, and his work provides us with several examples of esoteric exegesis.[26] The unfathomable and at times unsettling dimension of Scripture stems from the fact that it cannot simply be defined by the themes it addresses, nor by the way it addresses them, but rather by the ontological source of its manifestation. The essence of the Book is neither a matter of content nor one of style; it is a matter of ontological origin. This origin determines both the content and the style, but not in a way that is *outwardly* evident to the reader. Speaking of the Qur'ān, Schuon has no qualms acknowledging the fact that its immediate content is neither always sublime nor even without apparent incoherence, and the same holds true for the Bible. The Qur'ān deals with a wide spectrum of realities, from the legal realm to the eschatological dimension, and not a few of its passages are a challenge to commonsensical understanding. It is precisely, and paradoxically, in this unevenness and abruptness that, among other ways, the very identity of the text as sacred may be revealed. This disproportion must dispose both to a sense of awe—a sense of the sacred, and to a reliance on traditional exegesis, without which much of Scripture remains an enigma.[27] In a way, the disproportion between the Divine origin and the human text is such that it makes it impossible for the supernatural to manifest itself in a direct, clear, absolute manner in the terrestrial substance of the Book.

This should serve as a reminder of the fact that one cannot approach Scripture as one would approach a human text, however sublime and inspired it may be. The notion of Revelation, without which the very idea of Scripture becomes moot, entails a totally different relationship with the text, not that the latter is endowed with a transparent authority resulting from the words themselves, but rather on account of that which, beneath and between the words, bears witness to a Reality that cannot be confined within the nets of grammatical and historical determinations. The relationship with the Book partakes of the sense of the sacred which, according to Schuon, may best be defined as the sense of "the Center within the periphery." God is mysteriously present in the Book, and the obscurity and incoherence that we may encounter in it, far from being reasons for dismissing its message, are among the evidence of the transcendence of its origin. A clear awareness of the symbolic nature of the Book flows from that sense of mystery; literal intelligibility, as claimed by a modern consciousness informed by rationalistic categories, is indeed irrelevant to such a sacred view of reality. In this context, Schuon, like Corbin, distinguishes the symbolic from the allegoric, the latter being a mere indirect figuration, whereas the former involves an essential identity between the symbol and the symbolized. The symbol, and the Book as such, is not one element within a mental correlation but the emergence of an ontological unity, an opening onto the Divine that transcends its formal "contours." Any verse from the Book is in that sense the very appearance of the divine Word. This amounts to saying that, from a subjective point of view, the Book is the language of the Self that is mysteriously immanent in the soul.

As we have mentioned above, Schuon conceives of the Book as the outward manifestation of the Divine Intellect, whereas intellection is like a subjective revelation. This amounts to saying that the Book is a projection of the universal Intellect, or a crystallization of the Logos. Its reality cannot be separated from the human manifestation of the Logos, which is expressed by the fact that 'Ā'isha, when asked about the Prophet, answered that his nature (khuluq) was like the Qur'ān. The Book is, in that sense, a mold into which all the faithful are summoned to enter. The sacred text is first of all a spiritual reality, a spiritual perfume as it were; in the absence of a sensitivity to

that perfume, any approach to the scriptural literality is fraught with dangers
and "risks engendering grave doctrinal, psychological, and historical errors."
For Schuon, the molding and informing quality of the *Qur'ān* is like a flux
adapted to the needs of the rhythm of the soul:

> The soul, which is accustomed to the flux of phenomena, yields to this
> flux without resistance; it lives in phenomena and is by them divided and
> dispersed—even more than that, it actually becomes what it thinks and
> does. The revealed Discourse has the virtue of accepting this tendency
> while reversing its movement thanks to the celestial nature of the content
> and the language, so that the fishes of the soul swim without distrust and
> with their habitual rhythm into the divine net. [28]

As the *Sunna* of the Prophet consists in a multiplicity of actions and attitudes
that serve as an exemplar and a mold for the entire life of the faithful, so
does the *Qur'ān* espouse the plurality of the soul's needs, as it were. In fact,
the *Sunna* and the *Qur'ān* converge in the multiplicity of the Islamic *formulae*
stemming from the *āyāt* and the customs and actions of the Prophet. These
formulas, such as *subhana Allāh* (Glory to God), *in shā'Allah* (God willing), *al-
hamdu li'Llāh* (Praise to God), and so forth, are woven into the entire Muslim
existence. In all cases, however, there lies a unity of essence behind the multiplicity that mercifully envelops the diversity of human existence. Just as there
is an essential *Sunna* that consists in the fundamental virtues of the Prophet, so
there is a sense in which the whole *Qur'ān* is absorbed into the essential unity
of the Divine Name. For Schuon, the Name *Allāh* is the "quintessence of all
the Quranic formulas" and it contains, therefore, the whole Book.[29] This is
another way of saying, methodically speaking, that the remembrance of God
that is crystallized by the utterance of this Name is "greater" (*wa lā dhikru'Llāh
akbar*) and in fact recapitulates the whole religion. The Name is the essence
of the Book and it is, as such, mysteriously indistinguishable from the Self. In
Schuon's integral perspective, which reconciles the devotional depth of the
Psalms and the metaphysical principles of *Advaita Vedānta*, the Book is a priori
the very sign of God's transcendence vis-à-vis mankind but also a posteriori,
and above all, the sacramental symbol of His deepest immanence.

The metaphysical, mystical, and hermeneutic principles that Massignon,
Corbin, and Schuon highlighted provide us with a background that makes it
possible to address some of the problematic concepts and practices of Quranic
reading that have emerged during the last decades. The lessons that we draw
from these works may also be valid, *mutatis mutandis*, for contemporary Christian hermeneutics and Bible reading.

　　There is, first of all, a sense in which our "mystical ambassadors" caution
us against the dangers of linguistic trivialization and abusive historicization

of the *Qur'ān* and Scriptures in general. Whether it be a question of perceiving the *Qur'ān* as a verbal exteriorization of the Intellect, a supra-historic
realm of archetypical layers, or an engulfment in the instantaneity of the
transcendent, it needs to be stressed that the function of the Book is to take
us above our relative conditioning instead of confirming us in our horizontal ways. Scripture is not intended to reinforce our attachment to terrestrial
biases and ideological leanings by giving this attachment a seal of sublimity,
as it were. Scripture should contribute to dissolving our egoistic subjectivity,
not hardening it by a misleading identification of our passions and habits with
the absoluteness of its message. Massignon's *fiat* inspires an attitude of humility and receptivity toward the Book, and the disproportion, highlighted by
Schuon, between the Divine meanings and the human words that are their
means of expression should also infuse our relationship to the Book with a
sense of awe and humility.

As an expression of the divine "otherness," the Arabic substance of the
Qur'ān—with the whole wealth of its semantic associations—must be fully
taken into consideration when one wishes to apply specific verses to current situations, whether apologetically or critically. There is much danger in
bringing Scripture down to the level of linguistic familiarity, if not triviality,
thereby bypassing the symbolic wealth of its raw language and the devotional
sense of mystery that it inspires. Moreover, the "objective hardness" of the
sacred text, if one may say so, should guard one from any facile instrumentalization of isolated verses for the sake of individualistic whims or ideological causes. The type of inner "recollection" that Massignon associates with
the Semitic core of the Book is moreover incompatible with an excessively
analytic conceptualization. It is also deeply incompatible with the kind of dis-
cussant activism and democratic debating that informs the spirit of contemporary Bible groups and Bible readings. A sort of "virginity" or unjaundiced
receptivity is required on the part of the reader, for only such a *vacare Libro*
can bear authentic spiritual fruits. This is the highest meaning of the mystical
practice of *lectio divina*, which is less an active deciphering of concepts than
an increased, silent, receptivity of one's soul to the unexpected lessons of the
Book. A sacred Book is not a source of ideological and moral recipes, but
rather an urgent invitation to live our life on God's terms.

Corbin's emphasis on spiritual hermeneutics reminds us that Scriptures are
not to be apprehended as mere literary or philosophical texts, for they demand
from us a latent intuition of the realities to which they point. Reading Scripture should neither limit nor reify the text. Reading Scripture independently
from the metaphysical and spiritual context that it presupposes is like trying
to read the letters and characters of a text without knowing the language in
which it is written: One may describe the shape of letters, or even identify
these letters, but any real understanding of the meaning of the text is nonetheless precluded by one's fundamental inadequacy to the language and context
in which it makes sense. Consequently, an alert and humble sensitivity to the

depth of meaning of the Book is intimately bound to any degree of awareness of and receptivity to its subjective, transformative, and unifying function. A lack of contemplative attention to the Book, or an ignorance of the exegetic traditions that foster an indirect participation in that contemplative awareness, may lead to hasty literalism and thereby open onto fanatic blindness and religious "idiocy," the term being understood here in its etymological connotations of individual arbitrariness. In fact, Corbin teaches us that such a reductive approach confines the reader to no more than a religious type of idolatry. Such idolatry has always been latent, or even at times manifest, in religious history, but the contemporary context makes it all the more dangerous in that it sets it perilously independent from all traditional and spiritual safeguards. Literalism is an unfortunate limitation; but an ideological reading of the literal meaning is more than that: It is a betrayal of the very spirit of the text by means of a kind of hijacking of its literality.

Such unfortunate—and not infrequent—inclinations are but a caricature of the recognition of the Book as Revelation that Schuon emphasizes as a precondition for any understanding of scriptural ends. Moreover, a clear awareness of the symbolic dimension of Scripture, which is the complement as well as both the consequence and the evidence of its revelatory status, makes the reader unlikely to indulge in a flat and one-sided reduction of the text. The main lesson we may draw from Schuon is that a real contact with the Book amounts, first of all, to an awakening of the Intellect (al-'aql) in us, that is, that which binds one to the Divine Reality at the very core of our intelligence. The Intellect is as if unveiled by the Book and this is, in return, a promise of future unveilings of the Book itself by means of an intellective contemplation and meditation of its verses. Ultimately, the scriptural text leads to contemplative prayer because it is essentially none other than the Word, as crystallized in the Divine Name that sums up the entire Book and avers the immanent reality of the Divine Self.

Chapter Four

THE PROPHET

It is not possible to delve into the inner dimensions of Islam without considering the role of the Prophet in the spiritual economy of the religion. In our context, such a consideration is unavoidably related to an understanding of the notion of prophethood. It is also to be situated in contradistinction with the Christian outlook on the Man-God and the Incarnation. As has been written on many occasions, the spiritual status and function of the Prophet in Islam is by no means analogous to that of Jesus in Christianity. Although both figures are central to the human economy of the respective traditions, the centrality of Christ in Christianity is already evident in the very denomination of this religion, whereas the religion that emerged from Muhammad's message is not intrinsically connected to the name of the Prophet. The word Islam refers to a metaphysical and spiritual reality, not to the carrier of the Message. The term *islam* refers to a state of submission or conformity to God that is intrinsically productive of peace, and it is in itself independent of any historical figure, be it even that of the Prophet. There is no Christianity without Christ, that is without the Incarnation, but there is an *islam* without Muhammad as testified by the fact that the *Qur'ān* refers to ante-Islamic prophets and faithful as *muslimūn*.

The apprehension and interpretation of the Prophet by Western intellectuals cannot but be situated against the Christian background of the Man-God. Louis Massignon and Henry Corbin were both Christian thinkers whose interiorization of Islam was, in important respects, akin to their spiritual genealogy. However, the relationship between Massignon and Corbin was, in this regard, more discontinuous than continuous. Massignon's perspective appears much closer to the Christian traditional understanding of the Incarnation than Corbin's. This difference accounts, as we will see, for the fact that Massignon's acknowledgment of the spiritual greatness of the Prophet was considerably less than Corbin's. Besides this important difference, the two Islamicists share in an analogous vision of Islamic prophethood as being somewhat incomplete, although the term must be understood, in each case, in quite a distinct way. While the incompleteness of the Prophet is reflected, according to Massignon, in the incompleteness of Islam, his incompleteness—or rather the incompleteness of prophethood as such, does not result, for Corbin, in any sense of lack in the spiritual economy of Islam taken as a whole. For Henry Corbin, the incompleteness of prophethood is confined to the domain of Sunni Islam, but brought to a resolution in the context of Shī'ism.

It is clear that Massignon tends to approach the phenomenon of Muhammad in a way that emphasizes its specificity vis-à-vis the Christic manifestation. The key concepts, here, are the inaccessibility of the Divine, and the consequent exclusion of the Prophet from the "surrounding walls of Union."[1] These traits contrast sharply with the immediacy of the Incarnation in Jesus, and the discipline and path of mystical union through Divine Love that constitutes His central teaching. In this connection, Massignon focuses on the mystical accounts of the vision of Mt. Hirā, which initiates the cycle of Quranic revelation, and the *Mi'rāj*, the nocturnal and celestial ascent of the Prophet, in order to highlight what he conceives of as the religious value and greatness, and the intrinsic spiritual limitations, of Islam. One of his most important texts on Islam, which was rewritten several times over a period of fifty years—between 1912 and 1962, the year of his death—includes considerations that allow us to delve into the essence of Massignon's Christ-centered Islamology: this text was initially entitled "L'Exil d' Ismaël," then "Prière pour Ismaël," and was ultimately published under the title "L'Hégire d' Ismaël."[2] It is important to understand that the "Hegira of Ismaël" is only one panel within a triptych that is also composed of "La prière sur Sodome" and "Le Sacrifice d'Isaac." These three texts are centered on the three groups upon which Abraham, father of monotheism and "apotropaic" figure par excellence, is described by the Bible as having prayed in the manner of an intercession: the inhabitants of Sodom, who stand—in Massignon's spiritual vision—for all those who close themselves to the other, whether this "other" be foreigners or the other gender, the descendents of Hagar, that is, the Arabs and, by extension, the faithful of Islam, and finally the Jews, or Isaac's lineage. In the spiritual system of Massignon, these three groups are understood within the context of the particular mystical relationship that Christians are divinely assigned to entertain with them. This relationship is one of substitution, the central concept in Massignon's mystical thought, the meaning of which is subsumed under the idea that the suffering of Christians may be offered as a way to fulfill the Divine Promise in others. The Hegira of Hagar and Ismaël is understood, in this context, as indicative of an exclusion that is only partially compensated for by Muhammad's mission among Ismaël's spiritual progeny. This is why Massignon understands the Prophet's mystical vocation in light of, and in parallel with, Hagar's hegira. Both are situated within the context of a distance, a hegira precisely, that prefigures the spiritual identity of Islam, and calls for a completion.

Massignon meditates on the text of the *Sūrah* of the Star (*al-Najm*) in the context of this distance and this inaccessibility. The *sūrah* refers to the two major mystical events in the life of the Prophet. The first passage is traditionally considered to refer to the Prophet's vision on Mt. Hirā, and the second to his *Mi'rāj*. The first event is referred to in verses 6 to 11:

> (. . .) and he grew clear to view
> When he was on the uppermost horizon
> Then he drew nigh and came down
> Till he was (distant) two bows' length or even nearer,
> And He revealed unto His slave that which He revealed
> The heart lied not (in seeing) what he saw.[3]

This passage expresses three dimensions of the relationship between God and the Prophet: the "visibility" of God on the metaphysical "horizon" of his Essence, this visibility being associated with, or mediated by, an angelic manifestation—a divine or angelic motion, or descent, toward the human servant (*'abd*) that is the Prophet, and finally the permanence of a distance between the Lord as such and the servant. The verb *istawā*—used in verse 6—implies a firm settlement or establishment that is the prerogative of the Divine: It is the "sitting" position of God, as it were. It is interesting to note that the various translations of this verse offer distinct interpretations of the meaning of this verb in context. Massignon confirms this polysemy, or ambiguity of the term, by noting that the text of the *sūrah* is "very elliptical." While Pickthall insists on the "visibility" of God ("and he grew clear to view"), Yusuf Ali combines the notions of glory and manifestation ("for he appeared—in stately form"), while Shakir pushes the meaning of the text toward a notion of completion ("so he attained completion"), which is indeed present in the verb *istawā* when referring to fruits which ripen, or a food that is well cooked. Bringing together all these various denotations and connotations, Muhammad Asad, who translates "who in time manifested himself in his true shape and nature" indicates in his commentary that "manifested in its true shape and nature" is, according to Zamakhshari,[4] the meaning of the expression *istawā* in this context. In addition to the meaning of *istawā*, one should not underestimate the notion of "supreme horizon" (*ufuq al-a'lā*), which is cardinal here, since it suggests a possible analogy with the sun appearing in all its glory, coming to fruition so to speak, on the infinite expanse of the horizon. Since this passage is generally interpreted as referring to the experience of Revelation (*wahy*) through the mediation of the Angel Jibril at Mount Hirā, which took place in 610 of the Christian era, it is likely to be connected with the relative cognoscibility of the Divine Mysteries, in an episode that is reminiscent of Moses' encounter with God at the Burning Bush in the Book of Exodus. Eastern Orthodoxy refers to the "miracle" of the Burning Bush as to an indication that Moses was given to witness the Divine Glory itself in its Uncreatedness,

before he heard the Word of God through the Angel. The Quranic horizon seems to refer to the same level of Essential Uncreatedness from which
emerges, as it were, the voice of the Word, or the *wahy*, in the form or through
the mediation of the Angel. The Angel is clearly the "visible" form of God
without which God would remain invisible. It is the *barzakh*, the intermediary between the human and the Divine. The term *tadallā*, which is translated
by "suspended in the air" in some English versions, implies the state of being
"hung" between two states as it were, an expression that is perhaps suggestive,
here, of the intermediary status of the Angel. Curiously, Massignon conflates
this episode of Revelation on the horizon with the second Quranic account,
which immediately precedes in the text, and which refers to the prophetic
access to "the lote-tree of the furthest boundary" (*jujubier de la limite, sidrat
al-muntahā*), using the textual presence of a small tree as a thematic connector
between the Muhammadan and Mosaic episodes. He describes the Prophet
as being transported beyond the "supreme horizon" up to the lote-tree of the
furthest boundary.[5] However, the two contexts are different, since one suggests a descent, the descent of the Angel of God or the Revelation, whereas
the second refers to an ascension to the very limit that is allowed to a prophet.
These two motions correspond to the two Nights, *Laylāt al-Qadr* (The Night
of Power or Destiny) and *Laylāt al-Mi'rāj* (The Night of the Ascension). The
"supreme horizon" is mentioned in the context of the descent, while the lote-
tree is referred to in the narration of the ascent. It is significant that Massignon
situates these two events in the perspective of an ascension—whereas only one
is actually akin to such a motion. The reason for this questionable conflation
is no doubt related to an intention to situate these two important moments of
Islamic sacred history within the spiritual context of the inaccessibility of the
Divine. The fact that the *Qur'ān* insists, in the first account as in the second,
on the privilege of vision bestowed upon the Prophet, shows clearly that the
distance between the Prophet and the Divine is not exclusive of an actual spiritual perception. Corbin will develop this point in the context of a profound
meditation on the beauty of the Angel and its role as theophany or means of
spiritual manifestation and perception of the Divine. Significantly though,
Massignon does not enter into this question of the vision of God, or he does
so only obliquely and negatively, by assuming on the part of the Prophet an
initial temptation to "worship God through the angelic nature" that would
finally have been overcome.[6] The phenomenon of vision is approached by him
from the point of view of potential idolatry, thereby extolling the perspective of utter transcendence that Massignon tends to emphasize in his readings
of the message of Islam. But it is with respect to the second motion, that is,
the ascension, that Massignon's perspective on the Prophet reveals its clearest
intentions. For him, the covering of the lote-tree forbidding the Prophet to
enter the divine mysteries and the precinct of spiritual union is indicative of
the limitations of the Islamic tradition. Whereas the *Qur'ān* insists upon the
Prophet's vision and its unflinching character ("the eye turned not aside nor

yet was overbold" LIII, 17), Massignon understands the *Mi'rāj* above all as an intimation of the incapacity of the Prophet to enter the Divine Life itself. A curious passage from "L'Hégire d'Ismael" gives us the keys to an understanding of this particular perspective on Islam:

> No, Muhammad did not know what he refused, he had not seen yet; being virile, he was not inclined to conceive the *Fiat* of the Immaculate; placed under the power of an angel, he could only identify and proclaim the divine inaccessibility; (. . .) His exclusion from divine union, as Moses' exclusion from the Promised Land, may have prepared an access to it for others by leading them to desire the supreme hegira.[7]

Muhammad's vocation is exclusively "virile" in that the Prophet does not conceive, inwardly, the passive submission, the utter and secret consent to the divine Word. In this regard, the contrast drawn between the Immaculate Mary and the Prophet is all the more striking in that a clear analogy can be perceived, and has actually been perceived, by Massignon himself, between the virginity of Mary toward the Word, and the "illiterate" receptivity of the Prophet to the divine dictation of the Angel. As has been suggested on occasion, the Prophet of Islam is functionally much closer to the Virgin Mary of Christianity, as receptive "conceiver" of the Word, than to Jesus himself, whose function in the economy of the tradition would be better equated to the *Qur'ān's*. It is therefore unmistakable that by emphasizing the active and masculine ascension of the Prophet, and his initiation by an angel, Massignon underestimates the feminine aspect of Muhammad in the very reception of the Word in the context of the descent of the Revelation. The overemphasis on the role of the guiding Angel, and the extreme "masculinization" of the latter, are parallel to an understanding of the Prophet's function in the exclusive context of a distance vis-à-vis the Divine Presence, in sharp contrast with the intimacy of Love conceived of as a feminine reality. The Angel "circles" around God, as it were, without ever gaining access to the precincts of Union with Him. This is akin to a "circumambulation" that Massignon understands less as a centering than as an incapacity to dwell in the Center in Love, a turning around the Center without ever being able to reach it. Such an interpretation is confirmed by the curious notion that the episode of the lote-tree would suggest a kind of turning motion on the part of the Prophet:

> (. . .) al-Najm (. . .) shows Muhammad taken beyond "the supreme horizon", up to a bush, "the furthest lote-tree" (. . .) as if Muhammad had turned: circumambulatory motion that reminds one of the *tawāf* at the Ka'ba, or the complete circle traced by the lost nomad, caught in the sand storm that hides the sun from him, when he turns around an insignificant bush, his only means of orientation, without wanting to come closer to it nor being able to separate from it tangentially.[8]

It is significant to note that Massignon is less interested in the symbolic suggestion of proximity implied by the Quranic expression "two bows' length or even nearer" than in the remaining distance that it explicitly denotes. Early Sufi meditations, by contrast, have tended not only to highlight the inaccessible Mystery of the Divinity but also the ways in which the Prophet was, as it were, "clothed" with Divine Attributes, thereby providing an exemplar for actual states of mystical union.[9] For the French Islamicist, unable to enter the Garden of the Abode, which is the "consummation" of Divine Presence, the Prophet only bears witness to transcendence, as a second Abraham that has not known Christ. The Christian outlook of Massignon detects in this distance, symbolically expressed by the "two bows' length" that separates him from his vision, a sign of the incomplete character of the way that he opens for his community. This is, paradoxically perhaps, the source of a spiritual nostalgia for union, which Massignon will pursue in the spiritual paths of *tasawwuf*. Massignon's Sufism is entirely situated within the space of this distance, and the lack that it entails, a remark that has ponderous consequences for the way in which he approaches Islamic mysticism. Let us add that the contrast between the masculine Prophet and the feminine Virgin also has major implications in this context since it places mystical Union within the confines of a sanctity made exclusively accessible through the co-redemptive function of the Holy Virgin.[10]

Be that as it may, it is clear that for Massignon the Prophet of Islam has failed to realize the "supreme hegira" in the sense of not having entered the "personal life of God which would have sanctified him."[11] This limitation of the Prophet's vocation is thereby connected with the two essential theological "deficiencies" of Islam in Massignon's view: the rejection of the Trinity, and union with the Divine through Love. Muhammad remains a "spectator" of the Divine Nature but he does not enter the spiration of Love that is the internal life of God. Hence the insistence, on the part of Massignon, on the analogies between the Prophet and Moses: In both cases, a religious awe exclusive of an experience of the immanent and mystical flame of the Divine condemns the monotheistic communities of these two prophets to the limitations of the Law. The "perfect life" is not reached, since only its prefiguration through obedience to the Law constitutes the definition of the religion itself. Interestingly, Massignon accounts for this "failure" in terms of a lack of spiritual audacity on the part of the Prophet, an audacity that only love can lend:

> If he (Muhammad) engraved in his memory the tablet of the creative decree enjoining worship to all, he does not unveil the ultimate meaning of this precept; his will does not dare to adhere to the counsel of a perfect life, he declines the mystical engagement of love; thereby keeping its enigma secret, under threat of death, from all Muslims, in the future.[12]

The Prophet's worship is Abrahamic in that it refers back to the prime covenant that is still inscribed as *fitrah*, the primordial norm forever "engraved" in man's spiritual "memory." Massignon's Islam is Abrahamic, and his understanding of Muhammad cannot be dissociated from this patriarchal heredity that marks both its nobility and its limits as the Prophet of exclusive transcendence. The "lack of audacity" that enters the spiritual identity of the Prophet defines the contour of a collective religious consciousness and sensibility that is entirely defined by its relationship with the Law. The Prophet's silence on the dimension of immanence, and the mystical union that he has himself declined, according to Massignon, must moreover be understood in the context of an emphasis on testimony as a primary mode of mystical experience. Witnessing is central to the spiritual world of Massignon: It appears in two forms, one masculine, one feminine. The first type is the oath, or the swearing of allegiance that is verbal, outwardly manifested, and relates—globally speaking—to the regimen of the Law. The inequality of the Islamic Law relative to the weight of masculine and feminine testimony in court alludes to the masculine affinity with this outer dimension. The second dimension, however, pertains to a much deeper zone of human conscience; it is encapsulated in the concept of vow, a secret, inner reality of which only God is the "other" witness, as it were. This is the "feminine" consent, the silent vocation that determines, most profoundly, the "curve of life" traced as destiny. Now, some particular witnesses, defined by Massignon as "apotropaic," that is, taking upon themselves—sacrificially—the suffering and evil of others—have the spiritual privilege of externalizing this vow in order both to transgress, and thereby to "accuse," and complete the domain of outer commitments and laws. Such was the sacrificial role, in Islam, of the tenth-century mystic of Baghdad, Mansūr al-Hallāj, whose torture and execution because of his alleged threat to the theological and political order of the day was a determining inspiration in Massignon's life and scholarship.[13] His famous *"Anā al-Haqq,"* as other "theopathic" statements that bear witness to a spiritual "disappearance" of the egoic consciousness in *fanā'*, constitutes, for Massignon, the epitome of such a mystical testimony in Islam, since they may be read as the very antithesis of the Prophet's silence. By entering the flame of Divine Love, and being consumed by it, Hallāj perfects Islam by crossing the boundaries that define the Prophetic mission. It is as if the Prophetic forbidding had become, in mysticism, the source of a spiritual audacity to transgress. Likewise, the mention of a death threat is closely connected, in Massignon's personal encounter with Islam, to the figure of Hallāj understood as the epitome of a spiritual nostalgia that *must* be struck by the Law. The mystic of Baghdad who literally introduced Massignon to Islam, at least spiritually, bears witness to the limits of Islam, and to the perfection that it contains in its "secret." It goes without saying that Massignon's interpretation of the Prophet is highly consonant with his Christian outlook on the function of Christianity as perfection and consummation of the Law. Hence the emphasis placed on martyrdom as a means of mystical testimony, and Massignon's paradoxical affinity with the family of the Prophet, as perceived in the spiritual perspective of a Shī'ism that bears witness to the limits of what Frithjof Schuon has called "dry Islam," that is, legalistic Sunnism. Massignon's Prophet of Islam, if such an expression be allowed, is therefore akin to an Arab Abraham that would have ignored the central message of the Incarnation while keeping perfect allegiance to the original Covenant. The paradox, not to say contradiction, of Massignon's view of the Prophet lies in his reduction of Muhammad to the function of a distant and silent witness of God's transcendence, which seems at odds with the central thesis of his major contribution to the study of Sufism, *Essai sur les origines du lexique technique de la mystique musulmane*, in which he defends and supports the idea that Islamic mysticism, far from being indebted to external borrowings, is to be found in the very language and concepts of the *Qur'ān*. Hence, we are left with the paradox, or the contradiction, of a Book containing the precepts of the "rule of perfection," that is to say the seeds of the mystical way, conveyed by a Messenger whose spiritual function remains foreign to this domain of pure grace and union. There is, in this distance, the odd suggestion that the human side of prophethood remains somehow inadequate to the full potential of the message, by virtue of a choice on the part of the Prophet not to enter the fullness of religious life. This is another way of saying that the Prophet's Islam can only be perfected by the acceptance of the Incarnation, the only way leading within the precincts of amorous union.

Henry Corbin takes on this problematic adjustment of prophecy and mysticism from a very different perspective. His is not a priori an existential, mystical encounter with the climate of monotheistic prophethood in its Abrahamic bareness and jealous concentration on transcendence, but rather a philosophic progression leading into the immanent mystery of prophethood. While Massignon's approach to the Prophet may appear as the philosophical, or at least intellectual, expression of an a priori mystical perception of reality through the prism of the Incarnation, Corbin's angle of vision on the Prophetic reality could be defined, conversely, as a mystical understanding of the philosophical issue of prophethood. Corbin's approach to Islam is indissociable from a prophetology, that is a philosophic discourse on, and a philosophic experience of, prophethood. Prophethood is here quite clearly distinguished from prophecy, the latter being too easily associated with a superficial view of a prophet as one who foretells, or proclaims the future, whereas the deepest nature of prophethood is actually to unveil what is ontologically original, therefore *prior* to any chronology, albeit a sacred one.[14] The Western tradition has, by and large, been extremely reticent to address the question of prophethood philosophically. There has been, as early as the Renaissance and even in the Middle Ages, a clear separation between the domain of prophetic experience and that of philosophical reflection. Theology has indeed included a rational discourse on the prophets, among other religious realities, but it cannot be said that Western philosophical discourse as such has delved into the ontological and epistemological reality of prophethood as such. Aside from marginalized elements of visionary philosophy that have manifested primarily, and ironically, in the eighteenth century, Western philosophical discourse has been much too detached from religious realities to focus on a philosophical theory of the prophetic substance and prophetic knowledge. By contrast with this long Western exile of visionary philosophy, and in direct opposition to the intellectual axioms that have been at the root of this exile, one of the thrusts of Corbin's contribution was to highlight the centrality of the philosophical reflection on prophethood in the spiritual economy of Islam, particularly in Shī'ism.

By envisaging a priori the reality and function of the Prophet of Islam from a philosophical vantage point, Henry Corbin modifies the usual approach to Islam by looking, behind the historical account of the prophetic mission, at the ontological and epistemological realities that are its foundations and constitute its ultimate meaning. The ontological reality of the Prophet is not exhausted by his terrestrial mission—far from it. In fact the historical dimension of the Prophet is only the epiphenomenon of a metaphysical principle that transcends any data that a historical science may take as its object. The historical and exclusive unicity of the Prophet of Islam is here both founded on and transcended by the inclusive unicity of the Prototypical Form that lies at the core of gnostic prophetology. Let us specify, in this context, that the term gnostic is understood by Corbin as referring to an inner, spiritual knowledge that coincides with both self-knowledge and God-knowledge, in conformity with the oft-quoted *hadīth*, "He who knows himself knows his Lord." Such knowledge is not rational, since it comes about through spiritual identification, and not by deduction, without being "irrational," since it may be expounded, not certainly in its ineffable core, but in its formal modalities through conceptual means. The essence of this prophetology is encapsulated in Corbin's quotation of the sixth Imām of Shī'ism, Ja'far as-Sadiq:

> The human Form is the supreme testimony by which God bears witness to his Creation. It is the Book which he wrote with his hand. It is the Temple which he erected with his wisdom. It is the collection of the Forms of all the universes. It is the compendium of all knowledge issued forth from the Well-Kept Tablet (*lawh mahfūz*). It is the visible witness bearing witness for all the invisible (*ghayb*).[15]

The reference to the human Form must be understood, in this context, as referring to the prototype of the human as expressed in the norm to which bears witness the first human, Adam, who is also, in Islam, the first Prophet. This reality is not first understood in the historical sense, because it actually transcends history as a pattern of temporal successions; it has first and foremost an ontological status, since it coincides with the very form in which the

Divine Perfection mirrors itself *before* any existentiation. Corbin, in the wake of Shī'ite and Sufi prophetology, identifies this prototypical reality with the Muhammadan Logos, conceived as the foundational, essential nature of prophethood as such. This mystery is made manifest in the paradox, irreconcilable for the exoteric religious mentality as well as for what Corbin decries as contemporary "historicist reductionism," of the *hadīth*: "I was already a prophet while Adam was still between water and clay." It is clear that the Adam who is referred to in this prophetic *logion* is not the principial reality to which we alluded above, but rather the terrestrial manifestation of the human norm. The prophetic Reality is therefore eternal, not in the sense of an indefinite extension of time, but in the sense of a reality that transcends the very realm characterized by sequential concatenation. This ontological understanding of prophethood is essential to Corbin's understanding of the Prophet of Islam because it posits both the exclusive unicity of Muhammad as reflecting the unicity of the Prophetic Logos, and its inclusive unicity as participating in the latter. In other words, Muhammad is both the exclusive Prophet that Islam extols as human perfection by virtue of his reflecting, in his terrestrial reality, the one supreme Prototype of Humanity and Prophethood, which Corbin also designates in various metaphysical idioms as *Adam haqīqī*, *Homo maximus*, *Haqīqah Muhammadiyyah*, First Intelligence, the Pole of Poles; but he is also all of the prophets, encompassing the universal horizon of prophethood through which he is merged, as it were, with the universality of the Perfection of Creation by virtue of his identification with the Primordial Logos.

This Logos, which Corbin refers to in other contexts as *Haqīqah Muhammadiyah*, must not only be understood in relation to the terrestrial realities in which it finds its reflections, but also with respect to the entire chain of being that constitutes the unfolding of the Divine Mystery, as it were, or the exteriorization of the Innermost Reality. In Islam, the Prophetic Reality, and a fortiori its continuation in the initiatory chain of the Imams as they are envisaged by Shī'ism, remains under the constant suspicion or danger of confining to an Incarnation, or a Divinization, what would be contrary to the spiritual economy of the tradition. This is not only a matter of hyperdulia, that is, an excessive devotional attachment to the figure of the Prophet that would amount to conflating him with the Supreme *subjectively*; but ontologically and *objectively* there is also the danger of a metaphysical identification of the Prophetic nature with the Divine Reality. Corbin is quite aware of the problem, and it is remarkable that his Christian, namely Evangelical, background does not seem to interfere with his ability to differentiate a metaphysics of Presence (*al-hudūr*) from a metaphysics of the Incarnation (*al-hulūl*). The philosophical key to this conformity with the metaphysical perspective of Islam as a whole lies in an interpretation of Shī'ite theosophy, particularly in the nineteenth-century Shaykhī School, that prevents the very possibility of an idolatry on any level of the onto-cosmogonic chain. This interpretation is bound to an understanding of being as pure act, and therefore as best expressed in the imperative mode of the Quranic "*Kun!*," the divine command (*'amr*) by which every being is brought into existence. This is, to some extent, parallel to the distinction between the two notions of *Sein* (Being) and *Dasein* (existence) in German phenomenology, and particularly Heidegger's philosophy.[16] Such a distinction, which is at the very center of Corbin's thought from his early years as a mediator and translator of Heidegger, is also suggested, albeit less directly so, by the two French concepts *être* and *étant* and the Arabic *wujūd* and *mawjūd*. Whatever the insufficiencies or biases of the terms available in each idiom, it remains that being is, on any level, an act; it is therefore best to be apprehended in the imperative mode of the creative act.

When God wants to create He does so through his "*Kun*," the existentiating act, the divine command through which every creature is brought into existence according to the words of the *Qur'ān*: "The Originator of the heavens and the earth! When He decreeth a thing, He saith unto it only: Be! and it is (*kun fayaqun*)." (Pickthall, 2, 117).

The world of the command (*'alām al-'amr*) refers, in that sense, to the divine realm in its generality. However, the only dimension of this world about which we may say something, and of which we may preserve a concept, is that which is in the imperative only passively. In other words, on the basis of such an understanding of being, an integral theosophy, such as envisaged by Corbin, must further distinguish between the active and the passive meaning of the divine imperative. This is what Corbin refers to on several occasions as *significatio activa* and *significatio passiva*. According to the first meaning, the Divine Imperative transcends any manifestation of its Act; it is the inner and transcendent "energy" that animates any being as "passive imperative." As for that which is "primordially placed in the imperative by the K-N which commands it (. . .) it is the *haqiqat Mohammediya* (. . .) it is in fact to this that such terms as First Being and Light of Lights (. . .) apply."[17] Corbin proposes the image of incandescence as a symbol of this inner energy that remains hidden while being at the principle of all energetic manifestations: Although the fire remains invisible it manifests itself to our senses through the effects of the incandescent energy. The Prophetic Reality, or, in Shī'ism, the Muhammadan and Pleromatic Light, is none other than the first manifestation of the energy of the *Kun*.[18] It cannot be taken as an idol, or as a God, nor confused with the *Absconditum*, the Hidden Mystery that lies beyond all beings while being their principle, precisely because it is not a being in the sense of a *mawjūd* that could be reified and therefore worshipped. This is the key answer to what Corbin calls the "paradox of monotheism," that is, the permanent danger, on the part of the monotheistic consciousness, of confusing the Supreme Act of Being that is also Pure Transcendence with a Super-Being that would be ontologically analogous to a horse or a table. Understanding God in such a reifying way amounts to absolutizing the duality between Creator and creature, thereby confining one to an unconscious idolatry preventing a true understanding of *tawhīd* (unity) as a "unification" of each and every being through its existentiation by the One Act of Being, in the mode of the multiplication $1 \times 1 \times 1 \times 1$. Such a multiplication is a mathematical symbol of the unicity of the Principle through—and in spite of—all of its manifestation: There is no way to indulge in any "associationist" polytheism,[19] as long as one remains aware of this principle of metaphysical *tawhīd*. God is not a Super-Being to be added to an indefinite sum of monads $(1 + 1 + 1 + 1 \dots)$ since such an addition would amount to weaving a thick theological veil upon *tawhīd*. God is not a Supreme Being in that sense, but an Unfathomable Existentiating Act transcending all that It places in the imperative of its being. As for the Prophetic Reality, which is our focus in this chapter, it is identifiable *in divinis* with the Supreme Being taken in the sense of *significatio passiva*, and as such the Prototype of all that is. However, the Prophetic reality is neither God—taken in His Essence, nor a veil upon God, thereby satisfying the strictest vein of Islamic monotheism and opening the way to the theophanic vision implied by such *ahādīth* as "I am Ahmad without the *mim*, I am an Arab with out the *'ayn*; who has seen me has therefore seen the Truth."[20]

The ontological aspect of prophethood that we have just sketched is immediately linked by Corbin to an epistemological function that is at the very core of Shī'ite prophetology. It is here that the sense of incompleteness that we discussed in the context of Massignon's Islamology manifests itself in a way that is both analogous and profoundly dissimilar. The analogy has to do with a sense that the spiritual, inward dimension of Islam is somehow not wholly manifested by the external prophetic mission as such. But this "incompleteness" is of a significantly different nature from the one argued by Massignon. What had to be "imported" by Massignon into Islam through the mediation, or rather the substitution, of a Christic, if not Christian, apotropaism, *beside* the Prophetic mission—in a way that one may deem to be tantamount to a surreptitious Christianization of Islam, was to be found by Corbin in a Shī'ite imamology that completes the prophetology without presupposing, nor implying, a sort of deficiency of the Islamic tradition itself, nor narrowing the scope of the Prophet himself as understood in his integral spiritual stature. Such is the case because the Prophetic Reality that we have described above is in fact envisaged as an ontological "bi-unity" that opens the way to an epistemological configuration that integrates the legal and the mystical, the exoteric and the esoteric. This means that the ontological differentiation between a general or absolute prophecy (*nubuwwat mutlaqa*) and a particular prophecy, as manifested in and through the various "epiphanies" of the latter along the history of all prophets that finds its seal with the Prophet of Islam, must be complemented by an epistemological differentiation that associates an exoteric, prophetic mandate, and an esoteric, "imamatic" function. This association is epitomized, in Islam, by the kinship of the Prophet Muhammad with his son-in-law 'Ali Ibn Abī Tālib, fourth Caliph of Sunni Islam and First Imām of the Shī'a. It is important to stress that this association is not, for Corbin, compatible with any sense of duality, even less with the intimation of an opposition, since it presupposes a principial prophetic unity, the differentiation of which does not alter the fundamental completeness of the Primordial Prophethood. This "bi-unity" is envisaged, rather, as a gradual bipolarization of the self-same Light that was, and is, *in principio*. In other words, it is suggested that the spiritual reality of 'Alī is included in Muhammad as the Muhammadan Logos. According to a second perspective, corresponding this time to the epistemological "actuality" of Islam, the two figures are like the complementary dimensions of the tradition taken as a whole. In this epistemological context, Islamic prophetology calls for an imamology without which it remains, not in itself, but from the standpoint of those to whom it is addressed, as an undecipherable letter. The Prophet enunciates the exoteric, legalistic framework of the tradition through the external and literal meaning of his Message, but this enunciation is as it were "closed" and needs to be opened by the Imam, whose function is to unveil the esoteric meaning of this same Message. Corbin continues in the tradition of Shī'ite imamology by claiming that the closure of the cycle of prophecy with Muhammad coincides in fact with the opening of the cycle of sanctity (*walāyah*) with 'Alī and the whole series of the Twelve Imams that he initiates. The relationships between prophethood and sanctity are complex, and have given rise to a diversity of understandings in various Sufi and Shī'ite contexts, but it is important to emphasize that it can be envisaged from two vantage points: one that focuses on the degrees of *nubuwwah* (the function of *nabi* or prophet) with respect to the externalization of the prophetic knowledge with which they are endowed, and the second laying stress on the interiority of the spiritual reality to which the prophetic figure must be identified. The first vantage point tends to give precedence to the *rasūl*, or *mursal*, the Messenger who brings a *risālah* (message) to the world, the second emphasizing the definition of *walāyah* as the "inner, esoteric aspect of the prophetic message".[21] Corbin follows in the line of Shī'ite inspiration according to which the *nabī* is a prophet as defined by his spiritual state, not by his message, which amounts to saying that those who were called *nabī* are henceforth called *walī*. The relationship between "friend of God" (*walī*), prophet (*nabī*), and messenger (*rasūl*) is therefore suggested by Corbin in the form of three concentric circles, the innermost one referring to the *walāyah*, the *nubuwwah* corresponding to the median circle, and the *risālah* to the most external. This means that the privilege of interiority results in a reversed privilege of inclusion, in the sense that every *rasūl* is ipso facto a *nabī* and a *walī*, every *nabī* is also a *walī*, while a *walī* may be such and no more.

Concerning the *wilāyah* of every *nabī*, Corbin suggestively states that "in each prophet, his *walāyah* is his 'face turned toward God', whereas his prophethood is his 'face turned toward mankind." This amounts to saying that the *walāyah* is both the "point of origin" and the "point of return" since God is both the First (*al-Awwal*) and the Last (*al-Ākhir*). The *walī* as such, considered in his being as centered on the inward reality, is superior to the *nabī*, envisaged in his being as outwardly missioned to a particular community. However the *nabī* is in fact a *walī* in his inner dimension, while the *walī*—although not necessarily a prophet *stricto sensu*—is at times referred to as a *nabī*, as exemplified in Corbin's study of the *Dabestān-e Madhāhib*, a seventeenth-century Persian encyclopedia composed in India, or at least as endowed with a *nubbuwah bātinah* (esoteric prophecy), albeit not as a *nabī mursal* or a *rasūl*, that is, a messenger. Spiritually, the relationship betwen *walāyah* and *nubuwwah* involves the following analogy: "the *walāyah* is in same relation to *nubuwwah* as the *nubuwwah* is to *tawhīd*."[22] In other words, the status of "friend of God" complements and perfects prophethood because it brings out its inner meaning as prophethood brings out the meaning of *tawhīd*. However, this analogy is not without involving a reversal of direction in the sense that *nubuwwah* relates to *tawhīd* along.the arch of descent or revelation (*tanzīl*), whereas *walāyah* or *wilāyah* refers to the arch of ascent that brings revelation back to its ultimate meaning through *ta'wīl*.

From the point of view of the relationship between Islamic prophetology and Christian theology, Corbin's thought is remarkable in that it relates Islam, albeit fairly elliptically, to early Christian interpretations of Christ as "True Prophet" (*Verus Propheta*), and not as God, as expressed, for example, in the so-called Pseudo-Clementine literature. In this line of consideration, his life-long study of the eighteenth-century Swedish visionary Emanuel Swedenborg, who rejected the dogma of the Trinity within the context of a Christ-centered theology, is clearly indicative of the continuity, postulated by Corbin, of a gnostic tradition whose central figure is the inner prophet. The spiritual guidance of this prophet constitutes an epiphany of the true self. In this context the separation between visionary knowledge and philosophical knowledge tends to be blurred in the sense that the Angel of Knowledge and the Angel of Revelation are conceived of as one and the same. This is the major convergence of religion and philosophy in gnosis that calls into question the fallacious Western and modern axiom of the disconnection, or even opposition, between matters of faith and matters of knowledge:

> The Greek theory of knowledge which Avicenna and Suhrawardi drew upon was translated in accordance with their prophetic philosophy, thereby enabling it to account for both prophetic revelation and the inspiration of the holy Imams, as well as the knowledge granted to philosophers.[23]

It is the same Holy Spirit that "leads both prophet and philosopher to that supreme state of the human soul-intellect known as *'aql qudsī*—*intellectus sanctus*." Corbin invites us to realize that the questions raised by the Islamic, and particularly Shī'ite, reflection on the nature and function of the Prophet of Islam open the way to a redefinition of philosophy that calls into question most of the presuppositions of the secular *epistēmē*.

Aside from its philosophical implications, the theme of the *Verus Propheta* refers to the unfolding of the cycle of prophecy into its "place of repose," which is, in Islam, the Prophet Muhammad as appearance of the mystery of prophecy in mid-heaven. In other words, there is a "motion" of prophecy throughout sacred history, a gradual unfolding or epiphany of the prophetic reality. This is epitomized in Semnānī's theme of the "Prophet of one's being." Without entering into the details of Semnānī's complex phenomenology of the seven subtle centers (*laṭā'if*) of human individuality as corresponding to the seven major prophets of the cycle of *nubuwwah*, we would simply like to stress that the Muhammadan reality is epitomized in the seventh, deepest center of the human microcosm, the "Muhammad of your being" (*Muhammad wujūdi-ka*) or "subtle center of truth" (*laṭīfah haqqīyah*), which is also identified with the "center of the true Self " (*laṭīfah anā'īyah*). Thus, this chain of correspondences associates the prophets Adam, Noah, Abraham, Moses, David, Jesus, and Muhammad with the respective seven *laṭā'if* of the human microcosm: the "mold," or subtle body (*qālab*), the vital and sensory soul (*nafs*), and the five properly speaking "spiritual" centers, which are the heart (*qalb*), the "secret" (*sirr*), the spirit, or *pneuma* (*rūh*), the "mystery," or arcane (*khafī*), and the "truth," which is also the true selfhood (*anā*).[24] Now, the most important aspect of this esoteric doctrine of the correlation between prophetology and self-knowledge lies not, for Corbin, in the exoteric specificity of the Islamic mythology and the hierarchy of prophets that it entails, nor even in the eschatological meaning that it unveils, but in the equilibrium between the human and the divine that it ultimately highlights. Because the sixth level, that of the "Jesus of your being" involves the assistance of the Holy Spirit and the access to the status of *nabī*, it also gives rise to the danger of a premature identification of the individual with the Divine, thereby abusively substituting the incarnation to the theophany of presence. It is revealing that Corbin would follow Semnānī in emphasizing that the "*Anā al-Haqq*" of Hallāj, as the Christian dogma of the Incarnation, constitutes a premature collapse, or a metaphysical confusion between the personal, theophanic locus of manifestation and the divine nature itself. Corbin's "docetism," that is, his emphasis on the purely spiritual nature of Jesus and the treatment of his physical reality as insubstantial, resonates with the esoteric Islamic critique of Christian incarnationism by stressing the nonhistoricity and "nonhumanity" of Jesus, as epitomized in the Muslim rejection of the crucifixion and Jesus' direct ascension to heaven. This is in keeping with Corbin's repeated caution against the spiritual temptations of "annihilating" the human self into the Divine Self by ignoring the divine "face" of the person and the personal "Face" of the Divine. By contrast with such a confusion, the Muhammadan reality represents the perfection of metaphysical and spiritual equilibrium. Thus, the prophetic statement "He who has seen me has seen God" is not to be taken in the terms of an incarnation (*hulūl*) but in those of a theophany, not as meaning a divinization of the human in the flesh but as an allusion (*ishārah*) to the divine reflection in the mirror of the human. The true selfhood (*anā'īyah*) is the "Muhammad of your being" in which the theomorphic reality of mankind planted as a seed in the heart of man, the "Abraham of your being," bears the ultimate fruits of an " identification of the different" and a "differentiation of the identical." This is not to imply that the Isawian reality of the sixth *latīfah* of the divine arcane does not constitute a perfection of its own when properly understood; it merely points to the danger of identifying this perfection with the natural identity of the carnal individual, thereby condemning the latter to an utter disappearance contrary to the metaphysical meaning of the personal self in God's creative intention. In other words, the Muhammadan reality, which constitutes the integral maturity of the theomorphic seed of prophecy, brings the Isawian reality to its perfection in and through the restoration of the personal self to its normative status of theophanic mirror of the Divine.

In their essential reality, or *haqīqah,* the various prophets of the cycle of monotheistic prophecy have all been the theophanic manifestations of the same Light. However, following the prophetology of Twelver Shī'ism, Corbin asserts that what differentiates Muhammad from other prophets as seal of the prophecy is the perfect equilibrium between unity and multiplicity—avoiding both "abstract monotheism" and "polytheism," between the exoteric and the esoteric, between *tanzīh* and *tashbīh*, between the human and the divine. In a sense the "lack of audacity" with which Massignon "reproached" the Prophet Muhammad for not entering the "precinct" of the Divine is what Corbin extols as the supreme spiritual eminence of Muhammad. This is a most suggestive synthesis of two very distinct spiritual apprehensions of the relationship between the human and the Divine.

The philosophical presuppositions against which Corbin fought in his efforts to present the intellectual model of a genuine prophetology to Western audiences were also directly confronted by René Guénon, whose entire work has been defined as an attempt at restoring "a genuine intellectuality" in the West. The intellectual perspective of Guénon constitutes a formidable framework that confronts modernity on the basis of a radical critique of its *Weltanschauung*, one that Guénon characterizes as being utterly deprived of real principles. In fact, the modern world, as it has been shaped since the Renaissance, is characterized by Guénon as a "monstrous anomaly" in the history of civilization. This is the first time in human history that a whole civilization has developed without being rooted in the primacy of the transcendent and the invisible, nor being steeped in the climate of the sacred. Guénon's work can be defined as an attempt at reawakening, among the spiritual wasteland of modernity, a sense of Reality and a realization of the primacy and integrality of metaphysics. Accordingly, Guénon's perspective is defined by him as metaphysical, a term that he characterizes as referring to "supra-rational, intuitive and immediate knowledge (. . .) (of) universal principles," these principles including

not only "pure being" but also and above all "reaching beyond being."[25] On
the basis of such a definition, it must be stressed that Guénon drew a line of
demarcation between the domains of metaphysics, pertaining to intellectual
intuition, and religion, which he conceived as being intrinsically bound to
a "sentimental" point of view. This demarcation, which led him at times to
underestimate religious realities and mystical realizations, is essential to an
understanding of the fact that his considerations on the Prophet of Islam, and
prophethood in general, are marginal in his works and can almost exclusively
be situated within the framework of metaphysical expositions of a universal
character. Some connections may be made, secondarily, to the function of the
Prophet in his work within the context of general considerations relative to
the means and conditions of spiritual realization. The fact that Guénon does
not envisage the phenomenon of prophecy in its religious sense derives from
his consideration of metaphysical doctrine independent of the revelations that
may be its religious symbols. This is the reason why Guénon is not interested
in, nor sensitive to, the function of symbols within the particular contexts
in which they may appear, a context that undoubtedly affects their meaning given the divine "logic" of its specific spiritual economy. For Guénon,
prophethood is only the external, specific manifestation of a metaphysical
reality, and a degree of spiritual realization, that is, in itself, independent from
any given religious mythology.

If a doctrine of the Prophet appears, in Guénon's work, it manifests itself
as encased in the metaphysics of the Universal Man (al-insān al-kāmil), which is
expounded upon by the French traditionalist in several places of his work, but
most explicitly so in *The Symbolism of the Cross*.[26] It is significant that the very
idea of this book was given to Guénon by the Sufi Shaykh 'Abd al-Rahmān
'Ilaysh al-Kabir, to whom the volume is dedicated. The paradoxically Islamic
"occasion" of a book about the central symbol of Christianity, and its reoccurring references to Sufi concepts, suggest that Guénon's perspective disengages
the cross from its ordinary confessional associations and envisages it in a purely
metaphysical, thereby universal, way. The cross is considered by Guénon as a
symbol of a metaphysical and spiritual totality that is comprised of a horizontal
amplitude and a vertical exaltation. The former corresponds to "an integral
extension of the individuality (. . .) that consists in the indefinite development of a given group of possibilities subject to certain special conditions of
manifestation".[27] In other words, amplitude is the perfection of the human
individual possibility. As for exaltation, it defines "the hierarchy (. . .) of the
multiple states, each of which (. . .) is one of those groups of possibilities corresponding to one of the 'worlds' or degrees, which are included in the total
synthesis of 'Universal Man'."[28] It results from the above that the doctrine
of the Universal Man is not only independent from the religious contexts in
and through which it manifests itself but is also applicable—through vertical analogy this time—to all metaphysical levels of Reality. It is in this very
connection that Guénon quotes the Shaykh Muhammad al-Hindī according

to whom, "exaltation and amplitude alike have attained their fullness in the Prophet" who, adds Guénon, is thus identical with "Universal Man." Consequently, the Prophet of Islam embodies the junction of the horizontal and vertical axes of the Cross by presiding over both the "Lesser Mysteries," which are the prerogative of the King, and the "Higher Mysteries" placed under the spiritual jurisdiction of the Priest. The "Lesser Mysteries" refer to the primordial perfection of mankind within the limits of individuality, whereas the "Higher Mysteries" evoke the transcendence of individuality as such, and the realization of the universal Self that Islam envisages as the Supreme Identity, to use Guénon's term. In that sense, the Prophet of Islam manifests, in his very terrestrial function, the primordial norm of the *Rex-Pontifex*, which is characteristic of the Universal Man. It is interesting to note that Guénon, in one of the only passages of his entire work in which he engages in a specific inter-traditional equivalence, considers this doctrine of the Prophetic Reality as an unmitigated coincidence of doctrine between Christianity and Islam:

> This will (. . .) explain the words uttered about twenty years ago by a personage who then occupied a very high position in Islam: "If Christians have the sign of the cross, Muslims have the doctrine of it." We would add that, in the esoteric order, the relationship between "Universal Man" and the Word on the one hand, and the Prophet on the other, leaves no room, as regards the actual basis of the doctrine, for any real divergence between Christianity and Islam.[29]

This conception, which is not significantly different, in its principle, from the doctrine extracted from Shī'ite theosophy by Corbin, reveals the limitation of the theological debate that is supposed to open a most profound and unbridgeable chasm between the Islamic and Christian perspectives on the Man-God and the Incarnation. It allows one to meditate upon the levels of manifestation of the Universal Man and the various possible degrees of consideration with regard to the intersection of the Divine and the human. What is, however, lacking in Guénon's exposition of the esoteric convergence of the two traditions on this point is an ability to take into account the difference of perspective deriving from the specific religious situation and emphasis that define a given religion in its singularity and spiritual coherence, as it were.

Guénon has been rightfully characterized as a pure metaphysician whose whole intellectual emphasis has been placed on doctrinal exposition. This is to a very large extent undeniable. There is, however, a segment of his work that bears some significance in qualifying this reputation. If it is true to say that Guénon has not engaged in the concrete, moral, aesthetic, and spiritual modalities of the Path, leaving this task to those who had been mandated as spiritual masters, it must be added that his work incorporates a series of writings describing some of the formal requirements, means, and modalities of spiritual realization taken in an exclusively initiatory sense. In his two books, *Perspectives on Initiation* and *Initiation and Spiritual Realization*, Guénon examines such questions as initiation, the function of rites, and the nature of the spiritual master. What strikes one most in these texts is the conspicuous absence of any specific reference to the relevance of the Prophet in such matters. If one were to look for such references in the works of Guénon, one would have rather to look into some of his classical articles on symbolism such as "Al-Arkān" or "The Two Nights," in which may be found particular insights into some aspects of the Prophetic nature and mission (the *Laylāt al-Mi'rāj* and the *Laylāt al-Qadr* in the latter, the geometric and symbolic relationship between the Prophet and *al-khulafa ar-rāshidūn* in the former) within the general context of a study of universal symbolism. The absence of any direct allusions to the spiritual role of the Prophet is, in fact, highly representative of Guénon's focus on the technical means and modalities of initiation, independent of the specifically religious context in which initiation is actualized. Guénon has repeatedly asserted the need for an exoteric system as a requirement for any effective spiritual work, but it is clear that such a requirement is envisaged by him in a quasi-technical way, and without a direct consideration of the specific economy, emphasis, and perspective of the *barakah* of such systems. The lack of references to the Prophet in his treatises on initiation, and the exclusively metaphysical apprehension of Muhammad in the context of a discussion of the "Universal Man," bear witness to this emphasis.

Frithjof Schuon's contribution to a wider and deeper understanding of the Prophet is related, by contrast, to a consideration of both the metaphysical reality of the Prophet and the terrestrial manifestations of this reality in the concrete context of Islam as a lived religion. In a sense, Schuon's work lies at the convergence of Massignon's insights into the Prophet's personality and milieu of manifestation,[30] and Corbin's or Guénon's envisagement of his Prototype *in divinis*. For Schuon, the Prophet is both a metaphysical reality and a spiritual presence engaged in historical contingencies, and it could actually be said that one of the thrusts of Schuon's pages on the Prophet consists in an elucidation of the nexus between these two dimensions.

Schuon's understanding of the Prophetic Reality is not substantially different from Corbin's and Guénon's focus on its roots in God. References to the Muhammadan Logos abound in Schuon's opus. Besides this fundamental commonality of view, which is obviously to be situated in the tradition of the prophetology of metaphysical *tasawwuf*, as epitomized by figures such as Ibn 'Arabī and 'Abd al-Karīm al-Jīlī, several aspects of Schuon's perspective lend to this consideration a distinct character and flavor. First, the Muhammadan Logos is envisaged by Schuon, in a more explicit way than it is in Guénon, as one of the facets of the Universal Logos. In other words, Muhammad may be considered in his most profound reality as the Logos as such, but also as a specific mode of this Reality responding to the particular needs of a given terrestrial community at a certain time in history. This shows that the Logos may be envisaged both on a diversity of vertical levels within the onto-cosmological chain, and under a multiplicity of "faces." Vertically, one must consider what the term "God" refers to: When it applies to the Divine Essence (al-dhāt li-dhāti-hi, the "Essence which is Essence to Itself")—to which Corbin refers to by means of the terms *Absconditum* or *Ghayb al-ghuyūb* (Mystery of Mysteries), Guénon as Non-Being, and Schuon as Beyond-Being—the Logos is Being, that is, the first determination of the Principle; when God is Being the Logos is the creating Word; and when the Word is God, the Logos is the universal Intellect or Spirit that is at the center of the cosmic universe.[31] The term Logos, therefore, does not so much pertain to a degree of reality but to a "situation" or rather function within the chain of being. This vertical "relativity," so to speak, is complemented by a horizontal one. In this connection the Logos is refracted in different aspects. These aspects correspond, first of all, to the various faces of the Divine Reality and the multiple segments of terrestrial humanity that they address. Each of the great founders of the religions is identified in his substance with the Logos as such, but each of them takes on a particular coloration and style that accounts for, and responds to, human diversity. This particularization of the Prophetic Logos is also connected to the distinction, particularly significant in Schuon's phenomenology of religion, between a formal and an informal dimension of the Logos. The former is associated with the feminine dimension, akin to inwardness and essentiality, whereas the latter pertains to the masculine dimension, characterized by its outward and formal aspect. In this context, the Prophet Muhammad embodies the masculine aspect of the Logos, the main function of which is expressed in the revelation of the Law. In complement, Maryam represents the informal dimension of the Logos inasmuch as her only "law" is inwardness and love of God.[32] As Virgin Mother she is the "Logos under its feminine and maternal aspect," and she is as such envisioned by Schuon as the Mother of all the prophets: "She personifies supra-formal Wisdom, (. . .) it is from her milk that all the prophets have drunk."[33] Schuon defines her accordingly as *Umm al-Kitāb*, the Mother of the Book identified to the Wisdom that is the essence of all prophecies. This is the point of view from which she is considered principally by Schuon and with reference to the Prophet and in relation to the spiritual economy of Islam. The context of Christianity makes for a more complex relationship between the masculine and feminine poles of prophecy since, in addition to the above, she is also, as Mary "next to the adult Jesus" the prolongation of the "masculine and active Logos," hence the Christian association between Jesu and Maria in which Mary is envisaged as the *shakti*, that is, the radiating energy, of Jesus.

This diversification of the Logos is also expressed in terms of the "mode" of the prophetic mission in relation to the duality between this world and the hereafter. This is actually the opening point of Schuon's remarkable chapter devoted to the Prophet of Islam in his *Understanding Islam*. In it, Schuon remarks that one of the reasons why the apprehension of the Prophet is often difficult, for those who do not participate directly in the economy of Islam, lies in the apparent primacy of "his function as a legislator 'for this world.'"[34] This is particularly true for Christians whose sensibility has been molded by the otherworldly contemplativeness of Jesus. Such a misperception is an opportunity for Schuon to delineate two fundamental types of revealers: those whose otherworldliness and "pure spirituality" place them in the category of religious figures immediately intelligible outside of their own spiritual world—such as Christ and the Buddha—and those messengers whose vocational engagement in the contingencies of human endeavors and vicissitudes means that their "spiritual reality is wrapped in certain human and earthly veils" that "hardly compels recognition"[35] when it is not perceived within the overall spiritual economy and "logic" of the particular tradition. Muhammad belongs undoubtedly to this category, as do, according to Schuon, Semitic prophets such as Abraham, Moses, and Solomon, or a Hindu *avatāra* such as Rama or Krishna. In other words, the Prophet is characteristic of a type of messenger whose spiritual perfection pertains more to an inner substance than to a form. Whereas Christ and the Buddha present us with destinies in which the "human is at it were extinguished in the divine message,"[36] Muhammad's mission enters fully into the complexities of the human—from family involvements to military engagements—in a way that cannot exclude a measure of ambiguity. This is not at all to say that Schuon participates in a kind of skeptical, relativistic attempt at devaluating the nature and achievements of the Prophet under the pretext of "shadows" and uncertainties; in fact, the contrary is true, since what could be called the spiritual prophetology of Schuon aims primarily at unveiling the "substance" that constitutes a concrete and integral picture of human perfection in the context of Islam. Describing the nature and virtues of the Prophet amounts, in this respect, to describing Islam, and this is why a concrete apprehension of the spiritual perfection constituted by the Prophet is one of the most important tasks in any serious attempt at understanding Islam "from within" as it were, or phenomenologically.

Schuon proposes a spiritual portrait of the Prophet in the form of a geometric perfection:

> The virtues of the Prophet form, so to speak, a triangle: serenity with veracity is the apex of the triangle, and the two other pairs of virtues—generosity with nobility and strength with sobriety—form the base; the two angles of the base are in equilibrium and at the apex are reduced to unity. (. . .) The soul of the Prophet is in its essence equilibrium and extinction.[37]

Let us consider, first of all, the moral character of the Prophet as envisaged, not from the vantage point of an ethics of action, but in the perspective of a "Platonic" ethics of "modes of conformity" or "beauties of soul," in other words, where morality is envisaged in its inward dimension, as reflected in the intentions and orientations of the soul, which are themselves reflections of the Divine Perfections. There is no doubt that such an understanding of morality does not exclude a consideration of action inasmuch as the latter manifests outwardly the inner qualities of the person, but actions are only "approximations" that do not, in themselves, have any intrinsic meaning from the standpoint of a spiritual "science of virtues."[38] This principle is particularly opportune when dealing with a religious figure like the Prophet, whose manifold involvement in the world of men necessitated the performance of a multiplicity of actions within a diversity of contexts. It is therefore virtually impossible to be able to assess the spiritual substance of such a figure from the vantage point of specific occurrences as determined by a host of contextual factors that escape the analyst's purview.

This being said, it must be underlined that the spiritual portrait of the Prophet proposed by Schuon reproduces, in a different mode, the symbolic apprehension of Universal Man through the figure of the cross, as presented by René Guénon. The horizontal branch of the cross refers to equilibrium, the human perfection envisaged by Islam as the totality of the normative possibilities of the individual, whereas the vertical axis corresponds to the extinction of the individuality in the Divine, which is the ultimate spiritual meaning of Islamic tawhīd. In Schuon's idiom, horizontal equilibrium is differentiated along two poles, one being gentle, that is, generosity, and the other rigorous, that is, strength. These poles are further differentiated in dynamic and static modes, so that nobility is understood as the intrinsic, static aspect of generosity, as sobriety is an analogous dimension of strength. These polarizations and differentiations suggest the way in which unity penetrates human diversity by ordering it according to its highest finality. As most directly expressive of the latter, the apex of the triangle is constituted by a virtue, which is like the Prophet's crown, and expresses the essence of Islam as serenity rooted in the submission to God's command, 'amr. The association of serenity with veracity manifests the profound correlation between the sincere attachment to the metaphysical truth, as expressed by the shahādah, and the peace that derives from it. While the horizontal perfection of the Prophet refers to his function of khalifah, as representative of the Divine Perfections in human and terrestrial experience, his vertical perfection, being extinction, clearly manifests his 'ubudiyah, his status of servant ('abd) totally abandoned to God's will. From a slightly different point of view, it could be said that the horizontal base of the triangle refers to the Prophet as rasūl, inasmuch as strength and generosity were the two fundamental human virtues required to serve as messenger— indomitable courage in fighting for God's Word and indefatigable gift of self in transmitting it to others—whereas the apex evokes the walī whose inner sanctity is made of utter extinction in the Divine.[39] Within and beyond Islam, the triangle of the Prophetic virtues outlined by Schuon reflects, in a sense, the spiritual foundations of Semitic monotheism in its Abrahamic mode as defined by Schuon as an "equilibrium in view of ascension."[40]

To this triangular synthesis of the Prophet's virtues Schuon adds a quad-rangular complement in one of his later books.[41] Schuon specifies that the complementarity between these two approaches lies primarily in the fact that an odd-numbered series tends to emphasize the retrospective motion of manifestation toward unity—as expressed by the apex of the triangle of Prophetic virtues, an apex that points to a return to God as it were, whereas even-numbered realities suggest an externalization, or a motion toward manifestation, thereby fittingly expressing the terrestrial, or cosmic, perfec-tion of a given phenomenon. As is well known in traditional symbolism, the number three is associated with heaven while the number four evokes the realm of earth. Therefore, the second "portrait" of Muhammad sketched by Schuon corresponds, in a sense, to a more analytic, specific picture of perfec-tion as expressed in the fundamental virtues that determined the Prophet in his earthly manifestation. This fourfold perfection is summarized in the quaternity "serenity, recollection, fervor, and certitude." Serenity is akin to purity and detachment, and determined by divine transcendence and rigor, as is fervor, which involves "vigilance, initiative, and tenacity," but in a dynamic mode for the latter, and a static mode for the former. By contrast, recollec-tion and certitude pertain to immanence and inclusiveness, the first under the static aspect of peace and contentment, the second in the dynamic mode of faith and charity. These four stations (*maqāmāt*), which can give rise to other specifications as we enter further into the complexities of human action, are also detailed in a major chapter of Schuon's *Stations of Wisdom* that shares its title with the book itself.[42] The "stations of wisdom" are, in this context, presented as universal qualities that define the fundamental modes of human relations to the divine, independent of the religious context in which they may manifest themselves formally.

It bears stressing that the synthesis of the various virtues incorporated in the spiritual portrait of the Prophet, far from remaining theoretical abstrac-tions, are also envisaged by Schuon in their concrete manifestations. Thus, the specific traits of the Prophet such as "love of fasting" or "love of cleanli-ness" participate analytically in the triangular perfection that we have sketched above. Fasting refers to sobriety as a static dimension of strength, while cleanli-ness pertains to nobility, which Schuon characterizes as a love of beauty, which is a "sort of contemplative generosity."[43] The latter is eminently exemplified by one of the most controversial, and widely misunderstood, aspects of the Prophet, that is, the love of the feminine. Schuon refers to this dimension of the Prophet as "Krishnaite," thereby alluding, beyond religious borders, to an ability to experience the divine roots of femininity within the immanent con-text of terrestrial experience. This could not be further removed from hedo-nism and facility since it presupposes that the perception and experience of the celestial *barakah* of femininity be envisaged as a mode of remembrance of God rather than a dispersion in external phenomena. Moreover, and accordingly, the Prophet's love of woman cannot be understood separately from his love of

sobriety, vigils, and fasting, the two aspects being, as it were, the two sides of
the love of God, one in an inclusive way, the other in an exclusive mode.

As we enter the domain of an analytical recension of the manifestations of
the virtues of the Prophet in concrete occurrences of his career as a Messenger, the question arises as to the relationship between the multiplicity of acts
that punctuated his mission and the inner virtues that we have just discussed.
The *Sunnah* of the Prophet, that is, the tradition of his words and the minute
details concerning his behavior and actions, plays an important role in the
spiritual economy of Islam. Given that Islam can be understood as an imitation of the Prophet, what can, or should, this imitation be in order to realize
its most fundamental finality? This question led Schuon to distinguish an
inner and essential *Sunnah* from an outer and formal one. The reason for such
a distinction lies primarily in the fact that Schuon's interest in Islam stems
from an interest in Reality, if one may say so, and not conversely. Schuon's
intellectual and spiritual perspective is centered on what he diversely refers to
as universal gnosis, quintessential esoterism, *scientia sacra*, *philosophia perennis*,
or even—with a specific connotation—*religio perennis*: This is the sacred core
of spiritual wisdom that both founds and transcends the various religions.[44]
This focus appears most unambiguously in the very preface of the only book
he ever devoted exclusively to a specific religion: "What we really have in
mind in this as in previous works is the *scientia sacra* or *philosophia perennis*, that
universal gnosis which always has existed and always will exist."[45]

In this perspective, the question of the imitation of the Prophet unavoidably raises the issue of the relativity of forms with respect to their essence, or
let us say their intentions. Two aspects of the Prophet are thereby potentially
conflicting, not in themselves, of course, but in the understanding of Muslims: the spiritual intention in its simplicity, and the action in the world in
its multiplicity. The latter cannot be meaningfully integrated without a consideration of the former. Taking stock of the idea that the spiritual finality of
actions is their primary raison d'être, Schuon observes:

> What the *faqīr* (the spiritually poor) will retain of this Sunna will be, not
> so much the ways of acting as the intentions that are inherent in them, that
> is, the spiritual attitudes and the virtues which relate to the *Fitrah*, to the
> primordial perfection of man and thereby to the normative nature (*uswah*)
> of the Prophet.[46]

This gnostic envisioning of the Prophet cannot but be at odds, though, with
the overall climate of the tradition as centered on works and active conformation to the Law. Against the background of his universalist and decidedly
supra-confessional outlook, Schuon does not hesitate to refer to this Islamic
context as being characteristic of what the Hindu would call a *karma yoga*, or
a path of action—*karma yoga* is distinct from *jñana yoga*, the path of knowledge, and from *bhakti yoga*, the path of love. This characterization implies

a spiritual perspective that perceives the ultimate meaning and salvific out-
come of religion in and through action. It is incompatible with a perspective of gnosis since the latter envisages actions as such as unrelated to the
acquisition of spiritual knowledge. No action can, per se, take one closer to
the realization of gnosis, save through an intellective perception that lends
this action the value of a symbol, thereby participating in a higher degree
of consciousness. Accordingly, a gnostic apperception of the Prophet cannot
but take its distance vis-à-vis a strictly formal, or a fortiori formalistic, imitation of the Prophet.

Schuon's consideration of the Prophet reveals a keen perception of two
apparently distant dimensions of the founder of Islam: his metaphysical reality
in divinis, and his concrete, human manifestation in the world of terrestrial
forms. Schuon opens the way to an understanding of the Prophet that outlines
him as "a synthesis combining human littleness with the divine mystery."[47]
These two dimensions account for the tensions in Islamic history between an
extreme "humanization" of Muhammad in the name of the most zealous concept of divine transcendence, and a mystical devotion feeding on a metaphysical prophetology that amounts to an inclusion of the Prophet in the Divine
realm. This synthesis is in no way akin to what would be an Islamic analogy
of the Incarnation since the two dimensions, divine and human as it were,
do not intersect in the form of a doctrine of the union of two natures. There
is no "Christianization" of Islam in Schuon's approach, since the theological
economy of each tradition cannot be brushed aside in the name of an easy
syncretism. On the one hand the principial and human levels of the Prophetic
reality seem to run parallel to one another in a kind of harmonic correspondence that does not involve any fusion; on the other hand the Divine perfection of the Muhammadan Light (*Nūr Muhammadiyyah*) appears to project its
essentiality and totality onto the harmonious inclusiveness of the destiny of
the "best of creation" (*khayr al-khalq*) and the "best of those whom God has
chosen" (*khayru man ikhtāra 'Llāh.*) Schuon's pages on the Prophet proceed
from the two main thrusts of his work, that is, the esoteric universality of
the truth, and the traditional integrity of each particular expression thereof.
While the metaphysics of the Logos unveils the inner and universal dimension
of the Prophet, the spiritual science of virtues delineates the specific traits of
the Muslim "quality of being" that his mission has outlined. But these two
complementary aspects are not exclusive: The former also accounts for the
particularization of the Logos upstream of the specificity of each revelation
and tradition, while the latter is not without opening onto a general phenomenology of spiritual virtues. In a sense these two aspects correspond to the
figure of the Sage and that of the Prophet, as combined in the spiritual reality
of Muhammad: The Prophet of Islam is a sage as well as a prophet. As sage he
is "active by his discernment," and as prophet he is "passive in his receptive
function" as messenger of God's Will.[48] Thus, Schuon concurs with Ibn 'Arabī
to consider wisdom as superior to prophethood in the sense that it entails a

higher degree of universality. This is due to the fact that the Divine Will as expressed in a given religious message is necessarily a particular "formalization" of the Truth, and not the Truth as such. This superiority of wisdom over prophethood, or *wilāyah* over *nubuwwah,* should not veil the fact that Prophets are always sages, whereas the reverse is not true. In that sense, prophets possess the two perfections although they may not always manifest the perfection of wisdom outwardly. There might even be some cases in which the two perfections reveal a tension or an apparent opposition by virtue of the intersection of two dimensions of the prophetic consciousness, the universal norm of the nature of things and the specificity of the religious opportuneness. Schuon's spiritual pespective accounts for the necessity and the relative legitimacy of religious partiality and expediency while being essentially centered upon wisdom as an integral recognition of the "nature of things."

The prophetology that derives from the contributions of our four authors, beyond the differences that they spell out, has major implications for the understanding of the Prophet in modern times. The most important is no doubt connected to a sense of universality flowing from the metaphysical foundations of an understanding of Muhammad in God's intention, as it were. Even though Massignon eschews the metaphysical fundamentals of the notion of the Logos, he does, in his own manner, account for a certain providential intention of Muhammad's mission. In this view of things, Muhammad draws us back to the universal horizon of Abrahamic monotheism, while bypassing the sine qua non of the Incarnation and Redemption. In a definitely more encompassing way—one that is not bound by the mystical premises of a Christian sensibility, Corbin, Guénon, and Schuon show the path of an apprehension of the Prophet that not only situates Muhammad in the context of an overall Abrahamic "plan," but also in the framework of what could be called a "science, or philosophy, of revelation" involving an insight into the Divine roots of prophetic and salvific phenomena. The implications of the sentence "Who has seen me has therefore seen the Truth" become fully apparent in such a context. On this level of reality, the metaphysical and religious unity of Islam with other revelations becomes accessible, beyond the diversity of the scriptural symbols and theological "myths" in which they are clothed in specific religious universes. This goes well beyond the partial correlations that an external analysis may pluck from the narratives of each prophetic mission. Of course, this kind of apprehension of prophecy pertains to a metaphysical realm that may not ring a bell with most faithful. The all-too-human needs of sentimental exclusiveness, or even passional bias, make it impossible to envisage the perception of such a convergence *in divinis* beyond the relatively small circles of minds able to grasp intimations of metaphysical mysteries aside from exclusivist concepts and partial feelings, not to mention the human and "imaginal" limitations that all mainly "experiential" approaches of religion impose upon believers of all creeds. In this sense, Guénon was not unjustified in highlighting the "sentimental" nature of religious consciousness.

Considering this inherent limitation of mainstream religious adherence to the exclusivist dimension of forms, it is to be hoped that insights into the spiritual and ethical characteristics of the Prophet could suggest commonalities and convergences with other messengers and faiths. This would presuppose, however, that one be ready to transcend the polemical potential of certain facts in order to delve into the substance of the ways of being that they express or translate. To give a concrete example, one would have to consider such controversial facts as religious war or polygamy from the point of view of the spiritual virtues that they presuppose and ultimately express,[49] instead of envisaging them unilaterally from the vantage point of an expeditious moral a priori and sociocultural determinations.

From a more strictly Islamic point of view, the concepts and images of the Prophet that the preceding lines have evoked may constitute an effective antidote, when fully fathomed, to the formalistic, moralistic, politically minded, and at times pharisaic and quasi-nationalistic flattening down of the figure of the Prophet that has become all too sadly commonplace on the mediatic stage of contemporary, and particularly Arab, Islam. Far from denying the Arabian and Bedouin character of the modalities in which the expression of the Islamic *Weltanschauung* has been couched in and by Muhammad, the prophetological principles that we have reviewed and examined give shape to a living image of spiritual normativeness and perfection grounded first and foremost in a concrete, profound, and sincere consciousness of the Divine. In this inward and divinely dispensed light, the Prophet appears not only as an institutor of the Law—which he undoubtedly was on an immediate and binding level—but also, and above all, as a synthetic unfolding of the manifestation of the consciousness of the Absolute in human form. Reading Massignon, Corbin, Guénon, and Schuon, we enter into contact with a spiritual reality that has little, if any, proportion with the vociferations of religious nationalism and the platitudes of secular relativism. In this context, which takes us to the core of religious reality, Muhammad appears as an embodiment of this "recollection in God's hand, this silent, immaterial, and sacred intimation of a pure divine transcendence (. . .) 'in which one may recognize', in its simplicity, the patriarchal adoration of primordial times."[50]

Chapter Five

THE FEMININE

The question of the status of women in Islam has been at the forefront of most discussions of that religion in the last decades. In fact, it would not be an exaggeration to say that it has become a kind of cultural symbol of the deep civilizational chasm that is deemed by many to have widened between Islam and the West. The pervasive Western perception that Islam condones a social subordination of women, and further legitimizes their overall oppression, is no doubt the primary factor, together with the question of the religious use of violence, in the deep-seated unease of most non-Muslims vis-à-vis the religion brought by the Prophet Muhammad. It is on this point that the Western and modern consciousness appears to be the most focused, and it is upon these grounds that the Western understanding of Islam as a religion incompatible with modern values and as an obsolete witness of archaic stages of development thrives. Our intention is not to assess the validity or the limits of such perceptions against the background of the complex and often disconcerting stage of contemporary Islam. There is no doubt that such visions cannot but be founded on certain painful or uncomfortable realities; the real question is that of their overall representativeness and normativity and, above all, their consonance or lack thereof, with the tenets and injunctions of Islam as founded in the *Qur'ān*, the *Sunnah*, and the consensus of believers. The other no less important question is that of the normativity of Western discourses in such matters, and the philosophical, not to say metaphysical, premises upon which these discourses are predicated. These questions, as against more immediate ones having to do with the social, economic, juridical, and political dimensions of women's status and conditions in Islam, are not the purview of this study. One may well wonder, therefore, what can be the relevance of "inner Islam" to such acute and sensitive matters. The following pages will in fact be an indirect response to this question, at least in so far as they will help reframe within a much wider and deeper philosophical context the specific problems of women's identity and function in the spiritual and human economy of Islam.

The fundamental affinity of inner Islam with the domain of feminine reality is already apparent in Louis Massignon's work. Let us say that it first emerges from a meditation on the relationship between self-awareness and destiny. Massignon's spiritual crisis of 1908 had no doubt played an important role in the unfolding of this crucial consciousness of the intimate nexus between what is *received* and *conceived* inwardly and what is *given* or *expressed* outwardly. This concept is made manifest in a spiritual duality that contrasts the domain of external duties with that of inner vocation. These two poles are epitomized by the complementary notions of *vow* and *oath*. Here is the most concise and substantial summary of this polarity to be found in Massignon's work:

> The ultimate personality of each witness, coming from within, is his vocation, from outside, his destiny; it is expressed from within by the *vow*, it is imprinted outside by the *oath*. The vow is feminine sacralization, the oath is masculine ordination. The vow remains open to the unexpected, the oath closes itself on a legal (sacrificial) sanction.[1]

As for destiny, it is the "gradual emergence of the secret vow through one's public life." The introduction of two terms defining the "witnessing" personality runs parallel to the consideration of two *worlds,* which remain distinct in their very mingling, that of the law, which is the purview of masculine outward engagement and definition, and that of the inner conception, which is the realm of feminine inward consecration and inspiration. The relationship between vow and conception has an essential bearing upon Massignon's understanding of the feminine. Conception, the exemplar of which is the *fiat* of Mary, consists in the acceptance of an other within oneself, another that determines one's being in a purely private, secret, but essential way. This is a feminine prerogative the manifestation of which Massignon has illustrated through the examples of female figures such as the Virgin Mary, Fātima, and perhaps surprisingly to many, Marie-Antoinette. Woman is the priestess of hospitality, not only in the outward sense of a homemaker, but also and above all on the level of the soul's concordance with God's will as a "foreigner."

Aside from the exemplars of Mary and Fātima, but in the very same vein, Massignon has also traced the more modest, familiar evidences of a specifically female spirituality, in Islam, through his study of Muslim women's devotion in cemeteries, particularly in Cairo's "City of the Dead." What dominates these forms of female spirituality observed by Massignon in Islam is their deep association with seclusion, inwardness, and vow. He underscores the fact that women are exempted from a number of ritual obligations, at least under certain circumstances, but that these exemptions are, as it were, compensated for by an emphasis on the inward dimension of religious duties. This is the Islam of the catacombs, as it were, the underground Islam of women, whose relationship with the world of the dead makes explicit the function of continuity within the genealogical line, and of interceding grace, which is the purview of the world of pious women.

Massignon repeatedly refers to Islam as a "misogynous" tradition. He frequently highlights what he calls the social "humiliation" of woman in Islam. However, this misogyny is primarily, if not exclusively, confined to the domain of the law: It emanates from men, rather than the religion itself. It is, in part at least, a result of the formal crystallization of the tradition as *shari'ah*. It pertains to an external status, not to an internal reality. Woman remains a "minor" under the sanction of the Old Law, in Islam as in Hebraism: She does not fully attain the privilege of independence and autonomy that the *Qur'ān* recognizes as hers, on a spiritual level, when mentioning *muslimātun* in the same breath as *muslimūn*. We will see that this situation is, for Massignon, both the source of a rebellion on the part of woman, and the situs of a deeper inner realization the consequences of which are not only individual but also universal. Most immediately, even on the level of the law, this tension is an allusion to the distinction between woman as a *mu'minah* or *muslīmah*, that is, in her situation before God on an equal footing with man, and woman as a member of society, whose sphere of influence is mainly domestic, and whose modes of external realization in society are marginal. There is, however, in addition to these two distinct situations, a vantage point that places woman in a pre-eminent position, with a privilege of extraordinary proximity to the divine mystery. This privilege is enunciated in the *Qur'ān* when woman is envisaged as keeper of the Mystery—*hafizat li-l-ghayb bi mā hafiza Allāh*. It is on this mysterious and central connection between woman and the inner dimension of Islam that Massignon focused in virtually all of his writings pertaining to this theme.

The supereminent status that we have just begun to analyze is epitomized and concentrated in the figure of Fātima Zahra, the daughter of the Prophet, who occupies an ambivalent position in the world of Islam. This ambivalence is outwardly manifested in the Sunni/Shī'ite controversy over some important episodes of her life, especially those which immediately followed her father's death. She refused to obey 'Umar's orders of swearing allegiance to Abu Bakr, thereby attracting upon herself the ire of the official representatives of the community, those whom Massignon calls with some disdain the *"gendarmes de l'Ordre public."*[2] Her treatment by the community and her social obscurity, not to say humiliation and isolation, make of her, in Massignon's eyes—who follows in this the *pathos* of Shī'ite Islam—both a figure of spiritual eminence and one of terrestrial solitude and mourning. She appears to Massignon as a supereminent exception, but also a most significant symbol of the ultimate role of woman in Islam, and beyond Islam, within the general economy of the world. This role consists in calling for justice, both in resistance and silence, thereby foreboding the revelation of the truth and the final redemption of mankind through "feminine grace."

A particularly striking element of this exceptional spiritual destiny is inscribed in the fact that Fātima appears as the only woman in the pleroma of the fourteen figures of Shī'ite devotion. It is interesting to note that Massignon perceives in Fātima the one who, among the fourteen, "lays bare the Divine Truth" since "she is occultated by the five relations of kinship: paternity, maternity, marriage, filiation, sisterhood."[3] This occultation of the Divine Nature under the five family relations refers to a spiritual principle that Massignon discovered in Husayn ibn Hamdan Khasībī, a tenth-century 'Alawite Shī'ite, according to whom God occultates himself under the five family relationships, while manifesting himself, in reverse as it were, under the five deficiencies that are "humanity, poverty, sickness, sleep, and death."[4] The destiny of Fātima, framed by the various family relationships and the eminent figures of male heroism who "cover" her, but also subjected to the misfortunes of solitude, hostility, and mourning, recapitulates the occultation of the spirit under the bonds of nature, and its manifestation through the fissures that undo them. She is the secret hidden under the formal lineage of the family, and revealed in her misfortune and suffering. As the hidden center of the five relations, she is also the unifier, the origin, the symbolic figuration of the spiritual perennity of the *Ahl al-Bayt*, "silent permanence of wisdom between her parents, her spouse and brothers, and her children."[5] This is epitomized in the episode of the *Mubāhala* of Medina, the ordeal with which the Prophet challenged the Christians concerning the divinity of Christ.[6] On this occasion, she was the only woman among the five ("the five under the cloak") that the Prophet had chosen as guarantors for Islam and against the Incarnation, together with himself, 'Alī, and his two grandsons. Here again she appears as the feminine, inner, center that binds the four others. Let us note that she also converts the masculine evenness through her feminine oddity, thereby constituting the "retrospective" element leading back to the transcendent Unity—in a kind of reflected reversal of the outer relationship between man and the four wives that the Law allows to him under certain circumstances. This function of suffering and hidden center epitomizes Massignon's vision of woman in Islam, and also beyond Islam, in the economy of mankind's redemption. The consonance of these meditations with the psycho-spiritual climate of Shī'ite Islam is not fortuitous since it points to the reality of a defeated Islam, a hidden Islam that can only be expressed through suffering under the oppressive tutelage of the agents of the law. Massignon finds in this spiritual "drama" the thematic affinities with which his Christian mystical sense of redemptive suffering may vibrate.

The centrality of Fātima in the genealogy of the Prophet is moreover reinforced by the name of Umm Abihā, daughter of her father, which is often given her as a nickname (*kuniya*). Massignon's interpretation of this name is quite characteristic of his understanding of the role of woman.[7] On a first level, he perceives of Fātima as the only member of the *Ummah* who, at the time of Muhammad's death, conceived of the mission of her father as incomplete.

This incompleteness is particularly connected to the status of non-Arab converts in the community: While Fātima had been the host par excellence of this category of companions, the advent of Abu Bakr and 'Umar represented the crystallization of an Arab, purely agnatic, identity of Islam that the cognatic mode of adoption, exemplified by the relationship between the *Ahl al-Bayt* and the Persian Salmān Pāk, called into question. What is at stake, in a sense, is nothing less than the universality of Islam, and it is no coincidence that a woman be the guarantor of this ideal. It bears mentioning that, in his study on "the Umma and its Synonyms," Massignon noted that the term *Ummah*, which refers to the Islamic community of the faithful, is etymologically akin to *Umm*, the mother, and by extension, to the cognatic family, its domestic household, and those placed under its protection, in opposition to the agnatic clan, *sha'b*, the ethnic and nationalist character of which relates to male leadership. The spiritual affinities of the *Ummah* with the inclusion and protection of non-Arabs in Islam are in perfect consonance with Fātima's function vis-à-vis the *Bayt* (the Household) and its "clients" (*māwāli*).

In keeping with the Christian reading of Islam that we have highlighted in our chapter on the Prophet, Massignon understands Fātima's extreme mourning and resistance to the new order of things as a way of expressing her attachment to the Prophet beyond death, thereby hoping to "have him be reborn in her heart" and "having her father reenter the maternal bosom."[8] This is a particularly sibylline and delicate aspect of Massignon's thought that deserves some further examination. In his essay "The Temptation of the Ascetic Çuka," Massignon comes back once again to this theme, in the very last years of his life (1961), in the context of a meditation on the spiritual transmutation of erotic love as staged in the story of the Indian ascetic Çuka and the *apsara* (celestial woman) Rambha. The encounter between the most accomplished ascetic and the most beautiful *apsara* is envisaged as presenting the Indian popular and aesthetic imagination with a problem that can only be resolved by "an open look of mutual ecstasy" that makes Çuka aware of his desire to reenter his mother's womb as Rambha's, while it leads Rambha to realize "her 'virginally' maternal calling to Çuka."[9] Massignon makes use of this story, through an examination of a lithograph and the Marathi poem of Muktesvar depicting and narrating it, to provide his readers with a brief dismissal of the Hindu idea of transmigration, or rather here reincarnation (*tanāsukh*),[10] on the basis of a distinction between the (Hindu) concept of a reentrance into the flow of existence through a new birth, and that (Christian) of a spiritual re-entrance into woman's womb that is akin to a rebirth in the Spirit: "There is no indefinite number of rebirths, only the one in which one 'reenters the womb of his mother,' as Jesus tells Nicodemus."[11] This is the birth from the Spirit that amounts to a rebirth in the "womb of the Spirit," the celestial essence of maternal femininity. Fātima appears, therefore, through the "most naive form of belief in resurrection," as pregnant with the desire to give him a second life in her heart, that his descendents may give rise to a new Muhammad, a "Fātimī Mahdi" who will "take the name of her father and perfect his mission" in truth and justice. Shī'ite confessional mythology mixes here with Christian mystical eschatology to invest femininity with a quickening mission in the unfolding of *parousia*.

Some mystical speculations of Shī'ah Islam have interpreted the theme of the maternal role of the daughter toward the father, in Fātima, as an indication of the sublime spiritual station of Fātima Zahra, first in the Pleroma of mainstream Shī'ism, then in the divine hypostasis of her in some sectarian segments of marginal Shī'ism. Thus, the spiritual meditation on the function of *Umm Abīha* may go so far as to entail what amounts to no less than a divinization of Fātima Zahra in some "extremist" sectors of Shī'ite Islam.[12] Massignon specifies that "Nusayris, Ismailis, and Druzes venerate Fātima Zahrā as Divine Name (Fātir (. . .), (. . .) as first divine emanation according to the Qarmates."[13] This suggests to Massignon a parallel with Mary as Theotokos or Mother of God, a connection that is a priori founded on the status of Mary at the crucifixion, as *mater dolorosa* and *mater orbata* (bereaving mother). On the highest level of consideration, which is the reverse analogy of her terrestrial status of *mater orbata* (*thākla*), this makes Fātima participate in "all the privileges of Maryam, mother of Jesus, and archetypical Perfect Woman, in the *Qur'ān* ." At this degree of spiritual height, Fātima, like Maryam, is mother of all the prophets, since the latter all stem "from the same Perfect Femininity, Fitra, Kūni, with respect to their inspiration."[14] This primordial norm of substantial being "out of the hands of God," so to speak, is also expressed by the creative imperative in the feminine form *Kunī*, to which Fātima is metaphysically identified by some Shī'ite gnostics. It manifests the perfect receptivity of the universal soul, or the universal and virginal Substance in which, according to Massignon following Hallāj, all faithful souls participate.[15] This is the *"point vierge"* that connects mankind to grace, the *sirr al-asrār*. In spite of the archetypical coincidence between Maryam and Fātima, the parallel between the two figures stops here, at least on account of Massignon's Christian understanding of Mary. Massignon develops in fact a contrasted interpretation of Mary and Fātima based on the distinctive criterion of the Incarnation. This is a complex theology of femininity that we can only sketch in our present context. It is, first, connected to a distinction between temporal incarnation and pre-eternal destiny. The *fiat* is annunciation, the *kūn* of Fātima, reminder.[16] Fātima's "redemption" is thereby connected to the primordial nature of Islam as a restoration of the religion of the origin, whereas Mary's redemption (*coredemptrix*) is intimately connected with the unicity of the event of the Incarnation. Moreover, Massignon contrasts the respective spiritual function of the two women by defining Fātima as the "human hostage of the affirmation of the divine Inaccessibility," while Mary is characterized as the "superhuman host of divine immanence."[17] By denying the divinity of Christ, in the wake of her father, Fātima remains within the context of a purely transcendent concept of God of which she is the hostage, in the sense of being held captive to the Law, without being able to make Islam participant in the immanent grace of her love for her father. By contrast, Mary fully participates in the redemptive mission of her son, through the Incarnation that crystallizes divine immanence in his flesh, by offering herself as a "host" to divine Love. Just as Muhammad cannot enter the precinct of union, so Fātima remains powerless to experience the full meaning of spiritual parturition, and can only orient her suffering toward a deferred advent of the truth, which is dramatized by Shi'ite eschatology.

What is the relevance of these mystical meditations and speculations on the actual social and religious status of women in Islam? The first pertinent point to emphasize is that Fātima's vocation as *Umm Abīha* is directly connected, for Massignon, with a concrete sense for the need of an immanent justice in this world. This is actually one of the two essential components of femininity in Islam. The anger and rebellion of Fātima—"feminine impatience of justice"—at the death of her father, whom she cannot conceive as being succeeded by any other man, thereby manifesting both concretely and symbolically the unconditional demands of a pure spiritual Islam, epitomizes the warriorlike and vengeful aspect of spiritual femininity, the incorruptibility of a desire for purity "borne within." This is "the strong woman, who excites to action the wavering warriors, who shakes up the cowards."[18] The expressive picture of Fātima untying her hair, in anger, coming out of her home to confront 'Umar's authority suggests to Massignon the lyrical statement that this undone crown of hers, symbolic pointer to a spiritual liberation of woman, "unleash[es] in Islam the final indignation of Woman that will burn the world down."[19] Fātima "protests against the Law that rules the bodies;" she embodies a resistance to the law of gravity pertaining to outer Islam, outer religion in general, and she conceives within herself a new Law brought by the last of her offspring, the Mahdi:

> Above the Law, legated by the Prophet to be applied *tale quale*, why did Fātima keep a senseless hope in a more perfect Justice, a Grace of Ihdā, (*ihdinā* from the Fātiha, said for the dead, and for the coming of the Mahdi), Irshād, guiding the community toward a collective ideal left incomplete by the founder of Islam, toward the secret of her heart (*sirr al-ikhlās*)?

One may be puzzled by the coincidence, in Fātima, and in women in so far as they reflect her vocation, of a "spiritual insurrection" and a silent consent—a revolt against man's injustice, but an acceptance of God's message in and through it. This a paradox of which Massignon is well aware, and the resolution of which he claims to find in the "extreme point, the heroic apogee of non-violence."[20] Nonviolence is in that sense a consenting revolt against injustice that purposefully calls upon itself the reaction of the violent, thus redeeming their sin, in an apotropaic fashion. Offering oneself as a victim is a way to restore the law, and the terrestrial order marked by the Fall, to its perfection; a point that Shī'ite activism, in the expressions of its violent revenge against its oppressors, has failed to perceive, according to Massignon.

We have discovered, therefore, a deep connection between the function of femininity, the spiritual sense of history, and the meaning of inner Islam. The latter is conceived by woman as a perfection, through grace, of the approximation of the law, a perfection that emerges in full light toward the end of history, through "the final promotion of the female sex." This inner conception oriented toward a final consummation is characteristic of what could be called Massignon's "feminist" eschatology: It does not refer, lest it be misunderstood as a sociopolitical phenomenon, to an assertion of women over men, nor even to mere calls for social equality, but rather to a kind of prophetic witnessing inseparable from sacrifice and suffering. This is not only the expression of one woman's aspirations, in Fātima the Radiant; it also translates "a popular eschatological hope in the final advent of justice, silently preserved in the heart of women."[21] Fātima, as other Muslim feminine figures of Massignon's spiritual universe—such as 'Arūsah al-Sahrā, who died a virgin on the night of her betrothal; Saydah Nafīsa, the patron-saint of Cairo who was "while still alive, a source of graces for those suffering";[22] Saydah Nabīha Wafa'iya, an unmarried shādhiliya ascetic whose body remained incorrupt at her death; and the second daughter of Husein, Umm Salama Fātima, who shaped "the ascetic mahdist mentality" of Nafs Zakiya,[23]—all incarnate this inner and suffering tension toward justice.

The spiritual "feminism" of Massignon is not likely to stimulate the enthusiasm of most women engaged in contemporary feminine causes. Massignon was too perceptive not to be aware of it, as shown in the text of one of his lectures given at Toumliline, in Algeria, in 1957: "(. . .) Women often treat me harshly for my ideas. I went and preached among feminists, and they did not receive me well, saying: 'You have a way of admiring us that discards us.'"[24]

The lecture in question is centered on the theme of education, but its focus lies primarily in the place of women's education in Islam. Education is conceived by Massignon as a "civic duty", that is, a duty pertaining to the external realm of society. In this domain, Islam "has been fundamentally and very violently, even excessively, I acknowledge it, in favor of education being reserved for man in view of his civic training."[25] It bears stressing that, when making such a strong statement, Massignon qualifies it by mentioning that this tendency to exclude women from the realm of education was particularly virulent in the Maliki world, that is, primarily in North Africa, while some other areas of the Muslim world, particularly countries ruled by the Hanbali juridical madhdhab, have in fact encouraged the education of women, although it was done exclusively within the fields pertaining to their ability to perform their religious duties. Aside from such exceptions, Islam has by and large been extremely restrictive in matters of women's education. Massignon does not delve into the question of a comparative approach to this question, which may have revealed an analogous, if not similar, situation in other traditional religious worlds. Be that as it may, in mentioning the role played by women's visits to cemeteries in giving them access to the teachings of *fuqaha*—the condition being that the latter be blind in order not to give rise to suspicions of sexual ill-doing—Massignon suggests that women's education has had something private, secret, and occult that is the index of a social shortcoming on the part of Islamic societies, but also the symbol of a feminine specificity of approach to the things of the spirit. Massignon is thereby torn, as it were, between a call for an improvement to women's educational status in the Islamic world, and a recognition of a special spiritual quality of female inwardness. On the one hand, Massignon, as early as 1923, defends—in his own testimony—the idea of the creation of a school for girls before the prefect of Fes. On the other hand, he does not hesitate to say that a "certain igno-rance" is a "blessing" akin to a quality of "abandonment of the soul to God" and a mode of "inner purity" and recollection in God's presence, a thought with which, in his own words, some Muslim women reproach him. For him, the "systematization of school" tends to destroy this inner quality that is con-sonant with the contemplative essence of *tasawwuf,* and Islam at large. For him, "Woman is grace, in the deepest sense of the word, in this horrible life of men."[26] Grace lies beyond the letter, and modern education is primarily about "letters," explication, commentary, reflexive awareness—all characters that lead Massignon to object that "it is not necessary to understand everything we say." There is an understanding that passes understanding, and it is women's province; not only, nor primarily in the usual sense of the fairly superficial view of a psychological intuition, but, rather in the sense of an underlying communion with the essence of being, below or beyond language, in the unuttered presence of the *"point vierge"* that opens onto a spiritual declension of the human with the Divine. It is this grace that a Westernized infatuation with exteriorized knowledge threatens to dry up, in part because it remains totally unaware of the intrinsic limitations of the "world of men." Such a precipitation, and self-righteous obsession, with the outer dimension of edu-cation is a way of forgetting that "if there is something in education that is more than everything, it is to mock education," in the same way as, for Pascal, "the real philosophy is to mock philosophy." A real education, in other words, does not absolutize its own status *qua* education. It fully understands its own limitations and its utter contingency vis-à-vis the real goal of human life as realization of God's ontological dominion over the soul. There lies, for Massi-gnon, the deepest relation between the feminine and inner Islam. Inner Islam is "feminine" because it amounts to a realization that "the soul is feminine, the soul must keep silent, it must consent to its destiny, and God teaches much more in the heart of men than he teaches in the book, and through teach-ers." Many of the current deviations and disruptions of Islam in the world may very well derive from a one-sided, "masculine," and formal hardening of the message of the religion. If, as Massignon contends, and not without reason, man/*vir* is a "brute," it is because he does not know how, or does not want to, listen to the "feminine" grace that is in him, nor to the silence of woman as an inner focus on the perfection of truth and justice that is profiled on the last horizon of providence. Such silence is not a call to "passivity" in the usually pejorative sense that the term is given in our hyperactive societies, since it flows out into manifestations of truth and justice. For Massignon, the feminine vocation of inner Islam is therefore connected to outer realization in several ways: first and foremost, in the sense of providing women with modes of spirituality that are paradoxically both induced by, and liberating from, their frequently inferior social status; second by allowing them to make use of this inner vocation as a lever in their public testimony and action for justice; third in fostering the sensibility of mankind to the plight of those in need, particularly the foreigners and the displaced; and finally by transmitting to their children an education of the soul in the spiritual continuity of their tradition, both of these last two roles being finalized by a resolution of the collective aporiae of mankind.

Considering the importance of the feminine as support of contemplation in Sufism, as epitomized by Ibn 'Arabī's statement "(. . .) witnessing God in woman is more complete and more perfect (. . .),"[27] one could be surprised not to find any substantial account of this spiritual perspective in Massignon's works. In fact, however, the reason for this lack lies in his very negative or skeptical perspective with regard to this contemplative path. This appears, for example, in his somewhat dismissive treatment of one of the greatest names of Sufism, 'Umar Ibn al-Fārid, *al-sultān al-'ashiqīn*, the Prince of Lovers, whose poetry he defines as consisting in "artificial languors striated with cries, Platonic desire of going back to the sexual ambiguity before the creation of Eve."[28] Elsewhere, he criticizes the Neoplatonic dreams of "escalating to Heaven through the ladder of human love." For him, the contemplative "sublimation" of sexuality is only a dead end or a self-flattering complacency. It is based on two illusions: that of being able to dispense with the limitations of the flesh, and that of recovering an androgynic status preceding the sexual bifurcation. The ascetic, Augustinian, perspective of Massignon on human love is expressed, by contrast, in the ideal of "marriage, made sacrament, (to) reach together a spiritual union, by going through the physical union destined to procreation, (. . .) the duty of spouses being to contain, through an increased continence, the physical element of their union." Ultimately, this leads to the spiritual ideal of "Woman as Mother of man," which our meditations on Fātima have already suggested.

Henry Corbin's perspective on the relationship between contemplation, femininity, and inner Islam could not be further removed from such an Augustinian and ascetic outlook. In fact, Corbin has been instrumental in bringing out the profound originality of the envisagement of femininity in Sufism, in contradistinction with both Christian asceticism and exoteric legalism. The two contemplative figures who have had a central role in informing Corbin's thought on the subject are undoubtedly Ibn 'Arabī and Rūzbehan Baqlī. It is with the latter that Corbin has perhaps most clearly indicated his own affinities in devoting to him, not only pages from *En Islam iranien III*, but also a French translation of *Kitāb-e 'Abhar al-'āshiqīn* (*Jasmin des Fidèles d'Amour*).[29] In these texts, Corbin focuses on what he has come to refer to as "*amphibolie*" (*iltibās*), avoiding thereby the negative connotations of "ambiguity" while being faithful to the meaning of a co-presence of two degrees of reality at one and the same time. For Corbin, *amphibolie* is at the very center of the perception of beauty in the feminine form within the spiritual context of Islamic mysticism. Let us specify, first of all, that the choice of the human and feminine form as focus of *iltibās* is not fortuitous. The theomorphic privilege of the human form in Islam is expressed in the Quranic *ahsan taqwīm* (most beautiful of forms) to refer to the state in which mankind was created, a perfection that reflects in fact the Divine Perfection.

As for the specifically feminine aspect of this form, mention must be made of Ibn 'Arabī's point concerning the fact that "witnessing God in woman is more complete and more perfect, since he (man) witnesses the Real with respect to being both active and passive."[28] This amounts to saying that man is passive toward God but active toward woman, which means that, in considering woman, man contemplates God both in the active and passive mode, hence in the most perfect way.[29] Corbin situates this twofold aspect of the contemplation of woman in Ibn 'Arabī in the context of what he refers to as the "Creative Feminine." This concept is founded on the parallel—which is obviously not a literal equivalence—between the relationship that unites God and Adam, on the one hand, and that which unites Adam and Eve, on the other hand. God is a "Pathetic God" in the sense that He is defined by His Sadness, a metaphysical symbol of his aspiration to be known by "other than Himself": this is "the Sadness of the *Theos agnostos* yearning *to be known* by and in that same creature."[30] Analogically, Adam's sadness lies in his solitude "which is appeased by the projection of his own Image" in Eve. Adam's love for Eve thereby replicates God's love for Adam, and this love is actually knowledge, knowledge of self in the mirror of the other. In loving woman, man loves himself, which amounts to saying that he loves God since he is himself God's love for Himself. The central theophany of femininity appears, therefore, as the unfolding of God's projection into existence. It is in this very profound sense that woman is creative: by being "created" by man she is also "creating" him as "creator," "she is creatrix of the being by whom she herself was created."[31] She is thereby like the Breath of the Divine Compassion which creates by being "created."[32] God, man, and woman are thereby in an intrinsic "creative sympathy" that expresses the essence of the *hadīth qudsi*: "I was a Hidden Treasure and wanted to be known, so I created the world."

This triad, God, man, woman, is also fundamental to Rūzbehān's experience in so far as it ultimately leads to the consciousness that the contemplator, the contemplated, and contemplation are one. This is the esoteric *tawhīd* of human love, which Corbin encapsulates in the Neoplatonic formula, "the Divine Being is himself together love, the lover, and the beloved."[33] Now, taking account of the principles enunciated above, how does the experience of the contemplation of feminine beauty in love bring about the "amphiboly" that lies at the heart of Rūzbehān's Sufism? There are, in this domain, two pitfalls, the first being hedonistic license, the second ascetic zeal. For the hedonist, whose god is his own pleasure, there is nothing else to the contemplation of beauty than the physical beauty itself, or rather the self-contained delight that it inspires in the beholder. This is the trap of a purely sensual love that makes two gods out of the experience, thereby falling into polytheism: the first god is the form itself, and the second, ultimately, is the self of the beholder. By contrast, the "pious ascetic," jealous of God's prerogative as supreme object of human love, keeps his eyes to the floor by fear of worshipping the creature. This attitude is representative of the domain of the law, the primary objective of which is to lead humans toward what lies in their ultimate interest by providing them with protective guidelines, the purpose of which is not to unveil the ultimate meaning of human love, but merely to keep its dangers at bay. Between worldly indulgence and ascetic zeal, the experience of feminine beauty representative of the spiritual ethics of the *Fedeli d'Amore*[34] transcends the very terms of the duality. It consists in perceiving the Divine and human beauty *in the same gaze*, as two faces of the same reality. This means seeing the Divine in the mirror of the human, and the human in the mirror of the Divine. In Chapter One of the *Kitāb-e 'Abhar al-'āshiqīn*, Rūzbehān presents us with the development of this dialectics of love, in the form of a lively dialogue between the narrator, Rūzbehān, and a young woman who will play the role of his spiritual instructor in the mysteries and dangers of love. It must be stressed that the beginning of the story takes place at the time the spiritual wayfarer has already reached what Sufis designate as *fanā'* and *baqā*, extinction and permanence:

> My annihilation through my own unification of power was revealed to me; He (the Divine Being) extinguished me to the law of the condition of creature, made me such as I am in the gaze of the increate; He made of me a superexistent of superexistence.[35]

This is important to stress in three senses: first, because the experience of love that will follow is not to be held as a preparatory stage toward a purely spiritual flight; it is in fact rather a test of the depth of this flight; second, because the very experience that will be described presupposes a degree of death to oneself and rebirth in God as its inner prerequisite; and third, because it conveys the suggestion that the human condition is always the human condition, and therefore always susceptible to the emotional and aesthetic components of terrestrial existence. It must be added that the role of spiritual instructor performed by the beautiful woman evokes two distinct, and in fact complementary, aspects of femininity. This is the paradox of the changing "voice" of the young woman, at times warning of the dangers of the contemplative experience of her own femininity and its incongruity with the law, at other times opening the door to an esoteric understanding of female beauty and grace. The first aspect pertains to the dimension of fear and respect, the inviolable aspect of femininity that manifests itself outwardly in the boundaries of the law; the second aspect relates to the deepest vein of feminine reality as "presentation" of divine beatitude.

The first stage in the path of the *'ashiq* is described as the encounter of a young "fairy whose grace and beauty enslaved to the power of love all the creatures of the world."[36] The shock of this meeting leads the beholder to question the spiritual legitimacy of his delighting in the vision of the beautiful maid: "According to Sufism, is not paying attention to somebody other than God a sin of impiety?"[37] In other words, is this not *shirk* in practice, if not in theory? This pondering hesitancy, and scruple, is reinforced by the response of the maid herself: "To turn one's gaze away from the divine world is a sin of negligence." She thereby gives word to the very objection that exoteric doctors and ascetic Sufis would not miss raising: To look at, and pay attention to, human beauty is *ipso facto ghaflah*, negligence, forgetfulness of the Divine. Coming as it does from the young beauty, this is probably a way of testing the degree of spiritual insight of her admirer, for upon his insisting question, "such as you are in God's gaze, who are you?" she replies, in turn, as a subtle metaphysician: "The secret of the divinity (*lāhūt*) is in humanity (*nāsūt*), without the divinity undergoing the trouble and damage of an incarnation (*hulūl*) (. . .) Beauty in the human creature is the reflection of the divine nature. (. . .) Creation begins with me; in God it finds its consummation."[38] The relationship between the human and the Divine is mediated by beauty, which, as a reflection of the Divinity, is both *apparent* in the creature and *independent* of it. Moreover, beauty is creative, it is the very Word, as it were, from which all things are made. From the standpoint of its epiphanies, Beauty is like a ray of the sun that falls as a gift upon the creature but does not belong to her. The young lady is well aware of both aspects; she knows herself to be beautiful without making of this fact her *own* beauty. She is not unaware that beauty is also the principle, or the supreme archetype, of creation; in it everything is perfected as in "God's gaze." The utter freedom of the divine source of beauty vis-à-vis its situs of manifestation becomes all the more evident in proportion to the concentration of the lover. At the height of his recollection, "by dint of contemplating her, (. . .) that which in the outer human form constitutes her true essence became, for me, independent from the visible symbol."[39] This complete interiorization of feminine beauty, which reminds one of Majnūn's refusal to see the living Layla out of faithfulness for his adoration of the inner Layla that he bore in his heart, leads the young woman to intensify the test of her lover's spiritual resolve by trying to break her relationship with him. Hence the provoking statement:

"In my eyes, Sufism is incompatible with license." This rebuke prompts the lover to come to the essence of his experience by making explicit the meaning of amphiboly: "The love I feel for you is precisely the premise of divine love (. . .) the condition of amphiboly (*iltibās*) is indispensable for experiencing the ecstatic inebriation of divine love, for the beginner as well as for the most expert of mystics."[40] Following a final attempt, on the part of the young beauty, to prod the orthodoxy of her lover's certainty by suspecting him of wandering, the lover concludes his argument with a series of canonical quotations, including *ahādīth,* such as, "He in whom lie a love and an overwhelming obsession for God, through God and in God, loves beautiful faces." This *hadīth* enunciates a principle which is all too likely to sound like an enigma, if not a scandal, to the conventional religious consciousness: How could the love of God translate into the love of beautiful faces? Corbin likes to refer to the depressing realities of the modern context in which "unconscious profanations committed in the name of advertising or sports-related mores, so-called 'demythologizations' or 'demystifications,' have so totally 'desacralized' human beauty, that the *numinous* character that it presents for the faithful of love is maybe the strangest if not the most foreign thing for contemporary man."[41] By contrast, such quotations demonstrate, a posteriori, that the essence of the experience of human love and feminine beauty is in fact the inner meaning of Islam's perspective on sexuality broadly defined. If Islam accepts the latter as an integrating part of human existence, it is, ultimately, because it is one, in essence, with the Divine nature itself.

Now, the *tawhīd* that derives from the spiritual experience that is at stake allows one to dwell on the question, likely to be raised, of the feminine experience of beauty in such a mystical scenario. Is not this path of access to the Divine through human beauty an exclusively masculine affair that reifies woman, reducing her to the status of an "object," while perpetuating her social status of subservience in the name of a mystical exaltation of her most external features? This is the most likely reaction to be expected from the vast majority of contemporary readers of Corbin's spiritual foray in Rūzbehān's wake. In fact, however, the inner reality of *tawhīd* as lived through the experience of erotic contemplation, which is here our focus, is potentially as much spiritually illuminative for women as it is for the man involved in this mystical scenario; although it may be so in a different, and complementary, way. The anecdote of Rūzbehān's contemplative love encounter with a young woman in Mecca, told by Ibn 'Arabī in his *Futūhāt*, tells of the effects of the intrepid sincerity of the young mystic upon the object of his ecstatic devotion. Ibn 'Arabī specifies, and Corbin insists on this fact, that Rūzbehān's transfigurative love for this young singer leads to her spiritual transformation as well.[42] Rūzbehān remains silent of his love, in keeping with the *hadīth* "He who loves and keeps his secret dies as a martyr." But his beloved is so shaken to hear about the depth of the devotion he has for her in silence that she herself converts to the way of Sufism. Having become the object of an adoration that has been freed from the attachment to her external contingency, she can become aware of the beauty that, within herself, escapes all relativities and all alteration by time: "the theophanic function with which she has been vested by the lover, leads her to the inward truth of her beauty (. . .)."[43] This is indeed parallel to the most profound meaning of Dante's final verse in his sonnet "*Amor e'l cuor gentil*", "*E simil face in donna uomo valente*" (and so does man awake love in the lady). An objection may be made that a woman has only a very passive and reactive role in this path toward self-discovery, since she de facto depends upon her lover's gaze to awaken to herself. But this passivity is only apparent; she is indeed the active magnet that draws to her the eyes that will unveil her *sirr*. Man's activity is for its part quite passive, deriving its power from she who becomes the focus of his contemplation. In both cases the supreme activity consists in detaching the reflected light from what it has made visible. Thus is realized the *tawhīd* of the lover, the beloved, and love itself, transcending the polarity of the two lovers to realize the unity that is the real fuel, and meaning, of their love. This mystery is beautifully expressed in the *Kitab-e 'Abhar*:

> If we are not ourselves love, the lover, and the beloved, then who is it? All that is not this indivisible instant is no more than the world of duality. Meditate on this strange fact: it is myself who, without myself, is the lover of myself (*man bar man bī-mān āshiq-am*). I do not cease to contemplate myself, without myself, in the mirror which is the existence of the beloved. So, *myself*, who am I?[44]

The connection of this theophanic experience of love and femininity with Corbin's inner Islam may, by now, have been intimated by the reader: The beloved is none other than one figure of the Angel, the mediating being whose appearance on the horizon of the soul unveils the self to the self. This Angel often bears the marks of a feminine identity: He is akin to the "spiritual sister," the twin, the alter ego whose nature is symbolically feminine inasmuch as it evokes the other half of oneself. His femininity also lies in his participation in a more "informal" domain of reality than the terrestrial soul, enmeshed as it is in physical reality. Ultimately he/she is also the inner face, the esoteric dimension of the self, the soul "in heaven."

All these considerations lead us to infer the fundamentally feminine identity of inner Islam for Corbin. This is best illustrated, perhaps, by his discussion of the Ismaili hermeneutics of the foundational narrative of Adam and Eve. In this interpretation of the Quranic story, Eve is conceived of as a compensation given to Adam for the betrayal, or lack of submission, of Iblis. The refusal of Iblis to prostrate before Adam, as taught by the *Qur'ān*, is, in this context, a symbol of a rejection of the intimate connection between the exoteric and the esoteric.[45] By claiming his superiority as a "being of fire" as opposed to Adam's "clay," Iblis asserts the superiority of the esoteric, while separating it from the exoteric that he refuses, in disdain, to acknowledge. If

Eve is a compensation for this rejection it is in so far as she represents the inner reality of Adam, an inner reality that proceeds from him and is one with him. Complex Ismaili meditations on the topic identify Eve as one of the twelve "spiritual ribs," *lawāhiq,* "who had been chosen to surround Adam and help him."[46] This spiritual interpretation of Eve's function is evidently connected, in Corbin's Shī'ite imagination, to a parallel between the law and the spirit on the one hand, and Adam and Eve on the other hand:

> (. . .) The esoteric is essentially the Feminine, and (. . .) the Feminine is the esoteric (the Self that is deep and hidden from man); (. . .) That is why, in the bi-unity, the couple or dyad, that forms the prophet and the Imām, the prophet who is instructed to state the exoteric, the Law, symbolizes the masculine; the Imām invested with the esoteric and the spiritual sense, symbolizes the feminine.[47]

This identity between the inner and the feminine appear to us to be the major convergence between Massignon's and Corbin's meditation on femininity in Islam. Although the informing principles and spiritual flavor of the two approaches greatly differ—mystical and redemptive in Massignon, gnostic and theophanic in Corbin—it remains nevertheless true that both Islamicists have highlighted the essentially feminine character of Islamic spirituality. Such an association is neither arbitrary nor fortuitous; it actually stems from an intuition of the metaphysical roots of the feminine, within the context of a tradition highlighting the masculine (*Huwa,* He) identity of God as he manifests himself in the *Qur'ān* , that is, as a prescriptive Master (*Rabb*) and Legislator. There is, therefore, a feminine Islam that may not always be visible but assuredly nourishes (*Qur'ān* 2, 212) and transmits, most often in silence, the secrets of *tawḥīd* and the grace of *ittihād.*

Given its essentially esoteric character, it may therefore seem particularly surprising that Guénon's work is so clearly devoid of any substantial references to the importance and meaning of femininity. This is all the more surprising when one considers what is perhaps the central concept of his metaphysical opus, that is, All-Possibility, the realm of non-Manifestation that transcends Being (Plato's "*epekeina tes ousias*")[48] and constitutes, in many metaphysical idioms, the supra-ontological roots of the feminine. Even Guénon's studies in symbolism, which one might have expected to touch upon certain aspects of the feminine, do not reveal any significant matter on which to meditate. For lack of any other possible consideration, one cannot but wonder why the feminine is so conspicuously absent from the spiritual world of the French metaphysician. Two answers may be put forward: First, Guénon's work has been characterized as mathematical and geometric. Its mode of expression virtually excludes all elements of musicality and grace whether it be the "science of symbols," which is presented in his books as a rigorous architecture of correspondences and analogies, or the "initiatory sciences," which pertain to rigorous modes of technical transmission that may easily give the impression of ignoring the imponderable role of grace. The second answer is related to the fact that his work is primarily focused on the purely doctrinal aspect of traditional teaching, thereby staying clear of any references to the living side of spiritual matters. Now this dimension, which pertains to the function of spiritual instructor, is precisely that which is most akin to the feminine modalities of inner Islam, being connected as it is to the immanence and freedom of inspiration.

Schuon's work could be envisaged as a comprehensive response to such a lack. It is really no exaggeration to say that his opus is literally innervated—as befits the dynamic aspect of feminine inspiration—by the centrality of femininity in his exposition of Islamic spirituality. This centrality is to be felt on all levels of consideration, from the metaphysical to the spiritual. It bears mentioning, at the outset, that Schuon considered himself to be determined by a *Maryamī* inspiration, meaning that his intellectual and methodical contributions were in fact marked by the spiritual imprint of the figure of Maryam. In the context of Islam this is, of course, closely bound to the lessons of the Quranic account of Maryam's mission, in the *sūrah* that bears her name. This account recapitulates, for Schuon, the spiritual qualities and emphasis that he has in view in his definition of quintessential Sufism. First, Maryam separates herself from the world: "And make mention of Mary in the Scripture, when she had withdrawn from her people to a chamber looking East."[49] She thereby embodies the otherworldly and hidden dimension of Islam, privy to the essential origin of the tradition symbolized by the East. She devotes herself exclusively to prayer, expressing by this choice the ultimate primacy of the remembrance of God (*dhikr*) over all other aspects of the religion, since it is their synthesis and essence. This concentration on orison, and utmost trust in God, finds its "divine complement" in her being fed miraculously, first in her oratory,[50] and second when finding a palm-tree in the desert ("And shake the trunk of the palm-tree toward thee, thou wilt cause ripe dates to fall upon thee").[51] For Schuon, Maryam represents, therefore, the perfection of the soul in adoration of her Lord, and thereby the ultimate meaning of inner Islam.

On a metaphysical level, the relationship between the feminine and inner Islam is also most significant in bringing out the question of the gender-specific designation of God in monotheistic traditions. This matter revolves around the debate over the genderless definition of the Essence. The divine essence is understood by Schuon as Beyond-Being, a concept that refers to the principle that the Supreme Reality lies beyond all oppositions, and cannot therefore be equated with Being, which implies a potential polarity with non-Being. Now this principle quite obviously implies that Reality dwells beyond the polarity of genders, and cannot therefore be satisfactorily, or fully, apprehended by the use of either. To this first remark must be added the complement that monotheistic religions, including Islam, envisage God as a masculine reality, as flows from their sacred scriptures. This indicates, from a strictly metaphysical point of view, that these religions, do not consider a priori the Divine at its highest level of reality. They merely envisage it as Being, or Supreme Being, by virtue of the fact that their spiritual economy is based upon the *relationship* between God and mankind. However, the denomination of God as *Allāh* is not, in itself, exclusive of a higher degree of reality. In fact, Schuon asserts that this name is inclusive of all ontological levels *in divinis*, referring to Allāh as a Person—hence the anthropomorphic expressions of the *Qur'ān*—as well as to the Essence that bears no relationship whatsoever with man *qua* man. The "absolutely Absolute" can thus be designated in Islam as masculine, hence the masculine pronoun *Huwa*, sometimes used to refer to the Essence beyond the polarity of an I and a Thou, a designation that is in fact Quranic in origin since it is used, among other occurrences, in the *Sūrah al-Ikhlās*, a most central passage of the Book.[52] Schuon takes note of Ibn Arabī's reference to the Absolute as *Hiya*, She, but he also notes that this designation has nothing exclusive about it, for "God is indivisible, and who says 'He' says 'She.'"[53] Taking into account the fact that the Arabic word for the Divine Essence is the feminine noun *Dhāt*, it must be added that this designation refers in fact to a situation, that of Islam precisely, in which Being *qua* masculine reality is understood as the first determination of a Supreme Reality, Beyond-Being, considered, by contrast, as being feminine. The latter is then "synonymous with indetermination, illimitation, mystery (. . .)."[54] This Divine Femininity is none other than the Infinite dimension of the Principle, or the All-Possibility. Let us quote Schuon on the ways in which this Divine Potentiality can be envisaged:

> (. . .) There is (. . .) in the Real a principle of polarization, perfectly undifferentiated in the Absolute, but capable of being discerned and the cause of every subsequent deployment. We can represent this Principial polarity by an axis, either horizontal or vertical: if it is horizontal, it signifies that Potentiality (. . .), remains within the supreme Principle (. . .) as an intrinsic dimension of latent potency; if the axis is vertical, it signifies that Potentiality becomes Virtuality, that it radiates and communicates itself, and that consequently it gives rise to the first hypostasis, Being, the creative principle.[55]

This passage must lead us to specify that Schuon envisages dimensions, modes, and degrees in the Divine Order. The question of a "superiority" of the Masculine or the Feminine *in divinis* can be envisaged primarily in terms of dimensions or of degrees. The two main dimensions of the Divine are its absoluteness and its infinitude. The former is akin to masculinity inasmuch as it entails necessity and exclusiveness, the latter pertains to femininity in so far as it involves liberty, or potentiality, and inclusiveness. The Divine Essence is both the Absolute and the Infinite, which means that it can be conceived of either as integrating the Masculine and the Feminine—while being exclusively identifiable to neither—or as being primarily Masculine or Feminine depending on whether it is envisaged as the Absolute or the Infinite. On this level there is obviously no question of Masculinity or Feminity being "higher" or "lower," although relatively speaking the Masculine would be "superior" to the Feminine in terms of Necessity, and the Feminine "superior" to the Masculine in terms of Potentiality or Liberty. On this level of consideration, the Infinite is the *Shakti* of the Absolute, which is why the Absolute is normally considered to be the "first" dimension of the Supreme. Schuon tends to reserve the notion of *Shakti* for the second of two dimensions or aspects of reality that are situated on the same metaphysical level. He thereby distinguishes between metaphysical "pairs" or "couples" that "are horizontal when the second term is the qualitative and thus harmonious complement of the first, in other words, if it is its Shakti" and others which are "vertical when the second term tends in an efficient manner towards a more relative level or when it is already at such a level." This is parallel to the fact that, in Sufism, God can be referred to essentially as *Huwa* or *Hiya*, although exoteric Islam refers to God only as *Huwa* on the basis of its scriptural and theological point of view.

As for the degrees of Divine Reality, Schuon describes them, in descending order, as Beyond-Being, Being and the "existentiating Logos." Schuon refers to the relationship between Beyond-Being and Being through the symbol of a triangle, the basis of which is above and the top below. While Beyond-Being in itself can be represented by a triangle the basis of which is formed by the two dimensions of absoluteness and infinitude, the passage from Beyond-Being to Being appears in the form of an inverted triangle with its "upper" basis comprised of the Absolute and the Infinite and its "lower" top of Being. In this respect, because Being "proceeds" from the Infinite as All-Possibility, the Feminine is identified to Beyond-Being, and Being to the Masculine as the first autodetermination of Beyond-Being. It is as if the Feminine Infinitude and Indeterminacy of Beyond-Being were contracting or concentrating in the Determination of Being as the Principle of Relativity. The infinite space "becomes" the point from which proceeds all the rays and circles of Universal Relativity. The "passage" from Beyond-Being to Being is not, therefore, properly speaking a projection *in divinis;* it is an autodetermination of Beyond-Being, as the point is a determination of space. It is, in a sense, akin to the Kabbalistic *tsimtsum*, in that it can be conceived symbolically more as a "contraction" or "concentration" than as an "unfolding" or "development."

Schuon repeatedly asserts that Being is indeed part of Universal Relativity. It is the summit of *Māyā*, or what he refers to as the "relatively Absolute." Now Schuon also refers to the relationship between the Masculine and the Feminine as being epitomized by the relationship between *Ātmā* and *Māyā*, or the Absolute and the relative. Inasmuch as Being is part of *Māyā*, it seems plausible to consider the relationship between the two degrees of Beyond-Being and Being in terms of the Masculine and the Feminine, with the latter being from this vantage point at a lower degree and the former at the higher one. Now, in fact, we have been unable to find any passage in Schuon's work in which Beyond-Being would be envisaged as Masculine and Being as Feminine. Although Schuon considers the Absolute as Masculine and Relativity as Feminine, he does not seem, to the best of our knowledge, to use this model to refer to the relationship betwen Beyond-Being and Being. We believe that this is the case because even though Being « belongs » to *Māyā* it is normally envisaged by Schuon as the first Determination of Beyond-Being rather than as its Projection. In other words, Being is considered as "proceeding" from the infinitude of the Supreme Reality, rather than from its absoluteness, which is exclusive. This seems to us the reason why, even though it would be excessive to claim a superiority of the Feminine *in divinis*—since the Supreme is both Masculine and Feminine, the particular relationship between the two degrees of Beyond-Being and Being is envisaged in terms of a "higher" Feminine Reality and a "lower" Masculine Reality. Inasmuch as Beyond-Being is considered from the standpoint of its Indeterminacy and Inclusiveness, or as the Infinite, it is undoubtedly Feminine, and since the relationship of Beyond-Being to Being "proceeds" through the Infinite Dimension of Beyond-Being—and not *stricto sensu* from its absoluteness, it makes sense that the Feminine would be *particularly*—but not exclusively, associated to the Divine Essence *qua* Beyond-Being in relation to Being, without in the least negating its dimension of Masculinity in Itself as the Absolute, nor therefore its "relative" superiority over the Feminine from the standpoint of Necessity.

There is little doubt that when considering matters *in divinis*, Schuon emphasizes the Feminine over the Masculine—without this emphasis being in any way exclusive of a recognition of the masculine dimension of the Divine. This emphasis on the feminine is parallel to the fact that the Divine Essence has been "felt" as a feminine reality by many mystics. It also coincides with the reality of Divine Mercy as the most essential "layer," if one may say so, of the Divine. As we have mentioned above, the Infinite is the *Shakti* of the Absolute in the sense that it is the principle of what will become its projection on the lower level of Relativity, but the relationship between the two does not imply a vertical hierarchy since they are both dimensions of the same Principle. In one respect the Infinite is "superior" to the Absolute, as in another respect it is the opposite that is true. The same holds true, analogically, in what Schuon designates as the paradoxical "reciprocal superiority" of man and woman on the terrestrial level. When referring to the relationship between man and woman, Schuon envisages three points of view: that of friendship that implies equality, that of sexuality—in the widest sense—that entails "reciprocal superiority," and that of biological and social identity where man enjoys a privilege of relative superiority. The first relationship finds its metaphysical foundation in the fact that the Absolute and the Infinite are two dimensions of one and the same Reality. The second standpoint refers to the fact that the Absolute is "superior" to the Infinite with respect to Necessity, while the Infinite is "superior" to the Absolute with regard to Possibility, or Potentiality. As for the third angle of vision, it pertains to the affinity between the masculine and formal determination on the one hand, and the relationship betwen femininity and essential indeterminacy on the other: It can be conceived, therefore, as the reverse analogy of the corresponding relationship between the Feminine and the Masculine *in principio*.

These brief metaphysical considerations suggest a particular affinity between the super-ontological degree of reality and the feminine as inner reality pertaining to the supreme *Haqīqah*. This observation cannot be taken to mean that the Essence is feminine, as preceding considerations have demonstrated, but it does suggest the primacy of a certain angle of vision which is, perhaps, the specificity of Schuon's metaphysical outlook.

There is a profound connection between the metaphysical vision sketched above and the importance of the feminine element in Schuon's spiritual world. Going back to the spiritual portrait of Maryam in the *Qur'ān*, we can observe that she is envisaged both as Virgin and Mother. She is Virgin by virtue of her withdrawal and seclusion, and Mother with respect to her bearing the child Jesus. Now this twofold nature has implications both on the metaphysical and spiritual levels. With regard to the metaphysical aspect, let us recall that Schuon's metaphysical delineation unfolds as follows: Beyond-Being is the "absolutely Absolute," which is intrinsically Infinite and Perfect; Being is the auto-determination of Beyond-Being, and the principle of manifestation; as such, it corresponds to the Quranic Creator; Existence is the immanent dimension of manifestation that encompasses everything. In geometrical symbolism, Beyond-Being is infinite space, Being is the point that is the first determination of space, and Existence is the circle that radiates from the point. In this context, the twofold nature of Virgin and Mother refers to the feminine divine degrees of Essence, Substance, and Existence, since the Essence is both Infinite potentiality and Indetermination, while the ontological Substance is both productive of and untouched by its manifestation, with Existence being for its part the matrix of multiplicity and the underlying principle of its unity. According to Schuon, this double aspect of Virgin and Mother also manifests itself, accordingly, on the level of the spiritual life. As Mother, feminine "aid descends upon us from Heaven," while as Virgin, feminine "attraction raises us towards Heaven."[56] From the first vantage point, divine femininity initiates mankind into a second birth whereas from the second perspective it "offers liberating graces." In the spiritual economy of Islam these two functions are manifested by the divine names of Mercy, which Schuon relates intrinsically to the Virgin Mother. These are *Rahmān*, the Clement, and *Rahīm*, the Merciful. These two names correspond to different degrees and modalities of Mercy: *Rahmān* is a name of the Essence, which as such, is identifiable with intrinsic Divine Femininity, whereas *Rahīm* refers to Divine Mercy as it relates to the world of creation. Schuon notes that these two names derive from the root RHM, akin to *rahim* and *rahm* meaning "womb," which relate them suggestively to Divine Femininity. The *Basmallāh*, which includes both names, initiates and introduces the *Qur'ān* just as it introduces every pious and legitimate action. It thereby expresses a spiritual consecration to the feminine *Rahmah* that is immanent to all things. As for the "liberating graces" akin to the Virgin, they are connected by Schuon to the Islamic realities of *Barakah*, or blessing, and *Sakīnah* or gentle appeasement. The *Barakah* is the spiritual influx that radiates through sanctified presence. It is, therefore, connected to grace felt as a feminine reality, both immanent to and independent of the formal, masculine, texture of the tradition. As for the *Sakīnah*, related to the *Shekhinah* of the Kabbalah, it evokes the notion of peace as immanent to the heart, as expressed in the Quranic verse "*Huwa alladhi anzala as-sakīnata fi'l-qulūbi-l-mu'minīn*" (It is He Who sent down peace into the hearts of the Believers) (*Qur'an* 48, 4). On a higher level of consideration, this *Sakīnah* is none other than Wisdom, *Hikmah*, the seat of which is located in the human heart. If there is a certain divergence of emphasis between the two realities, this difference has to do with the fact that *Sakīnah* is conceived of as a descent from God into the heart of the believer, whereas *Hikmah*, while being divine, is a "supernaturally natural" reality that "we bear in our very essence." This reality is identified by Schuon with the Holy Virgin.[57]

The correlation between the metaphysical and spiritual aspects of Divine Femininity may not immediately present itself to Schuon's new readers. It is, however, a matter of profound relationship, and the opus modulates it in various ways and from a variety of perspectives. It is to be unveiled, first and foremost, in the association between the dimension of Infinitude in the Principle, which Schuon often characterizes as the Divine source of Relativity. It is not "Divine Relativity" itself, for this paradoxical characterization belongs to Being, which is both included in the Divine and also relative in relation to the Essence. Femininity *in divinis* pertains primarily to the supra-ontological degree of the Essence, but it represents the dimension of infinitude that "prompts" the Absolute to "go out" of Itself to realize its All-Possibility in a determinate, manifested mode. The Feminine in God is, therefore, that dimension that projects itself "out of Love." This is why manifestation is, in essence, feminine and merciful, below the crust of its segmentations, crystallizations, and accidental separation from the Principle. Reaching the core of reality means reaching the feminine, whence Schuon's repeated quote from the Song of Songs, "I am black but beautiful," a poetic statement that amounts, metaphysically, to pointing to the immanent mercy and beauty of reality beneath the surface of ambiguity and accidental ugliness and evil.

We must now complete this presentation of Schuon's considerations on femininity by emphasizing the central role that it plays in the spiritual alchemy suggested in his books. The term spiritual alchemy is used here very generally, in keeping with Schuon's own usage, to refer to the inner transmutation of physical realities experienced in terrestrial life, whether it be the reality of our own body or the phenomena that are part of our ambience. One will see that this alchemy is directly rooted in the metaphysics of femininity sketched above. There is, in effect, a sense in which the latter is the principle of the manifestation of forms. Such a function is akin to the notion of *Hijāb*, the ontological veil that both covers and reveals God's nature. The first aspect is related by Schuon to the mystery of Eve, the second to Mary. Femininity can be an obstacle to the perception of the Real, or it can be "an open door" to the Divinity. The first aspect is primarily envisaged by exoterism, the second by esoterism. However, the spiritual economy of Islam allows for the manifestation of gleams of Mary's aspect inasmuch as beauty and pleasure are envisaged in Islam as a kind of *barakah* by virtue of their participation in divine blessings. By contrast, not a few currents of Sufism overemphasize *zuhd* or asceticism in response to the potential dangers of Eve. In her positive aspect, terrestrial femininity is an expression of the liberating function of forms. Whatever may be the complex interplay of religious perspectives within the framework of Islam, the quintessential Sufism that Schuon has in view is characterized by a full integration of the interiorizing potentialities of femininity, both in its aspects of goodness and beauty, which are the two faces of mercy. This function of the feminine in the spiritual path is suggestively expressed by Schuon when he refers to feminine musicality as bringing "the segmentation of form back to unitive life, reducing form, which is a death, to Essence—at least symbolically and virtually—so that it vibrates with a joy which is at the same time a nostalgia for the Infinite."[58] To write that "form is death"—as the letter that kills—implies that the definition and segmentation of forms would constitute a sort of metaphysical and spiritual "dead end" were it not for the fact that forms may become as if liquefied by the vibration that emanates from their essential source. "The formal world is made of congealed essences"[59] but feminine forms are the eminent bearers of a musicality and "metaphysical eloquence" that make them specifically apt to melt the ice of this existential crust.

As we have been able to suggest through the preceding analyses of Massignon, Corbin, and Schuon's works, the function of femininity in Sufism and inner Islam is a fundamental and determining one. Whether in the silent or sacrificial testimonial of woman as witness of corruption and reminder of justice, the theophanic revelation of divine mercy and beauty, or the metaphysical implications of a "feminine knowledge," Islam hides and reveals at the same time the feminine core of its spirituality within the framework of a religious language outwardly characterized by the regimen of Semitic patriarchs and the formal Law. This characteristic is expressed both in a tension and its resolution, that is, the discrepancies that an outward and legalist focus unavoidably produces, and their inner cancellation, or reversal, in the *haqīqah*. It remains that this spiritual resolution, and its potential or actual outer consequences, presupposes that the avenues of inner realization be as wide open to the women who conceive of the inner reality of Islam as to the men still able to decipher the inward secret of the feminine. It is also to be feared that a primary, or exclusive, concentration on the outer approximations, flaws, and abuses of the world of society and action may precipitate both men and women into the blind alleys of a formal, superficial understanding of justice. Inner Islam offers the path to an acceptance of true self, and receptivity to vocation that is predicated on transcending the limitations of the complacent and vindictive ego. Such a transcendence is the true meaning, and fulfillment, of femininity in Islam, since it only reaches the inner shore of the *ghayb*, the divine mystery that opens the way to genuine freedom, *hafizat li-l-ghayb bi mā hafiza Allāh* ("Guarding in secret that which God hath guarded") (*Qur'an* 4, 34).[60] This affinity of woman with the *ghayb* is also a reminder, for men, of the ultimate meaning of woman, thereby guarding them against the self-assertive illusions of their temporary and circumscribed vocation to outer vice-regency.

Chapter Six

THE UNIVERSAL
HORIZON OF ISLAM

There is no world religion that does not claim universality for itself, at least in the sense of its being potentially accepted by all of mankind. Even autochthonous shamanistic traditions, as bound as they may be to a particular people and a particular land by virtue of their spiritual economy being intimately connected to a sense of sacred immanence in the most concrete natural and physical phenomena, presuppose a type of relationship to spirits and the Spirit whose objectivity guarantees the existence of other manifestations in different modes and different languages. Hinduism and Judaism, though undoubtedly grounded in a specific covenant, or a specific revelation that draws the boundaries of a sacred community into which it may be possible to enter only under very exceptional circumstances and on the basis of very strict conditions, envisage their respective traditions like a sacred basis that ultimately calls for a universal entrance into the precinct of Divinity. On more complex and subtle grounds all world religions have tended to develop, especially in the last century, theologoumena allowing for some latitudinarian interpretations of the faith, even though the exclusivist bent of collective mentalities and institutions has also curtailed the limits of such inclusiveness. In Christianity, and particularly in the Catholic Church, the concern for universality has focused primarily on the extent given to the redemptive promise of salvation, since the unicity of the Redeemer generally prevented taking account of a metaphysical unity independent of the Incarnation. Massignon's student and Dominican priest George Anawati has reminded his Christian readership that the theological position of the Church has been, for many years, that all men have access to supernatural grace through Christ, even outside of baptism and without entry into the Church, through faith and moral conscience.[1] There is therefore a distinction to be drawn between baptism as a sacrament giving access to the supernatural life and what Massignon has called the "baptism of desire," that is, the inner, implicit, and most often unconscious longing for baptism understood as a grace freely given by the Redeemer beyond the confessional boundaries of his Church.

As the last of the major religions on the world stage, Islam has benefited from its historical situation, retrospective identity, and encompassing simplicity in fostering its universal claims, not only in the general terms of the validity of its creed for all people, but also in the more specific sense of an ability to recognize and integrate prior faiths within its own sacred history. In other words, Islam is in a position to claim an eminent degree of universality by reason of being the last revelation and, as such, the synthesis of all previous messages, as indicated by the directness and "transparence" of its emphasis on divine Unity. One of the central tenets of the Prophet's predication lay in his assertion that his mission did not bring to mankind anything new. Islam is simply the reminder of the original religion, ad-dīn al-qayyīm (Qur'ān 30:30), which has been alternately known and forgotten by mankind since the origin of time. The specificity of Islam as a "new" religion is simply to restate, to correct misrepresentations of the one and only religion that has always been, and to bring the cycle of revelation to a close. This situation is already indicative of two potential hermeneutic poles of Quranic reading, which have in fact been taken as seeds of interpretation of the nature and identity of Islam. The first of these poles is characterized by an insistence on the coincidence of Islam with what has always been known, and it is as such the maximally inclusive horizon of Islam. The other, by contrast, has tended to sharpen the distinctness of Islam by emphasizing the fact that the new religion was indeed needed to restore the pristine authenticity of the primordial religion, without which the very mission of the Prophet would seem utterly superfluous. In the Qur'ān, these two ways of understanding the universal horizon of Islam are expressed in the double meaning of the word muslim, which can be taken most universally as referring to those who acknowledge divine Unity, like Abraham and the prophets, or in a more restrictive manner as pertaining to the disciples and followers of Muhammad. Islam is thereby in its very definition in a position most conducive to acknowledge the spiritual validity of other religions, at least in principio, being even potentially able to make of this privilege a paradoxical claim of superiority. Now, Sufism conceived as the inner core of Islam has most often capitalized on this universality of Islam to enter into fruitful contacts, or even convergences, with other spiritual paths. One of the most striking examples of this spirit of openness and spiritual exchange was witnessed in seventeenth-century Muslim India in the wake of the Moghul legacy. Shah Jahan and Mumtaz' son Dara Shikoh,[2] the grandson of the illustrious Akbar, had the remarkable insight of bringing together works and representatives of the main spiritual traditions of India, namely Vedānta and tasawwuf, in a symbolic junction of the "two oceans" of wisdom (majma'al-bahrain). Besides this most eloquent historical development, one could mention the two often-quoted verses of Rūmī and Ibn 'Arabī[3] "I am neither Christian nor Jew, nor Magian, nor Muslim" and "My heart has become capable of every form: (. . .) it is a convent for Christian monks, and a temple for idols, and the pilgrim's Ka'ba and the tables of the Tora and the book of the Koran" as exemplary expressions of the ability of Sufism to serve both as spiritual "container" for diverse manifestations of wisdom, and as inner ladder allowing one to transcend the exclusiveness of creeds. It is precisely this aspect of Sufism that today makes it particularly attractive in the West, albeit sometimes in a somewhat hasty and superficial manner. ·

Coming as they did from a Christian background that tended to limit the universal scope of religion because of an emphasis on the historical unicity of the Incarnation and Redemption, it comes as no surprise that our interpreters were, by and large, receptive to the opening of horizons provided by Sufism. As we will see, the extent of this receptivity varied greatly, from Massignon's substitutive ecumenism to Schuon's "transcendent unity of religions." In spite of sometimes radical differences of outlook and accent, it remains nevertheless true that the apprehensions of inner Islam that our authors have propounded have been among the most effective instruments of inter-religious understanding in the twentieth century and beyond.

The essence of Massignon's ecumenism is encapsulated in his famous spiritual motto, "*on se rapproche d'une chose non en nous, mais en elle*" (one comes closer to something not in ourselves but within it). Such a courageous conviction is at the core of Massignon's spirit of "decentering" that itself determines his practice of "compassionate substitution." The mystical motion of substitution (that Massignon called *badaliyah* in Arabic) consists, as we have already noted, in an experience of suffering in the place of others; it is best described in a letter of Massignon to his friend Mary Kahil:

> . . . They say that the *Badaliya* is an illusion because we cannot put ourselves in the place of another, and that it is a lover's dream. We must respond that this is not a dream but rather a suffering that one receives without choosing it, and through which we conceive grace. It is the visitation [by the spirit of God], hidden in the depth of the anguish of compassion, which seizes us as an entrance into the reign of God. It certainly appears powerless, yet it requires everything, and the One on the cross who shares it with us transfigures it on the last day. It is suffering the pains of humanity together with those who have no other pitiful companion than us.[4]

This "entrance into the other's system" is the basis for interfaith understanding, since there cannot be any real dialogue without a temporary suspension of one's belief and attentiveness to the spiritual "logic" of the other. Massignon favors an approach that is "without restriction" and involves an ability to live with the other in his own system of religious representation, so as to assess whether or not it is "livable." As a consequence, such an existential participation in the other's way is necessarily connected, for Massignon, to a willingness to "espouse in one's thought the claims for justice of the other."

Justice is, as it were, the ultimate horizon of universality, since it takes account of the particular claims of each community while situating them within an integral human finality. However, this "universalism" in action and justice does not sanction what Massignon designates as "pluralism de jure"; it simply takes spiritual account of a de facto pluralism, and makes it the "spiritual matter" of an inner transmutation. In other words, understanding and dialogue should not imply any kind of relativism with respect to dogma and creed; they simply involve a spiritual discipline of communion with the other within the psycho-spiritual framework of his own system.

Grounded in the soil of this kind of "mystical empathy," Massignon's "entrance" into Islam is accordingly predicated on the idea that Islam has been "suffering" because of its exclusion, since the time of Hagar and her wandering in the desert, from the full fruition of Abrahamic monotheism, the final and most acute evidence of this exclusion being Muhammad's rejection of the Incarnation. It is no doubt this emphasis on the sufferings of Muslims throughout history that accounts for Massignon's affinity with those he calls "Shī'ite legitimists." For Massignon, the apostolic gains of Shī'ism on the borders of Islam bear witness to the frustrated desire for justice that has been burning like a wound within Islam and which are showing clear signs of becoming infected with the poisons of political rancor—hence, for Massignon, the need to substitute oneself for Muslims to conceive and realize in them the perfection of Love within Jesus Christ. This means that Massignon's closeness to Islam is based both on his recognition of the genuinely monotheistic inspiration of this religion, but also on his acute sense of what he considers it to be lacking in terms of its fulfillment by grace. Massignon acknowledges a level of divine inspiration for the *Qur'ān*, and he considers Muslim faith, not only as a natural reality, but as a theological one. This is no small acknowledgment when one remembers that theological virtues are, in Catholic doctrine, directly infused by God, who is also their ultimate object. Acknowledging the theological nature of Islamic faith amounts, therefore, to identifying Islamic spirituality as supernatural, and not simply natural. Among other important consequences, this distinguishes it from Hindu and Buddhist forms of spirituality, which are deemed to be no more than natural—that is, expressing a merely "natural" thirst for the Absolute—by Catholic theologians and scholars such as Jacques Maritain and Louis Gardet, whom Massignon follows on this point.[5] Although being supernatural, Muslim faith "does not suffice for salvation according to Christian doctrine but it is still faith that is the root of justification."[6] It is on such complex and qualified foundations that Massignon can preach a brotherly respect for Muslims, this respect not extending, however, to the recognition of an essential unity of the two religions. It cannot come as a surprise, therefore, that Muslims' grateful appreciation of Massignon's Islamology has been, on average, mixed with a measure of unease, if not latent irritation. This cannot but be the case, given that Massignon's Islam, when reduced to its fundamental "architecture," is no more than an intimation of the promise of Christianity.

In characteristically paradoxical fashion, Massignon's ecumenism appears to be founded on difference rather than identity. In matters of interfaith under-standing, he believes in what he calls "singular numbers and signs" rather than in "common measures and common denominators," as he declared at the 1947 World Congress of Faiths.[7] In keeping with his mystical engagement into the life of his tradition, what matters most for him is a convergence of the authen-tic core and the most original specificity of each religion. Authenticity here refers to the concrete and active witnessing of saintly figures who have been ready to give their lives for their faith; hence the idea of an existential ecu-menism, as epitomized in Massignon's recognition of Gandhi's spiritual great-ness, notwithstanding the context of a tradition that Massignon has proved unable to understand in its full metaphysical implications. If Massignon can be legitimately suspected of reducing the whole of Hinduism to Gandhi's *satyagraha*, "spirit of truth," rejecting the non-dualism of Advaita Vedānta in the name of a devotional consecration to Isvara, the personal God of worship, the source of this partiality is to be sought in a heroic, mystical vision that cannot make sense of a spirituality that would not be centered on an amorous dialogue between the soul and her Lord.

Such a personal, dynamic, and engaged—Hindus would say bhaktic—understanding of religion, with its stress on the unicity of the existential tes-timony that it demands and the collective implications that ensue, cannot be consonant with what Massignon calls, in a somewhat derogatory fashion, the "theosophic point of view."[8] Behind this designation, it is easy to perceive a pointed reference to Guénon, and to what will later become known in the Anglo-Saxon world as the "perennialist school," that is, those authors who have asserted the existence of a universal and perennial wisdom underly-ing the various religious expressions of divine revelation. Massignon's objec-tions to this position are basically two: First, such a "theosophic" argument amounts to placing oneself above the religions themselves, and their explicit teachings; second, it implies that one is too far detached from the essence of religion, which is, for him, devotion.[9] The first objection manifests, in Massignon's perspective, a rejection of the principle, enunciated in various religious expressions of the path of knowledge, that there is something in man that transcends man *qua* man, being divine Light. It is this divine Light, and not the person as such, that makes it possible to consider the literality of the religious message "objectively," and as if "from above." Of course, Massignon's mystical point of view cannot be compatible with such a gnostic perspective since, for him, the essence of religious consciousness is a sincere and passionate identification, on the part of the believing soul, with the immediate, specific, grace attached to her faith. The "interchangeability" of religions that Massignon alleges to be representative of the perennialist outlook, seems to him to preclude the very possibility of an "exchange" or a "dialogue," hence its inappropriateness at a congress of world believers. A closer look at the matter may reveal these assumptions to be only partially true, in the sense that the "theosophic"—the term being used here to refer to the perennialist approach—point of view does not involve, contrary to what Massignon implies, the idea of a perfect equivalence of traditions in their forms and modalities, but only a convergence of goal, and a transcendent unity with respect to their ultimate object. Massignon is not unjustified, though, in perceiving this transcendent perspective as somewhat incongruous with the idea of a dialogue, at least when such a dialogue presupposes essential and irreducible differences with regard to the nature of Reality, and the means leading to it. However, the perennialist perspective may be a precious instrument of interfaith efforts when understood as an intellectual and spiritual framework allowing one to situate differences within an integral context that makes sense of their raison d'être: It does not amount to an obliteration of distinctions and divergences but rather opens one to the possibility of an understanding of their intrinsic necessity and limits. It is clear that for Massignon any kind of intellectual "distance" in religious matters entails a spiritual flaw in terms of sincerity and devotion toward the religion in its particularity, whereas the "gnostic" point of view postulates, by contrast, a perfect adhesion to, or identification with, the universal essence of the creed, transcending, thereby, its exclusive literality in order to embrace its inclusive depth. This does not in principle contradict the respect and devotion owed to saintly characters who are the spiritual exemplars of a given tradition, since these figures, like the traditions they embody, express in their being and action the universal principles of spirituality that their tradition conveys. It must be granted, and this is no doubt what Massignon had in view, that a primarily intellectual approach may result, not in itself perhaps but through an undue onesidedness, in an underestimation of the existential dimension of metaphysics and spirituality. Massignon's merit, through his caveat, is to alert one to the potential presumption stemming from a confusion between theoretical understanding and spiritual realization.

In this connection, Massignon had felt very early on, and his difficult relationship with Guénon bore witness to it, that Islam could be understood, especially in Sufism, as an ideal framework for the manifestation of what he calls "theosophy." This concept, needless to say, was deeply at odds with his own understanding and experience of Islam. Accordingly, he repeatedly objected to the premises of such an approach to the religion brought by the Prophet Muhammad. His first line of objection is related to a profound disagreement with the idea that Islam might be an initiatory, or as he put it, "secret" doctrine. In his lecture at Toumliline, he deplores the power of attractiveness of the initiatory view of Islam in French spiritualist circles:

We have in France the school of Guénon, a school of gnostics who say: "Islam is a secret doctrine." This is very seductive. Many Christians become Muslim by supposing that Islam is a secret doctrine. (. . .) I do not believe that Christianity and Islam are secret doctrines.[10]

The initiatory emphasis of Guénon's understanding of Islam is not consonant with Massignon's concept of a redemptive function of religion with respect to entire human collectivities, thanks to the public witnessing of sacrificial figures. If there is undoubtedly an "elitism" in Massignon's thought, it is precisely to be found in the notion of "real elite" that he assigns to those self-sacrificing heroes of the Spirit. In conformity with this sacrificial function, the main mission of Sufism is, for him, to bring out to the public the deepest layer of religious consciousness, as it were, in order to realize its liberating potentiality. There is no question that Massignon's affinity with the figure of Hallāj is very intimately bound to this call for an unveiling of the truth. The universality of inner Islam is conveyed by this testimony: It thereby radiates upon the whole community. If there is indeed a secret in this mystical manifestation of truth, it is the *"point vierge,"* the inner *sirr,* from which it springs forth; it could not be further removed, for Massignon, from the universal tendencies of Ibn 'Arabī's Sufism, which confines itself, in his view, to mere philosophical concordances and interferences. For Massignon, such universality is only superimposed *in abstracto* and does not do justice to the inner reality of Islam as an Abrahamic profession of faith. Set against the background of such an intellectual horizon, the so-called "theosophic" perspective appears to him predicated upon the view that religious teaching is dispensed through degrees of initiation proportionate to the aspirations and qualifications of its recipients. In Islam such a principle is founded on a series of *ahādīth* suggesting levels of predication on the part of the Prophet, and stressing the need to speak to each according to his own level of understanding. Upon close examination, and notwithstanding an undeniable bent toward initiatory secrecy in the background, personality, and stylistic mannerisms of Guénon, the author of *The Reign of Quantity* and his continuators have not actually reduced Islam to a secret doctrine since they have maintained with great clarity the coexistence of two dimensions of the tradition, as esoterism (*haqīqah*) and exoterism (*sharī'ah*).

As for the potential universalism inherent within Islam, Massignon perceives it more as a spiritual temptation than as a positive feature. He considers Judaism and Christianity to be better prepared than Islam to resist what he would call gnostic "infiltrations"; the former does not lend itself to Massignon's fears of "syncretistic" universalism, being so to speak protected by the Mosaic law; the latter is no less immune to such dangers, presupposing as it does, a "baptism of desire" that is the sine qua non of a participation in Christic grace. By contrast, Islam is particularly susceptible to "gnostic universalism" because of the very simplicity of its dogma and its focus on divine Unity, which can be all too easily reduced, in Massignon's view, to an intellectual abstraction. Given its emphasis on truth rather than life through the *shahādah*,

Islam appears to Massignon ill-equipped to counter the proponents of an esoteric universalism that he seems unable to differentiate from the position of
Deism. One cannot but think here of Corbin's puzzlement concerning Massignon's mysterious exclusion of certain spiritual phenomena "from the light of
his intuitive understanding." In a sense, Massignon's attempts at discovering
within Islam traces of a living mysticism of testimony, thereby fulfilling its
Abrahamic vocation in the obscure intent of a "baptism of desire," is in direct
contradiction with a perspective that conceives of Islam as a pure and direct
restoration of that "which has always been and always will be," to use Guénon's expression. Massignon's inner Islam evokes the seeds of a growth toward
the full unconscious recognition of the one Savior, while Guénon's esoteric
Islam stands as the inner truth of the last manifestation of a primordial religion
eternally inscribed in the Intellect.

If Massignon perceives a genuinely universal horizon in Islam, it can be
none other than the vision of Abraham's religion of friendship with God in
truth and justice. The most important function that Islam can fulfill is, in
this view of things, to "stigmatize" Christianity for having too often lost
contact with the monotheistic sense of primordial adoration. Islam, therefore,
is a constant reminder for Christians of the unconditional demands of the
Absolute: "It is the angelic spear which stigmatized Christendom."[11] In the
characteristic language of Catholic mysticism, "stigmatizing" amounts here
both to condemning and to inflicting a wound, as befits a term suggestive of
the wars of history and the contest of faiths. This purely spiritual function
of "stigmatization" reverberates in the geopolitical domain of contemporary
politics when "Islam threatens to lead a general insurrection of the exploited
against the superior technical, monetary, and scientific oppression of a Europe
without Messiah and without God."[12] These foreboding words suggest all the
complexities, ambiguities, and tragic consequences of a situation that blends
the innermost aspects of the desire for truth and justice with the external
sociopolitical symptoms of collective religious sickness. There is no doubt
that Massignon tends to perceive the universality of Islam in terms of an
eschatological vocation. He goes so far in that direction as to define Arabic,
the "liturgical language" of Islam, as the language of ultimate peace, which
"will be the language of promulgation of the second Advent."[13] It is suggestive to note that Massignon connects this proclaiming function of the Arabic
language to the Eastern origin of the Magi bringing offerings and prayers to
the child Savior. This clearly indicates the function of Islam, in his view, in
the completion of the cycle of Redemption, as if Muhammad's religion were
to universalize, so to speak, the promise that Christianity had conceived in
truth, by and through its ultimate gift of the spiritual fruits of its long and
hard story of faithfulness.

If it were possible to find a partial and rare convergence between Massignon and Guénon with respect to the universal function of Islam, it would
have to be sought in the eschatological realm. Both perceived Islam as a religion

entrusted with a specific role in the closing of this cycle of human history. The critical segments of Guénon's work are focused on the specificities of the current cycle of human history, and they actually convey the message that numerous "signs of the time" can be discerned in contemporary predicaments. These signs are systematically related to an all-encompassing character, which is the predominance of quantitative factors and measures in virtually all domains of contemporary human pursuits. The "reign of quantity" introduces in fact a first important distinction most relevant to the question of universality, since it entails a fundamental opposition between a form of universality based on unity, that of religions considered in their essential message, and another akin to uniformity, the principle of which is the reduction of all things to purely quantitative factors. The parody of unity and universality by means of uniformity appears in full light to the "extent that more uniformity is imposed upon the world" and is "so much less 'unified' in the real sense of the word."[14] This apparent paradox finds its source in the fact that uniformity is predicated on those characteristics of a being that are most severed from what makes it participate in the unity of being, that is, its quantitative and external aspects. In that sense, the uniformity introduced by the technological and social changes of the last century realize an inverted reflection of the organic unity that unites all beings within an intelligible whole, whether a priori metaphysically or in all other contingent domains of application. Such a fundamental inversion cannot but have implications for the religious level as well. With respect to Islam, one must recall Guénon's argument about the "counter-traditional" parody of restoration of a caricature of "quality" and universality toward the end of the cycle, posterior to reaching the extreme limits of the initial process of "quantification" that had hitherto characterized the modern world. On a formalist level, the so-called fundamentalist movements are an attempt at fostering a "universal Islam" based on a literal, formal interpretation of the religion, claiming to restore the religion to its full universal horizon beyond sectarian and "innovative" deviations or accretions. At the other end of the spectrum, the last decades have seen the development, particularly in the West, of a neo-Sufism that has argued for the severance of Sufism from its Islamic framework, thereby advocating a full development of its universal scope. Both movements, as contrary as they may appear on the level of their immediate positions, reflect in fact the type of reversal of principles that Guénon had in view when describing the way in which "counter-spirituality" would present itself as a return to authentic tradition. They both constitute unconscious attempts at uprooting Islam from its genuine, inner sap, in the name of a one-sided, superficial understanding of Islamic spirituality.

From another point of view, the cyclical perspective of Guénon, which is consonant with the general teachings of eschatological ahādīth, but extends beyond Islamic teachings in being primarily informed by Hindu traditional data that encompass a plurality of past and future worlds beyond the current cycle of prophecy envisaged by Semitic traditions, firmly asserts the terminal and sealing function of Islam in the economy of sacred history. An important article entitled "The Mysteries of the Letter Nūn" spells out the specificity of this function in suggestive symbolic terms. Following esoteric interpretations of *'ilm al-hurūf*, or the science of letters, Guénon observes the significance of the letter *nūn*, which follows the letter *mim* in the Arabic alphabet. The latter is symbolically associated to *mawt*, or death, and its graphic form actually evokes the prostrated station that expresses, within the cycle of the Islamic *salāt*, the point of utter extinction, or death, of the human subject before the divine Reality. While *mim* corresponds to death, *nūn* suggests rebirth, Guénon connecting this symbolism to the very shape of the letter—a lower semi-circle with a dot in its middle—as well as relating it to the shape of the whale, *al-Hūt*. The overall symbolism suggests, therefore, the protection and conception of a seed that will be the source of rebirth. By contrast, or rather as a complement, Guénon offers an interesting meditation on the symbolism of the Sanskrit letter *na*, the phonetic equivalent of *nūn*. *Na* is here envisaged as amounting (when "reduced to its basic geometrical elements") to the similar figure of a circumference and a point, the difference being that it is the upper half of the circumference, in contrast to the shape of *nūn*. The symbolic complementarity between the two letters suggests that their association fulfills the integral perfection of spiritual manifestation in this cycle. Together they recapitulate not only the entire development of the cycle but also the integrality of spiritual realization. It is worth mentioning that Guénon relates the upper half to the "upper waters" while referring the lower half to the "lower waters"; the latter referring to terrestrial perfection, whereas the former pertains to celestial realization. In his article, Guénon does not specifically refer to the respective analogy between the two religions and the two levels of existence of spiritual realization. A possible interpretation of these correspondences may be found in the fact that Islam emphasizes the total integration of the elements of terrestrial existence, whereas Hinduism may be deemed to be focused on the ultimate spiritual liberation from the cycles of existence. Another relevant correspondence is connected to an observation made by Guénon concerning the fact that the most recent religions are those which must express in the most explicit way, in their outer doctrines, the principle of metaphysical unity, this necessity being related to a decadence of metaphysical intuition leading to a growing tendency toward idolatry and gross polytheism:

> (. . .) The most recent traditional forms are those which must express the affirmation of Unity in a manner most visible to the outside; and in fact this affirmation is nowhere expressed so explicitly and with such insistence as in Islam, where, one might say, it even seems to absorb into itself all other affirmations.[15]

This "outward" manifestation of the innermost content of tradition, that is, the doctrine of Unity, corresponds, in a sense, to the reverse of the Hindu context in which the strictest affirmation of non-duality is as if hidden under the outer forms of apparent "polytheism." It goes without saying that these differences are matters of accentuation rather than exclusivity, as indicated, symbolically speaking, by the presence of the point at the center of both letters. Notwithstanding, the respective correlations between *na* and the upper world, and *nūn* and the lower world, point to the fact that Islam had to appear in the form of a law, that is, an exoteric system, whereas Hinduism constitutes *in principio* a purely esoteric doctrine. In parallel, Islam's religious egalitarianism lies in sharp contrast with the Hindu caste system.[16] It could be said, in this context, that Hinduism has manifested itself as an esoterism in the form of an exoterism—considering the social system and extreme religious diversity in which spiritual gnosis is encased, whereas Islam sprang forth as an exoterism in the form of an esoteric truth. This implicit distinction between the esoteric and exoteric realms as referred to Hinduism and Islam, respectively, has important implications for the presentation of the latter in Guénon's perspective. On account of the fact that Guénon, in another text, makes use of the symbol of the circle and its center to illustrate the relationship between the *sharī'ah* and *tarīqah*, it is instructive to consider the representation of Islam by the letter *nūn* as suggesting the role of the law as a protective ark for the transmission of the esoteric seed. This characteristic of Islam illustrates in a most striking fashion the ambivalence of the relationship between inner and outer Islam by highlighting both the instrumentality and the necessity of the law: The seed is obviously independent from the "ark" that protects and "carries" it, but the latter is still imperatively needed to guarantee the transmission of the seed.

Guénon's introduction of the notion of equivalence between the various religious traditions has often been equated to a syncretistic concept. The word syncretism is generally used in a derogatory manner to refer to the collection of disparate elements borrowed from a diversity of sources. Massignon made use of this term to refer to Ibn 'Arabī's gnostic concepts, which he considered to be informed by heterogeneous Neoplatonic elements. The Theosophical movement to which we have referred earlier could be described as syncretistic inasmuch as its philosophy is the result of associating concepts stemming from occultism, Eastern religions, and even modern science. For his part, Guénon is adamant that such is not at all the case with the traditional intellectual perspective that he represents and articulates. To the notion of syncretism he opposes that of synthesis. The fundamental distinction between syncretism and synthesis lies in the principle that the latter incorporates and relates a diversity of concepts originating in different religions from an inner point of view that proceeds from the metaphysical center to the religious diversity. In that sense, it could be said that the various elements that are brought into play in the metaphysical exposition of the doctrine are like words borrowed from a diversity of languages to refer to a reality perceived a priori and independent of any linguistic mediation. Certain words from a given language may be

richer in connotation and more adequate or encompassing than their approxi-
mate equivalents in other languages, hence their frequent and convenient use
as tools of metaphysical expression, but their use is purely instrumental to
the reality that they are intended to convey. By contrast, syncretism appears
as a heteroclitic assemblage of words, the meanings of which are not really
understood, in addition to their intended objects not being clearly perceived.
Syncretism consists in constructing a whole system by making use of a variety
of components of diverse origins that are articulated together as constituents:
It therefore proceeds from "without." By contrast, synthesis proceeds from
"within" since its starting point is the perception of the "essential unity" of
"different traditional forms."[17] This presupposes, as an important epistemological premise, that the various concepts and terms involved in the synthesis
be understood as formal and symbolic approximations of the realities they
intimate, and not as accurate and exhaustive representations of the latter. As
Guénon indicates in several instances of his work, "there is in any certainty
something incommunicable."[18]

    These principles of understanding being set, it must be clearly indicated
that the universal dimension of Islam cannot but be identified, in Guénon's
work, as the universality of "pure metaphysics" as such.[19] In fact, as we have
already suggested in a previous chapter, metaphysics is "pure" to the extent
that it deals exclusively with the universal. This amounts to saying that the
exposition of universal metaphysics amounts to the exposition of Islam in
its essential, inner dimension. Guénon actually refers to this metaphysics as
"Eastern metaphysics" in order to distinguish it as clearly as possible from
the post-medieval tradition of philosophical discourse routinely designated
by this term:

> (. . .) Why speak more specifically of Oriental metaphysics? The reason
> lies in that, in the current intellectual conditions of the Western world,
> metaphysics has been forgotten, generally unknown, almost entirely lost
> whereas in the East it is still the object of an effective knowledge.[20]

There are two main ways to approach the universality of metaphysics: one
by conceptual exposition, the second by symbolic suggestion or evocation.
Guénon proceeds through both means, since some of his works are particularly centered upon doctrine while others delve into the world of symbols.
In both cases, Guénon emphasizes the unicity of the truth underlying these
various expressions. His doctrinal approach takes two roads: It either proceeds through an exposition of universal, abstract concepts that are integral
to his metaphysical vocabulary, as in his *The Multiple States of the Being*,[21] or
else through a systematic, or partial, study of a given metaphysical idiom, like
Vedānta or Taoism, as in his *Man and His Becoming According to the Vedānta*.[22]
Let us note that, in both cases, the extent to which Islam is brought to bear is
somewhat minimal and marginal, mostly as references to Islamic principles or

phenomena appearing in footnotes as equivalent of Sanskrit or Taoist terms. Besides biographical evidence suggesting that the paucity of Islamic references is primarily due to the fact that Guénon's familiarity with the wealth of Islamic metaphysics was for the most part posterior to his settling in Cairo, it must be emphasized that the most decisive reason for this apparent paradox lies in the fact that Islam was not conceived by him as a pure esoterism, but rather as a composite tradition in which pure metaphysics was necessarily clothed in a religious language less immediately transparent than those of Advaita or Taoism. It may also be that the relative proximity of the language of Islam vis-à-vis that of Christianity made it a somewhat inconvenient tool for a restoration and dissemination of traditional principles, this being due primarily to the theological and historical interferences inherent in a consideration of Islam within a Christian context. However, we must conclude on this point that Guénon was also keenly aware of the fact that this proximity of Islam to the Christian world was equally indicative of a potential unfolding of the truly universal dimension of Islam, as exemplified by his reflection on the role of Islam as spiritual "bridge" between East and West. Spiritually situated between the world of Semitic monotheism and that of Eastern wisdoms, Islam, especially in its inner kernel, is in a privileged position to suggest the metaphysical convergence of all the traditional forms. In his first letter to Schuon from Cairo, in 1931, Guénon writes, "it is certain that not only is Islam the form least distant from the West, but it is also the only one for which the question of one's origin cannot be raised in any way nor ever constitute an obstacle."[23] There was never any sense, though, in his writings or correspondence, that Islam would be destined to play the role of the universal manifestation of the Primordial Religion at the end of time. The universality of inner Islam was only an intellectual and spiritual means of facilitating a restoration of metaphysical intellectuality in the West, and, for a few Westerners called to play a role in this restoration, the most adequate support of contemplation and daily framework for a realization of the principles of universal esoterism. As Guénon specified in one of his books, the change of traditional form that he undertook and advised a few others to envisage was by no means equivalent to a conversion in the usual sense of the word:

> Contrary to what takes place in "conversion", nothing here implies the attribution of the superiority of one traditional form over another. It is merely a question of what one might call reasons of spiritual expediency, which is altogether different from simple individual "preference", and for which exterior considerations are completely insignificant.[24]

In this connection, and in order to emphasize the fact that the universality of Islam that Guénon has in view is totally independent from any pan-Islamic objectives, it is interesting to note that Guénon actually wrote to Schuon—at the time the latter was staying in Algeria in the context of his receiving an initiation from the Shādhilī Shaykh Ahmad al-'Alāwī—to agree with him in deploring the confessionalist and propagandist tendencies of not a few modern Sufi circles:

> Here (in Cairo) the deplorable influence of politics is certainly less marked, but there exists also this unfortunate tendency to recruit as many people as possible and to congratulate oneself for this expansion; at least it might not have too serious inconveniences if one were to observe a hierarchy of degrees, but, in fact, it is not so at all. I think that, in these conditions, the best is to take into consideration only the essential, that is the initiatory transmission, and not to be too concerned by the rest; but one still must be able to accommodate oneself in such a way as not to be disturbed by it . . . [25]

It is clear that, for Guénon, inner Islam is an abode, and nothing else, hence its capacity to function as the innermost, silent, but spiritually determining core of the tradition without being compromised or adulterated by the growing confusions and ambiguities of the outer realm.

There is little doubt that Henry Corbin was also convinced that gnostic or Sufi Islam had an important role to play in bridging the gap between the West and Asian religions and cultures. He seems to have conceived of it primarily in terms of its ability to integrate the spiritual values of surrounding traditions. This is not to say, though, that Corbin's outlook is identifiable, *tale quale*, with the perennialist perspective of a Guénon. His perspective is not actually centered on the premise of a universal doctrine originating with the Primordial Tradition, but rather on a phenomenology of religious consciousness that places the "religious act" as the origin of all human modes of being and acting. This foundational aspect of religious consciousness "has always been itself since the beginning of all thought, feeling, will, etc (. . .) it is a transcendental Presence, inseparable from That which it renders present."[26] By focusing on the intentionality of religious consciousness, Corbin intends to unveil what constitutes the reoccurring features of a concrete relationship between the individual and the universal Absolute. What clearly distinguishes Corbin's outlook from Guénon's is the way in which this relationship is articulated, and the spiritual focus that results from this articulation. Paradoxically, it could be said that the universality of Islam, or rather the integration of Islam to a universal phenomenology of religion, is proportionate to its capacity to integrate the personal within the very process of spiritual realization as theophany of the Absolute.[27]

In order to understand the specificity of Corbin's outlook, and the characteristics of his understanding of inner Islam, there is no better way than to delve into a major theoretical text of his that recapitulates the limits of its recognition of a *sophia perennis*, and the requisites that he attaches to its proper definition. In his essay "Of Apophatic Theology as an Antidote to Nihilism,"

Corbin propounds a refutation of George Vallin's apologetic of Indian non-dualism as articulated in his article "The Tragic and the West in Light of Asian Non-dualism." Vallin's thesis, founded on a philosophical meditation of Shankara's Advaita Vedānta, asserts that the specifically tragic character of Western consciousness throughout its history is to be linked primarily to a Western emphasis on the notion of person as the "*permanent ideology* of Western mankind."[28] The de facto absolutization of individuality, which results from identifying the real man as ego—meaning here simply the individual reality *qua* individual, when confronted with the metaphysical limitations of the latter, cannot but open onto nihilism and produce anguish and despair. All the problems of Western philosophy and Western mankind stem, in fact, from its *belief in the reality of the ego*, the reality of the individual as such. It is important to note, and particularly so in our current context, that the non-dualistic perspective is often considered the most universal horizon of metaphysics, and as such the underpinning of the doctrine of the transcendent unity of religious forms. For Guénon, for example, the Akbarian school of *wahdat al-wujūd* is the Islamic equivalent of the non-dualistic school of Advaita Vedānta. Now Corbin rejects non-dualism inasmuch as he understands it as being incompatible with a recognition of the reality of the individual person. When Vallin, founding his meditations on Shankara, claims that individuation is nothing more than a superimposition that veils the fundamental and infinite Reality of Being as universal Subject immanent to the human subject, Corbin concludes that such a view amounts to affirming that "the individual is guilty of existing, guilty of his own existence."[29] This proposition is considered as "extremely worrisome" by Corbin, who deems it incompatible with the personalist perspective of Semitic monotheism, as well as with the spirit of Hellenic philosophy. It is interesting to note, as an indication that Corbin's concerns may not be warranted, that one of the most famous formulae of early Sufism, attributed to Rābi'ah al-'Adawiyyah, quotes her as having answered a man who was claiming not to have sinned for many years, "Alas, my son, thine existence is a sin wherewith no other sin can be compared."[30] Such a hyperbolic and perplexing statement cannot but have major implications with respect to Corbin's critique of Vallin's diagnosis of Western tragic "individualism." Here is a saintly ascetic of the second century of the Islamic era, steeped in the strictest religious language of monotheism, who does not hesitate to equate individual existence with the worst of human characteristic in the face of God. The monotheistic consciousness is led, in its loftiest mystical expressions, to draw the most integral consequences from its position of one God above all realities. In its most consequent expression, this cannot but amount to denying the reality of the existence of oneself as participating in the domain of "other than He." This means that non-duality proceeds from the very "logic" of monotheistic religion taken in its highest and most absolute sense. In this line of thinking, the great contemporary Vedantin sage Ramana Maharshi used to quote the Biblical "I am that I am" as evidence of the inherence of non-dualism in religion. If Ramana Maharshi is right in his connecting the God of the Bible and non-dualism, and if Georges Vallin is not wrong in ascribing to the West the unenviable privilege of an intimate association with the tragic, it must be inferred that a radical reduction of monotheism has been prevalent in the West. In this scheme of things, esoteric Islam could very well amount to a restoration of the most consequent and demanding dimension of monotheism, as epitomized in Rābi'ah's uncompromising response to righteous exoteric conscience. Now, this is not at all Corbin's reading of esoteric Islam. In keeping with his refutation of Vallin's "preoccupying" interpretation of the Western tragic sense as founded on an unenlightened insistence upon the reality of the individual self, Corbin does not hesitate to categorize such a type of mysticism under the heading of a "certain Sufism" that falls into "confusing the transcendent unity of *Being* (*wahdat al-wujūd*) and an impossible, contradictory and illusory unity of *being* (*mawjūd*, latin *ens*)."[31] In other words, the non-dualistic path advocated by Georges Vallin, and dangerously trodden by some *mutasawwufin*, consists in substituting the "Night in which all cows are black" derided by Hegel to the differentiated, stratified unity of Being as manifested in and through the theophany of beings. The latter implies the notion of Being as an act existentiating the multiplicity of beings while remaining transcendent to their appearance as phenomena. Now the extremely important consequence of this theophanic vision—meaning that the act of Being "epiphanizes" itself as it were in each of its "productions"—lies in that the individuality of each and every person is founded in God: Each soul has an "alter ego" in heaven. The matter, therefore, is not to "disappear" in the *Absconditum* of the Supreme non-dual Essence but to know oneself in its mirror. We are at the heart, as Corbin warns us, of the problem of the cause of individuation. Since Aristotle, this principle has been interpreted as matter, or unintelligible substratum, while the form, or *morphê*, or *eidos*, would be understood as the principle of universality and intelligibility. Now, Corbin proposes that it is in fact the contrary which might be true: Individuation results from the *eidos*, which means that each individual soul is "willed" by Heaven; each soul has an archetype that may be referred to in many ways:

> It can be called *Fravarti* (in Persian *forūhar*) in the Avesta, *Neshama* in Jewish Kabbalah, *'ayn thābita* (eternal haecceity) with Ibn 'Arabī, Perfect Nature (*al-tibā' al-tāmm*) with Suhrawardī and in the hermetist tradition of Islamic philosophy etc.[32]

So we are confronted with the paradox—which is only an apparent one—of a "religious universal" founded on the recurrence and ultimate permanence of the individual. It could be added that Corbin's defense of individuality is also, by the same token, a defense of religious particularity. Far from erasing the specificity of each tradition, the only act of Being is the very "producer" of each and every one of them. The universal is to be found in the individual. This principle is actually the core of Corbin's ecumenism. Nearly all of the correspondences that the French scholar establishes between traditions such as Christian Hermetism and Theosophy, Shī'ite or Sufi Islam, Zoroastrianism, or even Mahayana Buddhism are precisely centered on a recognition of the fundamental spiritual fact of the person. If we consider, for example, the spiritual tradition of Mahayana Buddhism, the outlook of which may seem prima facie quite foreign to Corbin's concern since it is oriented toward the realization of the ideal of *nirvāna*, we see Corbin manifesting an undeniable measure of spiritual interest in the figure of the *bodhisattva* inasmuch as it gives each person the potential status of a locus of perfect illumination, thereby universalizing the message of the Buddha, even to include the laity in its fold. Individual realization meets with, and ultimately means, "cosmic redemption," so that the eschatological horizon of Maitreya is itself related to the universal theme of a constellation of the spiritual persons forming a kind of chain of light in and through which all are both perfectly themselves and fully participant in the community of saintly beings. This is indeed Corbin's esoteric ecumenism: the ideal of an order of spiritual knighthood that would encompass, relate, and transcend all confessional universes.

Such a *futuwwah*, or spiritual chivalry, is predicated, as we have seen, on a full realization of the person in and through its relationship with its Lord. How should we understand, then, what appears to entail a rehabilitation of the ego, taken as individual locus of being, while most, if not all, spiritual disciplines are keen to emphasize the limitations and pitfalls of the latter?

There is, first of all, an ambiguity to dispel concerning the very notion of the ego. The term is often considered pejoratively in theosophic and mystical contexts, referring to that which, in man, denies, obstructs, or adulterates the immanent Divinity that underpins the human subject. In other words, the ego is an illusory center that strives to usurp the centrality of God. Now, the Advaitin concept is in this respect the most radical of all since it posits the radical unreality of this ego by contrast with the Absolute subject, *Ātman, Tat* (That). Corbin objects that the equation of the ego and the Absolute subject leaves open the question of knowing why and how the ego thus equated with *Ātman* remains an ego:

> In other terms, how is it "I" who has the power to say: "I am identical to that, the supra-personal Absolute", since one opposes the idea of the real man to that of the ego? Is it the real man, the illustrious ego who declares "I am that"? Is it enough to say: "I am that", for the ego to cease being illusory?[33]

It seems that these questions might have been be prompted, at least to some extent, by the frequently ill-sounding affirmation of the utter unreality of the ego in mystical literature. This extreme non-dualistic paradox is to be found, for example, in some currents of post-Akbarian Sufism, particularly in Al-Balabanī's *Risālatu-l-Ahadiyyah* (Treatise of Unity), where an elliptical and hyperbolic emphasis on the absolute unicity of God appears to lead to an utter negation of the reality of the individual self:

> (. . .) The Prophet said: "He who knows his soul (that is himself) knows his Lord." He also said: "I have known my Lord by my Lord." The Prophet of God wanted to intimate by these words that you are not yourself, but Him; Him and not you; (. . .) I mean that you exist absolutely not, and you will never exist neither by yourself nor by Him, in Him or with Him. You cannot stop being, because you are not.[34]

Understanding these statements in their literal, unqualified, and exclusive manner clearly amounts to the "impossibility" and "contradiction" that Corbin fustigates in Vallin's metaphysical statement. It seems prima facie impossible to understand Balabanī's statements as more than metaphysical shortcuts that have the spiritual, or methodical, goal of emphasizing the purely intellectual character of the consciousness of Unity. In other words, to negate in an absolute fashion the reality of the ego, without the least qualifications concerning its relative or illusory "reality," amounts to parrying any error of attribution that would illusorily empower the individual with an ability to realize the Absolute *qua* individual. In other words, how could the ego deny its existence without being existent, thereby affirming its existence? This is the fundamental self-contradiction that al-Balabanī wishes to debunk; and this is evidence, *a contrario*, that the ego is actually not.

Some considerations concerning the Advaitin perspective on this matter can be helpful to stress both the convergence and divergence between al-Balabanī's perspective and the point of view of Vedānta. In his classic *Advaita Vedānta*, Eliot Deutsch distinguishes three levels of being, which, reconstructing the system of Advaita, he defines as follows:

> Reality is that which cannot be *subrated*[35] by any other experience.
>
> Appearance is that which can be *subrated* by other experience.
>
> Unreality is that which neither can nor cannot be *subrated* by other experience.[36]

The first level of being is that of the absolute Subject, which would be designated in Sufism as the Divine Essence (*dhāt*) or *Allāh*, inasmuch as He can be identified as such. The second level of being refers to *Māyā*, the phenomenal veil superimposed upon the Absolute, which is strictly neither real nor unreal. It is not real because only *Ātman* is real in an unmitigated sense, but it is not unreal inasmuch as it can be the provisional basis for an intellectual act of subrating. The third category is that of beings such as "son of a barren woman" or "the horns of a hare," which are impossible, therefore unreal. This important difference in point of view is clearly stressed in classical Advaitin literature, in which the illusory, or unreal, nature of the self and the world is strictly predicated on a spiritual knowledge stemming from the vantage point of the absolutely Real. This essential qualification is unambiguously stated in classical Advaitin literature, as in the following passage by Suresvara: "(. . .) There is no reason to call the world unreal before the knowledge of the oneness of the Ātman (has been attained)."[37] In Sufism as well, al-Balabanī's absolute statement of unreality with respect to the egoic self could not be understood independently from an actual realization that "there is none but Allāh," as clearly indicated by the following passage from the Risālat:

> If somebody were to ask: "you affirm Allah's existence and deny the existence of anything (but Him); what, then, are these things that we see?", the answer would be: these discussions are pertinent to him who does not see anything except Allah. As for he who sees something else than Allah, we have nothing to do with him, no question nor answer, for he sees only what he sees.[38]

None can testify to His Unicity but Him, and no full and consistent attestation of His Unicity can be but by and through Him.[39]

Corbin's concern with the dangers of a nihilism that would result from the absolute metaphysical "disproportion" between the Divine Essence and the ego, and the complete disappearance of the latter "into" the former, *as he understands it* stemming from the Advaitin point of view propounded by George Vallin, is in fact not warranted when one has deciphered the meaning of metaphysical ellipses and clearly realized that the alleged "disappearance" is also, *eo ipso*, a "recovery." In his masterful chapter "The Servant and Union," Schuon writes that the supreme spiritual station is one in which "the ego, which is 'accident,' is extinguished, or becomes absolutely 'itself,' in the Self, which is 'Substance.'"[40] This statement is a most explicit development of the twofold aspect of any spiritual realization: Corbin is quite justified in writing that the loss of self, understood in an absolute, radical, sense, is either an impossibility or a dangerous illusion, but George Vallin is well-founded to advance the argument that an absolutization of the reality of the ego, deriving from a misunderstanding or a subversion of monotheistic personalism, cannot but be the premise of despair and nihilism since it does not account for the purely contingent reality of the self, which is "nothing" before the *Absconditum*.[41] Schuon's quotation allows us to understand why and how there needs be a distinction between the "ego" as a separative reality conceiving itself illusorily as independent from the One, and the "ego' as archetypical, "angelic" reality, being, as it were, what "really" distinguishes the self from nothingness.

It is particularly fruitful to relate this dialectics of the self and the Self to the question of universality in Schuon's work. It seems that the distinction

between a being as "accident" and a being as "no different from the Substance" is an essential key to an understanding of Schuon's view of the universality, and specificity, of each religion. There is a sense in which each religion
is universal, being binding by virtue of its "identity" with the Absolute source
from which it derives, while there is also another way in which the same religion cannot but be relative by virtue of its "accidentality," formal limitations,
and necessary difference from its divine Source. There is no religion that
posits itself as God and yet does not "understand" itself as other than He; but
there is no religion that draws, nor in fact can draw, all the consequences from
this distinction, without jeopardizing its own absolute claims. This is because
religion is both absolute in its essence, and relative in its form. This principle
of the "relative absoluty" of religions, if one may so put it, is further specified
in the following important passage by Schuon:

> If Revelations more or less exclude one another, this is so of necessity
> since God, when He speaks, expresses Himself in an absolute mode; but
> this absoluteness concerns the universal content rather than the form, to
> which it applies only in a relative and symbolical sense, for the form is a
> symbol of the content and so too of humanity as a whole, to which pre-
> cisely this content is addressed.[42]

What does it mean to write that the substance or content is different from
the form? It amounts to saying that the substance of a religious message perforce transcends the formal order, that is, the physical and psychic domains in
which religious dogmas, rites, and prescriptions necessarily participate by virtue of addressing mankind. The ultimate informal content of the message that
is its core pertains actually to a Reality which, at its peak, is not even appre-
hensible as an object since it coincides with the immanent Self. How should
we understand the principle that the form is a "symbol" of the content, and
of "humanity as a whole"? The word symbol is to be taken, here as elsewhere
in Schuon's work, not as implying at all a lack of reality—or pertaining to a
merely "metaphorical" status, but as referring to a dual (from the two faces of
the Greek *symbolon*) aspect as "real" and "illusory," depending on the vantage
point. It goes without saying that not all religious forms should be situated on
the same ontological level. Some are more "substantial" while others are more
"accidental." Obviously, the question of the criterion of distinction between
substantial and accidental forms cannot receive an absolute answer, since it
pertains by definition to taking into account the specificities of each objective
and subjective context in which it may be raised. Furthermore, when Schuon
writes that the religion can be taken as a "symbol" of "mankind as a whole,"
this is to be understood, along the same lines, as indicating that any given
religion, provided it is fully what it ought to be, is in actuality religion as such.
This allows us to approach the principle that Islam is "the religion with (or
for) God" (*inna ad-dīn 'inda Allāh al-islām*) in a decisive light.

The case of Islam is perhaps more transparent, but also and consequently more difficult, than that of other religions, in the sense that Islam presents itself as a mere restoration of what has always been known. If Islam is universal par excellence it is primarily because it appears as the religious form manifesting the substance of all religions through its simplicity, primordiality, and terminality. Islam acknowledges the inspiration and mission of up to hundreds, or sometimes thousands, of prophets. Its ability to integrate prophets into its perspective is about as remarkable, if not more, than Hinduism's wealth of avataric manifestations. The simplicity of the doctrine of *tawhīd* is no less striking, and Guénon's point about the maximal externalization of what is most internal is quite warranted on this ground. It is as if the final divine message needed to be as synthetic and accessible as possible in view of terrestrial circumstances, the aspect of complexity being left to the legal aspect of the religion, which is itself determined, but in reverse, as it were, by the extensive gravity of the human predicament. This dialectics of metaphysical simplicity versus legal complexity (which is already prefigured in the Judaic tradition) is at the core of the "dual" aspect of Islam, as both inner and outer religion. With Islam, therefore, we are confronted with the paradox of a "formalization" of the supra-formal essence of religion. While Islam is by all accounts more tied up with ethnocultural specifics than, say, Buddhism or Christianity, it is also the religion most centered on what defines religion as such, that is, a synthetic doctrine of the Divine Nature as One. The deliverance from existential suffering and the Incarnation, not to mention the Covenant or the "polytheism" of divine manifestations, appears as relatively extrinsic when compared with the divine Unity. On the other hand, the formal language of both Buddhism and Christianity, not to say Hinduism, is arguably more independent from cultural determinations than Islam. This paradoxical situation is evidently a key to the duality between the universality of the Islamic essence (*tawhīd*) and the limiting particularity of the Islamic form.

In his chapter "Form and Substance in the Religions," Schuon specifies that "Islam spread like lightning by virtue of its substance; but its expansion was brought to a halt on account of its form."[43] The substance of the message is its stress on divine Unity, a truth that is the dynamic power of Islam, and which alone can explain its extraordinary success in the first centuries following Muhammad's receipt of the revelation. As for the form, Schuon does not explicitly develop which aspects of Islam account for the limit of its spreading, restricting his remarks to "a religious imagery that clashes with Christian sensibility and renders the West irremediably refractory to the Muhammadan message."[44] Without entering into the details of this imagery, one may infer that it primarily includes in the religion all these elements, like the integration of political force, military means, and sexuality, which are formally foreign to a Christian spiritual ethos; this imagery is moreover intimately bound to a Bedouin way of being that makes it virtually inassimilable, at least on the collective level, by certain cultures. These elements, like other formal elements, may, and must be, appropriate within a particular context, but their formal aspect is necessarily exclusive of other circumstances. In other words, there is no absolute form in the framework of relativity.

.   Islam is not only, like any other religion, a form giving access to the substance, that is, a form in which the essence of all religions is couched; it is also *the* form *par excellence* of that essence: "(Islam) has given a religious form to that which constitutes the essence of all religions."[45] Or, in slightly different terms, "Islam (. . .) aims to teach only what every religion essentially teaches; it is like a diagram of every possible religion."[46] No religious form can be considered as *intrinsically* superior to others, since no form can exhaust the Essence, nor can any form do justice to all aspects and all points of view of Reality, but each and every form is superior to all others from a particular point of view or in regard to a specific aspect. This "contest" between the various religious points of view may be what the *Qur'ān* has in view when it states: "If your Lord had so willed, he would have made mankind one community. . . . So compete with one another in good deeds." (*Qur'ān* 5:48). As Heraclitus indicated in one of his fragments, the coming to existence of all phenomena occur as a result of a "war" among archetypes and possibilities in the religious realm, this "war" continues on the terrestrial level once phenomena have manifested. This is parallel to Ibn 'Arabī's theory of the Divine Names as manifesting "conflicting" tendencies within the realm of forms. Now, to say, as Schuon does, that Islam gives form to what constitutes the essence of all religious forms seems to imply, paradoxically, a kind of superiority that cannot be relativized from the vantage point of form in its intrinsic function, since the latter is to give access to the essence; it can only be relativized in terms of its extrinsic modes, that is, its 'imagery." If there is a difference between Islam and other religions, aside from the general extrinsic differences pertaining to the diversity of formal languages, it lies in this intrinsic "essentiality" of the Islamic form, if one may say so. Martin Lings has referred to this specificity of Islam as a "secondary universality" in addition to the primary universality that characterizes all religions, and particularly all mysticisms, as various forms of Religion as such.[47] This allows one to understand the most fundamental reason for the Sufi claim of a pre-excellence for Islam, despite the universal and "ecumenic" horizon of the highest *tasawwuf:* "(. . .) It is in this sense that some Sufis have said that, being the terminal religion, Islam is ipso facto the synthesis of the preceding religions—the synthesis and thereby the archetype."[48]

Massignon's intuition about the "theosophic" propensity of Islam (which he deplored) and the perennialist focus—not by any means exclusive, but still undeniable—on Islam as a means of expression and a religious vehicle of the *scientia sacra* must be accounted for in terms of this dimension of Islam.

Given this fundamental essentiality and universality of Islam, the paradox lies, as we have already suggested, in that the very "language" of the Revelation—understood both literally and figuratively—is intimately bound to the specificities of Bedouin culture and mentality.[49] There is arguably no "universal" religion (thereby excluding Judaism and the various autochthonous shamanistic traditions) that bears so deeply the imprint of a particular language and ethnocultural style. This formal duality of Islam may explain the critical chasm and extreme tensions in contemporary understandings and conceptions of this religion, as much among Muslims as outside of the Muslim world. The universal message of Islam is the focal point of many, while the formal characteristics and accretions of its formal structure are arresting for many others, to the point of blinding them to the essence of the religion. Schuon's intention in describing and explicating Islam is, first, to provide an insight into the foundations and characteristics of religion as such, what he calls the *religio perennis*, and second to introduce Islam in its essential dimension, thereby freeing the core (*lubb*) from the shell. There is little doubt that this is the best avenue to introduce Islam to non-Muslims in a way that is authentic and faithful to the message itself, without disconcerting them with external "clothings" that may shock their cultural imagination.

The paradox of the contemporary predicament of Islam is that the religion that is arguably the best positioned to foster a spirit of genuine tolerance and respect of other faiths has come to epitomize the sectarian spirit of fanaticism and bigotry. This, in itself, is an alerting symptom of the profound crisis through which Islam has been subjected by many of its most visible zealots. Islam came to free mankind from the fetters of tribal and national idolatry by announcing and preaching the most comprehensive and universal truth. It did so within the context of Arab culture and by means of the language of that culture: as long as the essence was—or is—clearly the informing principle of the tradition, the universality of Islam can radiate in the full range of its potentialities. It is only if and when the extrinsic form becomes an opaque veil on the intrinsic form and essence that Islam runs the risk of becoming compromised, by losing contact with its raison d'être. From that point on, the form becomes available for any ideological pretext, and the religion cannot but be reduced to a set of outward formulae. This is the situation, described by a *hadīth*, when "young people of weak mind (. . .) will speak well (of Islam) (. . .) but their faith will not go deeper than their throat (*lā yujāwizu īmānuhum hanājirahum*)."

Chapter Seven

THE QUESTION OF WAR

The use of force, and particularly military force, in furthering purportedly religious goals is one of the most sensitive and difficult issues that must be reckoned with in the contemporary world. This is obviously and primarily due to the high visibility of religious violence in the world of Islam taken as a geo-political force. However, this issue is not only a matter of political circumstances, even though the latter have certainly helped push it to the fore; it is also a question of understanding the role played by violence in religion, and its compatibility or integration with religious principles and values. Islam's integration of war within the religious domain, both historically and juridically, is perceived by many as the evidence par excellence of the militant and aggressive nature of this religion, irrespective of the fact that nearly all other religions, including those which are "philosophically" least prone to legitimize violence, such as Buddhism, have in fact made use of military means in some historical circumstance or other in order to foster their politico-religious endeavors. It is therefore no exaggeration to say that the Islamic concept of *jihād*, which has become synonymous with the ideological thrust of political Salafi movements and its military or violent modalities, has been at the center stage of the debate over Islam.

A number of contemporary commentators and apologists for Islam have rightfully emphasized the fact that the concept of *jihād* does not exclusively refer to war as such, but to any "effort," whether internal or external, toward the promotion of the good. A series of oft-quoted *ahādīth* establishes a fundamental contrast between *jihād al-asghar*, or the "lesser *jihād*," and *jihād al-akbar*, or the "greater *jihād*," the former pertaining to the outward, military, fight against oppressors and enemies, the latter referring to the inner fight against the centrifugal tendencies within the soul, in the manner of the medieval *psychomachia*. Leonard Lewisohn has rightly noted, in a recent essay on 'Ali ibn Abi Talib, that "the sword of merciful self-restraint" (*tigh-i hilm*), in Rumi's terms, "conveys in fact the subtler truth that the lesser holy war without the greater holy war is of little value, since the spirit of forgiveness and the exercise of self-restraint are in the end stronger weapons against one's enemies than the sword wielded in passion."[1] In the same vein, Reza Shah-Kazemi has argued, in an essay on the spirit of *jihād*,[2] that the *jihād al-asghar* cannot be severed from the *jihād al-akbar*, since the latter must inform the intentionality, modalities, and goals of the former.[3] In other words, the distinction between a lesser and a greater "holy war" implicitly points to the principle according to which the outer aspects of religious and moral striving stem from an inner source of inspiration that finalizes them, and informs their modalities and their "style." Lewisohn's and Shah-Kazemi's point is crucial to a full understanding of the crisis of Islamic *action* in the world today. It is no exaggeration to say that the neglect of this inner determination of action prevents any significant change in terms of the outer moral conformity and effectiveness of sociopolitical activism.

The engaged and "militant" aspect of Massignon's personality and destiny could not but lead him to delve into the meaning and implications of *jihād* in Islam. In this context, Massignon recognizes the outer and combative aspect of Islam as *justified* in the exact measure of its aspiration, and conformity, to the quest for justice. As we have suggested in a previous chapter, there is in fact a way in which Massignon conceives of this claim for justice as an eschatological sign of the times that paves the ground, as it were, for an integral, spiritually and heavenly determined, restoration of justice on all levels of reality. This is not only connected with the external modalities in which this quest may manifest itself—these being of necessity ambiguous given their enmeshment in political contingencies—but it is also related to the aspirations they express. Although Massignon's focus is on the thirst for justice, he never defines the latter in purely terrestrial terms, articulating it as the eschatological horizon of the unveiling of the truth and, perhaps even more profoundly, to the "*point vierge,*" which he conceived as the only zone in the soul to be exempt from any contact with sin and evil. Justice is an immanent secret of the soul that only the unfolding of the latter times will exteriorize in perfection.

By contrast with this genuine conception of justice, and the indignant war cries that it may inspire in a religious community, Massignon is adamantly opposed to the deceits of modern imperial wars. The French Islamicist makes use of very expressive and powerful words to refer to what he considers to be a betrayal of the "spirit of truth," as manifested in the geopolitical maneuvering of Western Europe, and the West in general, during the contemporary period. Looking back into the Medieval past, he notes, without seeking to justify the Crusades as such, that the primary, initial, motive of the latter was an authentic religious desire "to liberate the Holy Sites from Muslim occupation," while nevertheless deploring that Christendom "soon conceded to the Machiavellinism of annexionist political leaders avid to exploit and oppress their Christian brothers from the East." Today's situation is much worse, though, morally and spiritually speaking: Since being "modernized,

Americanized, (Christendom) does not believe anymore in the 'mystery of places of election' for its salvation," as shown by its entrusting them to "international technocrats (. . .) who have chosen the Holy Land as a field of experiences for stifling industrialization."[4] The "external" war of Massignon is one of resistance against these desecrating trends, as against the hypocrisy of imperial powers, including the most subtle ones, and their moral inability to hold on to their *"parole donnée,"* their failure to keep to their sworn word. In this connection, the phenomenon of secular and "national" war cannot but appear to him as a *travesti* of holy war, bearing witness as it does to a lack of rootedness in both religious institutions and people of real justice. As an evidence of this betrayal, Gandhi's statement that "official religions are very weak for stopping war" is connected by Massignon to the subservience of churches to the State, and their spiritual powerlessness to counter the naturalistic principle expressed in the rallying cry "right or wrong my country."[5] Massignon has a prophetic perception of the way in which this tragic situation places the Muslim world in a critical and potentially disastrous stance conducive to all the fevers, disorders, and rancors stemming from a sense of oppression and injustice:

> In the global strangling hold in which two monolithic machines, uncaring about their sworn word, will to strangle as "traitors" the last believers in Freedom, the first ones to be laminated between money and petroleum, in an eschatological ambience, before secular laymen and Christians, are the Muslims.[6]

Massignon's interest in Islam, at least from a sociopolitical angle, stems precisely from its being "laminated" by the New World of power, this world in which the masses find themselves unconsciously subjected to a "collective incarceration on site"—the industrialized, technological, and mechanically globalized alienation that Massignon poses as the antithesis to spiritual freedom. In fact, Islam is considered by him, until the years that followed World War II, as the last spiritual remnant of Biblical simplicity and adoration in God's hands, a remnant which he considered actually to be threatened by Western "simony."

Once this global and eschatological horizon of the struggle for the soul of the world has been outlined, what can be said of the methods used to work toward a resolution of the tensions and the victory of justice? First of all, it is important to note that tensions are not considered by Massignon as pure synonyms of negativity: Life is tension, and the essence of testimony for truth, in the sense of the Hindu *satyagraha* that he borrowed from Gandhi, is tension toward the good and the true. This positive tension, that need not result in outer war, is in fact the essence of the inner war that is at stake in "sacrificial testimony." By contrast, the outer, collective tensions that result from oppression and injustice erupt in destructive violence and war. It is precisely at the junction between collective wars and inner spiritual tension that the role of a "real elite" is called for. This elite is comprised of the apotropaic witnesses who are ready to give themselves up in sacrifice to resolve the aporiae of collective tensions. These are the Hindu mahatmas, the Muslim *abdāl*, the Christian *compatientes* who "bear witness to the same certitude about the efficacy of spiritual means (. . . .)."[7] Their spiritual "treatment" of human predicaments is, in fact, the "method" or the "technique" that Gandhi's *satyagraha* inspired in Massignon during the later part of his life. It amounts fundamentally to a nonviolent fight that offers its agent as a sacrificial victim to detract violence from its cyclic, spiral-like, evil perpetuation. Massignon further designates this type of action as a "holy war"; conceiving it as a "crusade in reverse" (*"croisade à rebours"*), he writes: "We will fight our holy war of non-violence, living our compassion to its limits."[8]

It is important to note, in this connection, that Massignon analyzes the appearance of the notion of "holy war" in Islam in an analogous context, through the figure of Fātima. As we have discussed earlier, the distress and rebellion of Fātima against "institutionalizing" Islam is understood by Massignon as a protestation against the injustice toward the oppressed, the poor, the foreigners, and "the pretension of administrations" to limit and regulate the devotion to the dead. In leaving her "house of mourning" to offer herself to the blows of 'Umar, Fātima's action prefigures Gandhi's gesture of self-sacrifice, which "provokes the effusion of blood, his own, leading his conservative adversaries, in their exasperation, to devise his death, which is a crime: because it will redeem them."[9] This redemption of others through a sort of self-sacrifice may very well appear problematic when considering that it *calls for* an act of violence which is simultaneously and consciously assessed as criminal. In the "spiritual technique" that Massignon has in view, this is actually a way, in keeping with Christ's redemption, of "clarifying" the reality of evil in order to "exorcise" its effects, "burning" it and transmuting it into the flame of sacrificial love, as it were. This mystical method is no different, incidentally, from the "transfiguration" of the Law by an inducement of its violent clash with Love, as in Hallāj's sacrifice precisely. Fātima's anger and provocation in the name of filial love and mystical faithfulness, not unlike Antigone's piety, appears as an intimation of this supreme act of surrender. This is why, for Massignon, her gesture provides the psychological paradigm for legitimate *jihād* in Islam. A very personal interpretation of *jihād* is in fact connected here to a very rigorous mystical notion that finds its full manifestation in Hallāj's self-immolation to the Law. In that sense, Fātima's gesture is only a prefiguration, and not a perfection, since its "provocative" violence does not quite concur with the psychological quality of a consummate abandonment; there is still too much indignation in Fātima for her "violence" to be purely "self-denying" and apotropaic, hence Massignon's remark that "in fact, it is in Hallāj that Muslim compassion will be, in fullness, oriented toward the universal."[10]

It is clear that Massignon's view of *jihād* is primarily centered on the *jihād al-akbar* in its most mystical dimension. The "supreme holy war of Arabian Islam" is none other, for him, than Mansūr's death at the hands of the doctors of the Law. Any legitimate *jihād* cannot but be the analogue of this ordeal, the term being taken here in its strictest acceptation as a test of love. Massignon quotes Attār, and his designation of Hallāj, as "this fighter killed by God in *jihād*," "this intrepid and sincere warrior."[11] Ultimately, the greater *jihād* is conceived as a paradoxical fight, or competition, between the servant and his Lord: "The warrior 'sells his life' in the fight to the death against the enemy, he ends up being killed by God after having killed the irreconcilable enemies of Divine Unity."[12] Metaphysically, the concept of such a holy war is predicated by Massignon on the "occasionalist" ontology that he attributes, perhaps too generally, to Islam. In other words, Islam's emphasis on the unicity of the Divine Act of existentiation entails, for most mystics and theologians, a negation of secondary causes out of an exclusive affirmation of the primary Divine Cause that the *Qur'ān* relentlessly extols. This would amount, in his analysis, to a strong tendency, within Arab and Muslim imagination, to apprehend terrestrial reality as a discontinuous chain of events in which miracles, upheavals, shocks, and surprising turns of events are, if one may say so, the rule. Now it is in this spiritual context that Massignon situates the essence of the Islamic *jihād*. In fact, *jihād* results, in Islam, from the absence of the Incarnation: Without the mediation of the Word made flesh, there is no possible participation—in the Platonic sense of *methexis*, or ontological "commonality"—between the Divine Essence on the one hand and human nature on the other. In the absence of the Word made flesh, holy war is the only mediation between these two incommensurable realities: the Divine Destiny, *Qadr*, amounts to a predestination that can only be humanly "fought," as it were, by the gift of one's life. War is a fight against God's predestination, it measures the extent of our freedom through which we "oblige" God to save us. The episodes of the holy war are inscribed into the discontinuous chain of the Divine Will; they express a coincidence between the latter and the human fight against it. God is the "best of tricksters," *khayr al-mākirin*, in the sense that He hides from man the finality of his predestination, leaving him with the liberty of fighting the latter in holy war. In Massignon's words, this is expressed as follows: "This stratagem is but the veil of His holiness, which attracts to Him through the violent sacrifice of life."[13] Massignon's view of *jihād*, whether understood outwardly or inwardly, spells the fundamental mode of relationship between the soul and her Lord in Islam. At its highest, this fight is nothing but a stratagem through which God hides Himself to Himself. The war, the apparent war, is but a veil, and it is through this veil that the human being is restored, as it were, to the Divine Unity. This is expressed most eloquently by Hallāj's supreme *shath* as translated by Massignon from the thirteenth-century *Qissa*: "God, God, no divinity but God. I see none but God. If I lose consciousness,

He spies on me,—if I recover consciousness, He loves me. O people, I am the Truth, I am the Truth."[14]

This is the supreme *futuwwa*, the heroic virtue of the Arabs that finds its culmination in mystical union. Massignon connects this virtue of the *fatā* to Abraham's destruction of the idols of Ur, in the same way as Hallāj's holy war is but a destruction of the idols of the soul. Linking the pre-Islamic connotations of the term *futuwwa* to its Islamic denotation, Massignon identifies in it an element of boldness and heroic resistance on the part of those "isolated" ones who, in the image of Fātima, and Muhammad himself, stand with an indignant temerity against injustices and privileges. Ultimately, *futuwwa* is therefore characterized by him as a gesture of opening toward the "other": "*Futuwwa*, in Arabic, is the antithesis of *Muruwwa*, 'consideration, worldly honorability' within the clan; it is an attitude of extreme hospitality to those situated outside of our own group, toward the foreigner, the enemy."[15]

Once again, this time through the implications of *jihād*, we are presented with a contrast between the national and conventional aspect of religion and its inner orientation toward the universal. Whether understood as a sacrificial gift of self to the supreme Other, or as an "extreme" hospitality toward those in need, *futuwwa* expresses both the essence of *jihād* and that of Massignon's spirituality. This opening onto otherness, be it essentially divine or terrestrially human, is what most decisively distinguishes authentic *jihād* from fanatic violence and self-destruction. In fact the fanatic is twice an idolater: first in regard to the world that he absolutizes, and second with respect to his own self, which he substitutes for the only Self. The fanatic negates and destroys the world and the other inasmuch as the latter resists his zealous attempt at reducing them to the forms of his mental idols, or ultimately to himself. Having denied the otherness of God through an exclusive and jealous identification with his own representation of Him, the fanatic is ready to deny and annihilate the existence of any human otherness. While the mystic's *jihād* is a sacrificial death in the divine Other through which may be expressed a fundamental Unity of witnessing, *wahdāt ash-shuhūd*, thereby a Union in love with the universal, the zealot's unholy war is a harsh and tragic fall into the abysses of obsessive self-affirmation. To those superficial analysts who venture to equate the contemplative death of mystics with the deadly explosion of fanatics, it must be answered that only he who absolutizes the world and its predicaments, even and especially with religious motives, can be so seduced by them as to destroy himself for their sake. Like Hallāj, the true *mujāhid* finds his life in his death, because his death is not chosen but found; it is not an act of denial but one of affirmation at the point of intersection between human freedom and divine predestination.

It is on this very concept of *futuwwa* that Corbin and Massignon converge, recognizing in it the divine predisposition to a spiritual testimony. However, Corbin's approach to *futuwwa*, or in Persian, *javanmardī*, is significantly different from Massignon's in its more exclusively spiritual definition, as well as in its most evidently gnostic bent. The spiritual companionship that this *futuwwa* involves is a community of consciousness that secretly sustains the world. Be it not for the existence, and action of presence, of this mystical sodality, the world of men would disappear into darkness: The companions of spiritual duty are, in Shī'ite parlance, "the eyes through which God still looks at the world." There is an inner war raging in the world of *malakūt*, the intermediary world of the imaginal that gives form to spiritual realities, and the transmission of spiritual principles until the eschatological conclusion of sacred history depends upon the inner warfare of a spiritual knighthood entrusted with this mystical mission. Corbin derives from ancient Iranian sources, particularly from the Zoroastrian wisdom that he finds reintegrated into Suhrawardī's spiritual synthesis, a cosmic vision of duality between the legions of darkness and the forces of Light. The latter symbol is quite crucial to his understanding of holy war: The holy knights are defenders and propagators of the Light, they are "men of Light." Alone among mankind they have not severed their bond from their Avestic Dāenā or their Mazdean *Fravarti*, the "heavenly partner of the man of light (. . .) essentially immune to any contamination by Darkness." It is this immunity, which is not so much a merit of the soul as a grace from the Spirit, that places the knightly *javānmardi* under the golden aura of an eternal youth. Eckhart's "One is ever young in the Intellect" captures the essence of this *javānmardi,* which permanently blooms through being nurtured by the source of all graces. Corbin specifies that, in its "technical" sense, this youth is one "upon which time has no dominion, for it is a reconquest of time and its sclerosis."[16]

What are the characteristics of this juvenile knighthood? It seems that the answer should include at least four aspects, that is, occultation, exclusive focus on the spiritual quest, ecumenism, and eschatological mission. The first aspect is evidently suggested to Corbin by the spiritual and dramatic climate of Shī'ism. It responds to a situation characterized by the scandal and disorder of spiritual usurpation. There is no doubt that, for Corbin, this usurpation amounts to a human rejection of the divine offering: There is a dramatic tension between the celestial reality of the Angel, or the Imām, as *phosphoros*, and the opacity of the terrestrial world of "organized powers" and institutions. The entire spiritual ethos that emanates from Corbin's works could be encapsulated as a response to this tension. Religious institutions and exoteric authorities often appear, in his essays, as sedimentations of an obscure will to obstruct the Light.[17] They are akin to the literality of a hermeneutics of idolatrous subterfuge, always unaware of denying the truth it claims to affirm. As Tom Cheetham has argued, "the spiritual combat of Shī'ism (and Corbin) is against all the literalizing, secularizing tendencies of any age."[18] The paleo-Evangelical, anti-institutional, and anti-ecclesiastic layer of Corbin's spiritual genealogy is crowned by a Shī'ite *pathos* that antagonizes the principalities of this world. The Light does not appear yet in its full glory; it is as it were hidden under the darkness of cosmic chaos. It must therefore be "liberated" from its imprisonment, and this is the function incumbent upon the knights of the Spirit, whose "Church" is invisible and "informal," like a mystical sodality of the elect. Moreover, Corbin's critique of the socialization and exoterization of religion seems to be informed by a consideration of the gradual exotericization of Imamism.[19] This development was characterized by a gradual decline of the consciousness of the spiritual consequences of the occultation of the Imam, and the progressive compromissions with the world. The personal and initiatory dimensions tended to fade if not disappear. This is a sort of "Sunnification" of Shī'ism, the dangers of which Corbin was well aware of, and which explains many of his positions.

The second aspect of *futuwwa* is related to the notion of a "preexistential" covenant between the spiritual knights and their guide, in the image of the relationship between the Imam and his faithful. The bond that unites the knightly soul to his Lord harks back to the ontological *sympathy* inherent in creation. The Creative Breath (*nafās ar-Rahmān*) that existentiates the Name of the soul is also the revelation of this Name as Lord.[20] This is the primordial recognition, the ontological initiation that commits the knights to fight with "their goods and souls" (*bi-amwalihim wa anfusihim*).[21] Such a commitment clearly distinguishes the ranks of the spiritual knights from those of other believers, the rear-guard, those who remain "seated" (*al-qā'idūn*).[22] The exclusiveness of *futuwwa* is also bound to the idea that a spiritual contamination is inherently associated with our time of external subversion and consequent spiritual occultation. In this inauspicious context, only an inner contact with the heavenly archetype, the ego *in divinis*, can protect the soul of the knight against the potentialities of his own earthly shadow. The cosmic extent of the current conflict—current to our cycle of existence, the age of Swedenborg's *Ecclesia Christiana*, the "Age of Iron," certainly accounts for the ecumenical scope of this holy war. Here we leave far behind, or below, the confessional and politico-religious fantasies, and hateful scenarios, of eschatological combats between Christians and Muslims; in fact, the cosmic reckoning that Corbin has in view transcends religious lines to oppose psychic and spiritual forces that have every opportunity to cross the formal lines of exoteric identifications. Corbin's *jihād* is thereby implicitly critical of two contemporary types of errancy: the neo-spiritual, New Age, sentimentalist negation of war on the level where it is unavoidable, that of the *malākut* and *mulk*, the formal, imaginal, and physical realms, and, at the other end of the spectrum of illusory literalism, the neo-fundamentalist, neo-millenarianist, or pan-Islamic pathologies of religious and polemical hallucination. By contrast, and this is the third aspect of our *futuwwa*, the knights of the Spirit may, and must, belong to a plurality of religious denominations. They don't identify with the color that affirms their exclusive individualness as a new layer of opacity, but embrace the Light that makes their coat of arms translucent to the most essential dimension of the divine Promise. It is no coincidence that Abraham is, according to Corbin, the "father" of all mystical knights of faith," nor that this chivalry is placed under the sign of expatriation: "Islam began in exile and will finish in exile; blessed are those who expatriate themselves in the name of faith."[23] In the Islamic spiritual tradition, this "expatriation" has been understood on a variety of levels, beginning with the hegira of Muhammad and his companions from Mecca to Medina. On the highest level, this sentiment of being in "exile" informs the gnostic sense of belonging to another world, nurturing both a feeling of being "out of place" in the framework of worldly concerns, and a deep nostalgia for another realm of reality. This sense of spiritual exile is a fundamental feature of the "knights of faith" that Corbin often contrasts with the consciousness of exoteric Christianity as characterized by its penitential focus on sin. Whereas the average Christian, and more generally ascetic, perspective remains centered on a sense of inadequacy and powerlessness akin to guilt and suffering, the gnostic consciousness tends to concentrate on the gap between the radiant identity of the spiritual self and the material limitations and obscurity of terrestrial existence. There is here also an element of suffering involved in the tension to free oneself from the latter, but this suffering is not so much an expiation for sins and errors as it is a spiritual fuel in the quest for a rebirth *on higher grounds*. The inner perception of the gap between inner aspiration and outer conditions orients the consciousness of the spiritual knight toward an *advent* of the Light at the horizon of terrestrial history; this is the fourth characteristic that we have mentioned as constitutive of the knightly soul. There is here, undoubtedly, a certain affinity between Massignon's and Corbin's eschatological orientations, but these should not veil us from the profound differences of outlook separating them. Two traits clearly distinguish Corbin's eschatological vision from Massignon's tension toward a redemption of history. First, there is no emphasis, in Corbin's outlook, on a sacrificial element akin to the apotropaic function of Massignon's *abdāl*. Second, the gnostic fighter of the Light is not directly involved in the tensions, oppositions, and wars of the outer, physical realm. He remains at a distance from those external events, not so much because they would be neglected by him as unreal or irrelevant to his predicament, but inasmuch as they are only shadows, or reflections, of the actual battle for the soul of the world, which takes place on the level of the *malākut*, the intermediary realm which is, in a sense, the principle, or the originating field, of oppositions and wars.

The use of the term "gnostic" may conjure up, in this context, suggestions of a dualistic outlook in Corbin's polemological and eschatological vision. His occasional use of Manichean and Mazdean concepts may further a sense of this dualism, and raise the suspicion of a subtle solidarity between Corbin's gnostic outlook and gnosticist tendencies characterized by a de facto absolutization of the duality at work in the formal realm.[24] It bears stressing, as an initial answer to this question, that Corbin's perspective can hardly be suspected of dualism in the most immediate sense of the word since it refers back to the primacy of a single, essential Reality that passes all understanding and dualities. It is clear that, for him, the supreme *Absconditum* of the Divine

Essence absolutely transcends any polarity or duality whatsoever, since it even transcends Being as a determination of the Divine. However, there is no doubt that Corbin's theoretical emphasis on the angelic and sub-angelic strata of the spiritual personality, and his spiritual affinity with the intermediary world of *mundus imaginalis*, makes him necessarily and quasi-vocationally engaged in the realm of spiritual war, *al jihād al-akbar*. In a sense this centrality of holy war is akin to the principle of duality inscribed in the very nature of subjectivity: It refers to the idea that any human subject lies at the crossroads between its spiritual identification with the man of light, and its psychic fall into the periphery of darkness. The polemical dimension of Corbin's thought is also derived from his philosophical solidarity with the early *Imāmī* emphasis on the double duty of devotion to the Imam and hatred toward his enemy. The historico-mythical horizon of Shī'ism is fundamentally informed by the two spiritual realities of Imamite initiation and cosmic combat, what Mohamad Ali Amir-Moezzi defines as the vertical and horizontal axis of Shī'ite spirituality. While the former is characterized by a complementary and gradual duality between the inner and the outer, the *bātin* and the *zāhir*, the esoteric and the exoteric, the latter refers to a violent polarity that opposes the forces of Intelligence and those of Evil. This is the perpetual combat that will only subside and finds its resolution with the final victory of the Mahdī.[25]

Given its strictly doctrinal aspect, Guénon's consideration of the significance of war is to be situated in a more exclusively principial context, which is only allusively connected to operative considerations. War is envisaged, in fact, from a purely metaphysical point of view, within the universal framework of a conception of the universe that articulates Unity and multiplicity. The production of multiplicity entails, from a relative standpoint, the introduction of an ontological distance from the Principle, which results in some degree of disorder or another. This distance is fundamentally unreal, insofar as it is considered from the point of view of the Principle, which already suggests that war can have only a contingent and provisional reality. In fact, strictly speaking, the domain of war encompasses exclusively what Guénon refers to as the cosmological realm. This means that it excludes metaphysics as such, the latter being defined as the science of the truly universal horizon of reality, beyond all polarities and oppositions. By contrast, cosmology relates to the procession of the cosmos from Being: It is thereby relevant to the domain in which dualities and contradictions appear, and indeed abound. Inasmuch as the entire manifestation appears as "external" to the Divine Reality, or let us say inasmuch as it seems to proceed "out" of it—albeit in a purely illusory mode, since nothing can place itself outside of the Real—it is characterized by an ambiguous status, particularly with respect to the domain of action. Contemplation can indeed transcend the plane of oppositions and contrasts, but action as such cannot, since it is enmeshed, by definition, within a network of determinations with which it has to reckon and compromise. Spiritual realization consists, therefore, in liberating oneself from this chain of determinations, or let us say, this concatenation of actions and reactions, from within the very domain of action, with the ultimate view of reintegrating multiplicity into unity. This makes it plain why, spiritually, war is considered by Guénon as being "concerned with the unification of multiplicity by means which belong to the world of multiplicity itself," whereas metaphysically, or rather ontologically, "it represents a cosmic process whereby what is manifested is re-integrated into the principial unity."[26] From this point of view, it could be said that war encompasses, so to speak, the domain of manifestation inasmuch as manifestation presupposes a procession out of the Principle. In that sense, there is no other peace than that which is found in, and in fact identified with, the "divine Station" (al-maqām al-ilāhī), which Guénon refers to, using Taoist symbolism, as the axle of the cosmic wheel, which is both the principle of all motion and the only "point" independent from any motion, or purely motionless. According to Guénon, only the person who has realized this station can be characterized as being immune from evil, and therefore independent from the realm of war, since war cannot be anything else, in its normative reality, or essence, as a combat against evil, or rather a reduction of evil as illusory separation from the Good. Guénon introduces this identification in such a way as to suggest a complete transcendence of the individual determinations of the human state. This is perhaps an elliptical way of referring to the fact that it is only the Divine Center that, strictly speaking, can be considered to be totally free of the ambiguities and tensions of the cosmological "battlefield." Now, of course, the individual portion of the human person remains, out of necessity, within the strictures of relativity, and therefore subject to the consequences of its separation from the Principle, if only in the form of death. It is only inasmuch as it is one with the Principle, in its ontological center as it were, that the human reality can be said to be free from the realm of war. Hence the categorical affirmation that "nothing can therefore harm such a one, since for him there are no longer any enemies, either within him or without."[27] Enmity and opposition presupposes "otherness," and the human being who has achieved union with his transpersonal essence cannot but be one, and at peace, with all other realities sub caelo.

What, specifically, is the way in which the "warrior" may be said to free himself from the domain of manifestation by means that are, in fact, part and parcel of this selfsame manifestation? Let us begin by stating that these means are the purview of those who are vocationally engaged in the field of action, that is, primarily the "warriors," giving to this term the widest possible acceptation as referring to the domain of action and "effort" (jahd). Guénon refers particularly to a Hindu classic, namely the Bhagavad Gītā, a text specifically designed for the instruction of kshatriyas, the members of the second varna, the royal or warrior "caste," to address this important question. In this Hindu treatise, the primary spiritual lesson amounts to carrying out one's actions with the utmost dedication and perfection while abandoning all self-centered interest in the fruits of this action. Now Guénon is quite aware that the lessons of the *Gītā* are essentially parallel, albeit couched in a different religious language, to the Islamic *jihād*. In both cases it is a matter of unveiling the deepest dimension of the kingly ethics of action in the world. This is the particular province of the second caste, or order, although the primordial perfection of mankind, or universal man, subsumes both the priestly and warrior perfections under its aegis, a fact that Guénon illustrates by reference to the order of Melchizedek, who is both supreme priest and king. If Melchizedek is presented as superior to Abraham, it is, according to Guénon, because his *sacerdotal* function encompasses a higher and more complete realm than that of the priests of Levi: In other words, the latter presupposes a disjunction between the priestly and the kingly, whereas the former unites both in a supreme synthesis.[28]

The essence of the function of King-Priest consists in consecrating the essential junction of justice and peace, the former being understood as spanning all levels of reality, and ranging from spiritual discernment to social equity.[29] The essence of such justice is founded upon an ability to discriminate between realities, and levels of reality, in a way that is fundamentally free from egotistical bias. This spiritual extinction with regard to one's interests and expectations is no different, in spirit, from the foregoing of attachment to the fruits of one's actions as highlighted by the *Gītā*. Independent of the profound convergence between these two inner attitudes, Guénon acknowledges Islam's "warlike aspect," while denying that it is "peculiar" to Islam and not found in other traditions, including Christianity. The terminality of Islam in the economy of prophecy is not without relationship to this aspect when one considers that the end of the cycle of revelation is also, by the same token, the most acute degree of disorder and chaos, as a result of the extreme separation of mankind from its spiritual roots, or origins. The destructive aspect of war is akin, in this respect, to a negation of that which negates the reality of the primordial norm. In other words, the destructive aspect of war is clearly subordinate to its deeply reintegrative function. In such a way the combative, and ultimately restorative, character of Islam can be understood. As a restoration of a sense of Unity veiled by the vicissitudes of human conformity to its spiritual covenant, and the concomitant rise of idolatry, Islam could not but appear in the form of the sword.

As befits its focus on metaphysical and spiritual symbolism, Guénon's examination of war focuses, precisely, on the meaning of the sword in Islam, and its various equivalents in other religions. The symbolism of the sword is connected, as suggested above, to the discriminative function akin to the definition of the *Qur'ān* as *furqān*, or to the scissorslike shape of the *lā* of the *shahādah*. In his important article "The Sword of Islam (*Sayf al-Islām*)" Guénon emphasizes both the axial symbolism of this weapon and its double-edged aspect, referring thereby to a "triplicity" involving the vertical axis and the two sides, right and left, that are determined by it. In terms of the first of these aspects, the sword of Islam evokes both a solar and a polar symbolism. In this respect Guénon quotes a passage from the *Book of Revelation* (19:15),[30] implicitly referring to the Prophet of Islam, in which a "sharp two-edged sword" issues from the mouth of a rider mounted on a white horse: This is both the sun of justice that extinguishes, and the pole that relates to heaven and earth. Moreover, the double edge of the sword is connected by Guénon to the destructive and re-creative, or restorative, aspect of "holy war," a function that Guénon associates with the dual aspect of Shiva in Hinduism as destroyer and revivifier, or renewer. Although Guénon does not explicitly develop the implications of this twofold aspect with regard to Islam, it appears quite relevant to the "corrective" and "restorative" mission of Islam within the context of the historical unfolding of Semitic monotheism. Islam, being both an essential confirmation and a circumstantial abrogation of previous faiths, appears conjointly as "destructive" of what had been corrupted and "affirmative" of essential *tawhīd*. The sword of Islam is therefore a direct expression of the dual aspect of the religion, as eminently expressed by the two parts, negative and affirmative, of the confession of faith, *lā ilāha ill'Allāh*.

In keeping with its greater emphasis on the more directly human and spiritual applications of metaphysical principles, Schuon not only considers the deepest roots of the cosmic reality of war, but also its social and moral dimensions. This dimension of his work presents, in a sense, a direct affinity with the spirit of Islam, and also Judaism and Hinduism, inasmuch as these religions are characterized by an integration of all levels and aspects of the human predicament within their sacred purview, whether on an individual basis or a collective one. Throughout his work, Schuon makes use of the paraphrase "everything human is ours," which alludes to the integrality of the traditional outlook that he propounds. Such an integral understanding of the meaning of tradition could not leave out, or neglect, a reality as pervasive in human history as war. It is therefore envisaged, on the most immediate level, within the framework of a "spiritual realism" that situates human realities, including limitations and evil, at their proper degree of reality. Such a realism does not shy away from acknowledging the necessity of a margin of "scandal" that Schuon equates with the strictures of the "law of the jungle." The realm of terrestrial manifestation being what it is, that is, a state of disorder in which more often than not the law of moral gravity has precedence over the imperatives of spiritual verticality, spiritual values—and above all institutions that are, in one way or another, the repositories of these values—must of necessity participate in the ambiguities and even disorders of the world of men. This pragmatic principle leads Schuon to acknowledge the legitimacy of an "imperialism of the good" that presides over the development and strengthening of terrestrial and collective frameworks for the manifestation of the sacred.[31] This is the normative foundation of any just war, in a way that does not take mankind above its own frailty and imperfection but makes use of the latter *ad majorem Dei gloriam*, as it were. This situation, in which ambiguous means are decisively oriented toward a spiritual end, does not imply an unqualified justification of any war presumably entitled to tend toward the promotion or defense of a relative good or a lesser evil. In fact, Schuon is careful to emphasize that such paradoxical and ambiguous possibilities presuppose a decisively religious context within the ambience of a great "civilization of the sacred." Such principles could not, therefore, be applied to secular and contemporary contexts without a grave measure of distortion.

This is not to say that war, in its external dimension, cannot also fulfill, less obliquely, a spiritual function for some particular individuals, within the context of specific vocations. This is particularly the case for active and passional men whose way to God has to entail violently sacrificial paths of sublimation of the ego.[32] The early historical development of Islam undoubtedly shares in this type of human modality. Schuon stresses that the human mentalities that were involved in the early definition of human virtues in Islam were in part the product of a combative vocation akin to the way of the warrior. This sacrificial mentality, and the type of permanent association with death that it entails, represents a compensatory response in the face of worldly passivity and the spiritual law of gravity. Moreover, war cannot but enter into the economy of religious life, at least inasmuch as the affirmation of Reality cannot but be realized by overcoming illusion, most often with some degree of violence. The climate of war that characterizes the beginning of Islam is therefore akin to the law of contrast and opposition that characterizes the domain of manifestation. It is also predicated, as such, on the Islamic metaphysical perspective inasmuch as it asserts the transcendence of divine Perfection over the realm of terrestrial imperfection. This emphasis on transcendence is deemed by Schuon to be consonant with a codified legitimization of holy war.[33] It is, however, relative in two senses: first, inasmuch as it affirms itself as a response to the denial and persecution of truth, thereby a posteriori, and second, in so far as it is oriented toward the horizon of peace, without which it would have no meaning. Even with these qualifications, a polemical reduction of Islam to this dimension would gravely miss the point "that persuasion played a greater part than war in the expansion of Islam as a whole."[34] This is so to the extent that war, even though it be justified by sacred goals, is always a form of disequilibrium and pertains to the periphery, or the extrinsic dimension, of reality. Schuon describes the Kaaba as the center of Islam, which expresses the Absolute intrinsically, as it were, whereas the sword, symbol of holy war, manifests it extrinsically, or toward the periphery.[35] This is no doubt one reason why, as Massignon reminded his readers, the pilgrimage, *hajj*, is often considered, in Islam, as the outer *jihād* of women: The latter do not participate in the extrinsic aspect of the affirmation of the Divine by virtue of their innate affinity with its intrinsic dimension.

The sacrificial dimension of *jihād* appears most clearly in the context of the disputes of succession and competition between spiritual perspectives that mark the emergence of the polarization between Sunnism and Shī'ism. This is all the more clearly expressed in the fact that the opposition between Sunnism and Shī'ism does not so much contrast truth and error, good with evil, as it confronts various forms of, and perspectives on, the good. For Schuon, the competition between various adequate, albeit partial, perspectives of reality enters into the very nature of things. Sunnism and Shī'ism correspond to actual archetypes, the manifestation of which cannot but lead to oppositions and conflicts akin to the Heraclitean *polemos*.[36] Such a possibility does not only manifest itself within the fold of Islam, but also in the context of outer oppositions between Islam and Christianity. In this respect, the sacrificial dimension of *jihād* brings warfare, at its highest level of consciousness and rectitude, to the heights of a mystical ordeal. While the Crusades can be considered, on an all-too-human level, as the consequence of human imperfections, partiality, and greed, they have also provided opportunities for the manifestation and cultivation of heroic virtues. Schuon goes so far as to perceive a summit of heroic sacrifice for the love of God in which terrestrial oppositions become the highly paradoxical occasion for a kind of mystical union in and through the love of the One God.[37] This presupposes an integral context and an inner rectitude, exclusive of natural hatred and vile or inordinate means, that clearly clashes with the ideological counterfeits of *jihād* with which the contemporary stage has provided all too numerous examples. Short of idealizing the manifestations of holy war in the past, it must be recognized that the excesses and abuses that they entailed, out of necessity given what Schuon refers to as the "human margin," did nothing but reflect the raw and gross limitations and passions of "natural mankind" without, however, confining it to the inversions and subversions of the spirit upon which modern ideological "crusades" have thrived, and which manifest their tenebrous inspirations in the immoral, sinister, and counter-traditional modalities that they espouse in pursuit of their terrestrial, political ends.

Notwithstanding the relative importance attached to the concept and practice of the "lesser" holy war in Schuon's traditional outlook, it comes as no surprise that his fundamental focus be on the spiritual meaning of *jihād*. With respect to this inner dimension, *jihād* is none other than the rigorous aspect of the active perfection of the soul. This perfection is characterized by Schuon as follows:

> Since the spiritual act must assert itself with force against the lures of the world or of the soul which seek to engross and corrupt the will, it involves the combative virtues: decision, vigilance, perseverance; (. . .) what gives victory is the divine Presence which is "incarnate" as it were in the sacred act—prayer in all its forms—and thus regenerates the individual substance. The symbols of this spiritual station—that of combat, victory, pure act—are lightning and the sword; it is, *in divinis*, fulgurating and invincible Perfection, and in man, holy anger or holy warfare, but above all the inward act as affirmation of the Self.[38]

This passage highlights the way in which spiritual life must be considered, from a certain perspective, as consisting in a position of active determination with respect to the domain of universal passivity, which encompasses both the psychic *materia* and the outer diversity of forms. The most immediate manifestation of this active perfection is akin to the will, rather than to love or intelligence. It may, however, evoke the latter inasmuch as it is perceived, or lived, as a consequence of a metaphysical discernment akin to the *Qur'ān* as *furqān*; and in point of fact the *Qur'ān* can be characterized, in many of its passages, as an uncompromising reminder of the need to fight one's lower self, the *nafs al-ammārah*, and the world, inasmuch as it is an arena of expression and expansion for the latter. However, the passage that we have just quoted makes it plain that the source of this affirmation of the will against the lures of the soul and the world is ultimately to be found in the pure Act of the divine *'amr*, the divine Command, which is in essence the very radiation of the Divine Self. On this level, combative perfection can be considered, beyond its aspect of discriminative separation, as a mode of spiritual knowledge by identification. On such a profound level of consideration holy war is as if transmuted into the Peace from which it proceeds and to which it leads back. This is otherwise expressed by Schuon in his statement that "the goal of inward Holy War is perfect self-knowledge, beyond the veils of passion . . . ,"[39] this perfect knowledge being none other than Peace. Now, one must still ask about the ways in which this spiritual knowledge may be achieved through spiritual warfare. In conformity with most of the mystical tradition of Islam, Schuon answers this question by referring to the methodical centrality of *dhikr*, the remembrance of God. *Dhikrullāh* is active, determinative presence of the Divine; it is the spiritual sword forged in heaven.

None of the four authors we have considered could rightfully be considered a "pacifist," even though all of them certainly take the state of peace, at whatever level it may be envisaged, as being the goal and ultimate destination of human life. For them, peace is an intrinsic and essential reality that reflects the divine nature in the equilibrium of its infinite possibilities, whereas war is but the extrinsic response to a state of disequilibrium brought about by what Lurianic Kabbalists would refer to as the "breaking of the vases", that is, a rupture of balance in the economy of Creation. It is this irruption of "scandal" in the form of evil, and the correlative rejection of prophetic messages, that leads to the necessity of war, on whatever level and in whatever form one may consider it. While it is undeniable that entering the domain of outer war amounts to entering a field of oppositions and ambiguities, it remains no less certain nevertheless that a clear horizon of truth and justice can limit the interferences of the "human margin" and the manifestation of inordinate passions within the context of conflicts.

The main lesson that we can draw from our meditation on *jihād* in the preceding pages lies in the fact that any kind of outer *jihad* must ultimately be oriented by an inner *jihād*. It may be so either indirectly or directly. Indirectly, it could be said that outer *jihād* can only be justified to the extent that it strives to protect the framework and means of higher *jihād*, or contemplation. In other words, *jihād* as an outer reality refers to the defense of a civilizational and sacred space in which *al-jihād al-akbar* may flourish. This, by and large, is what Guénon and Schuon have in view when they affirm the legitimacy of traditional, social means of a violent assertion of the truth in the face of a subversion of traditional order. The question remains of knowing whether current conditions, within the Islamic world as elsewhere, can warrant such a traditional legitimacy of war in adequate circumstances. This would obviously presuppose that a given society retains a sufficient measure of conformity to traditional standards to be the bearer and protector of this "space of contemplation" that forms, normatively and ultimately, an authentic civilizational and religious ambience. It is doubtful that such is the case for any predominantly Muslim country in the contemporary world, and no less so outside of Islam, with the possible exception of some residual "pockets" of traditional ambience to be found in certain limited areas of the world still relatively untouched by the unflinching drive toward outer development.

In a more direct manner the "lesser *jihād*" must be conceived both as a reflection, and an opportunity for the flourishing, of a "greater *jihād*." This is perhaps the main conclusion to be drawn from a careful reading of our four authors on the topic. The correspondence that links outer macrocosm and inner microcosm provides one not only with a doctrinal understanding of the analogy between outer war and *psychomachia*; it also suggests the ways in which outer war may function as the arena par excellence, in which an ability to overcome the tenebrous and centripetal aspects of one's soul may be educated and refined. In that sense, inner warfare is the precondition for abiding by the external, moral norms and codifications of outer warfare, the latter being the "battlefield" upon which the former may be experienced and sharpened. The domain of conflict is—by definition, since it deals with oppositions—that in which the disequilibrium of the soul may be most patently revealed. It is in this domain that the ego is most likely to protrude and interfere since it finds in it an immediate field of expansion by contact with a hostile "otherness" and in the context of a dynamic affirmation of self. This allows one to understand why Schuon characterizes the warrior's path as "subjectively objective," in the sense that it envisions the objects of its quest from the point of view of individual striving. This is why the primary virtue of the warrior is self-control, domination of self, the epitome of which can eminently manifest itself in the midst of outer conflict. The maximal potential for the expression of the ego becomes the ideal framework for working against its untimely and inordinate infiltrations.

Now, while they make it evident that there could not be any genuine outer war without inner war against the soul, all the preceding considerations leave open the question of knowing whether the Islamic "greater *jihād*" necessarily entails "outer *jihād*." By contrasting the two figures of the Amir 'Abd-al-Qadir al-Jazairi and the Shaykh Ahmad al-'Alāwī, both of whom had to confront the threats of French colonial power in the nineteenth and twentieth centuries, respectively, one in "lesser *jihād*" and the other by exclusively spiritual means of resistance, Reza Shah-Kazemi suggests that no absolute and definite answer can be given to this question, since it can only be approached in a particular objective and subjective context. Subjectively, this matter pertains to individual vocation, and outer engagement, including the military path, clearly falls under the purview of those whose nature is akin to it. Objectively speaking, it is very unlikely that the chaotic and mixed predicament of the contemporary context could lend itself, save perhaps in specific situations that are geographically and culturally very circumscribed and the moral circumstances of which are crystal-clear, to a spiritual assumption of the way of outer combat. If the latter retains some legitimate meaning in our current era, it is more likely to take the form of Corbin's inner chivalry, outwardly expressed as a philosophical and spiritual resistance to the pressures of the times by dint of a daily struggle for survival and testimony in the midst of forgetfulness and negation. In a cosmic and human ambience that is as little conducive to a perception of the sacred as can be, to strive to remember the Divine and one's human vocation for transcendence with one's whole being is the greatest *jihād* that is.

Chapter Eight

EPILOGUE

The preceding pages have provided us with glimpses of a rich and integrated, if diverse, vision of Islamic spirituality; a metaphysical and mystical picture of inner Islam has emerged from an overall converging and often complementary set of insightful works of meditation and spiritual interiorization of Islam and Sufism. In the wake of Louis Massignon, Henry Corbin, René Guénon, and Frithjof Schuon, we have been able to trace the lineaments of a genuinely inward understanding of Islam while "reconstructing" the organic coherence of a distinct view of this religion that sheds light on the most profound layers of its spiritual universe, the universal horizon of its tenets, and the urgent relevance of its lessons for the modern world, East and West.

In a sense Massignon and Corbin, on the one hand, and Guénon and Schuon, on the other hand, belong to worlds of meaning that are clearly discrete and even at times divergent. The academic context, premises and modi operandi of the former strike a sharp contrast with the esoteric inspiration that nourishes the latter. In that sense, moving from Massignon and Corbin to Guénon and Schuon is like changing planets. This impression must be qualified, however, by the strong existential and spiritual undertones of the former's scholarship. To a large extent, Massignon and Corbin initiated the very possibility of a new kind of Islamic studies informed by the categories and framework of reference of religious faith and spiritual commitment. The spiritual "substitution" of Massignon, with its emphasis on a sympathetic understanding of Islam from within, and Corbin's phenomenological thrust have contributed to revolutionize and fertilize a field of studies that had shown signs of "scientific" sterilization and reductive historicization. Massignon's and Corbin's works launched a bridge of renewed and liberating scholarship that allowed some to reach to the spiritual and mystical side of understanding Islam. It is on this "other" side that Guénon and Schuon have worked to illuminate the innermost and universal strata of Islamic spirituality. As such, their works may be perplexing, challenging and perhaps even unsettling to many academic readers.

Moreover, inasmuch as Massignon and Corbin considered their object of study from a point of view crystallized around Christian points of reference, they also tended, as a result and as if in contradistinction, to perceive Islam in the perspective of its confessional specificity—albeit obviously not irrespective of its common grounds with other religions, while Guénon and Schuon's consideration of Islamic spirituality *sub specie universalitatis*, as it were, have offered, by contrast, a unique point of view from which to understand Islam "top down" or "inside out." These differences of outlook amount less to irreducible differences than to complementary enrichment. There are many bridges from Massignon's work to Schuon's output, for example, not one of the least being a certain "resonance" of the spiritual meaning and function of the feminine in the modern world, a Marian flavor so to speak. Thus, our authors may provide a wider range of readers, academics or not, with convergent insights and fruitful connections, thereby affording access to a wealth of metaphysical and spiritual teachings and practices.

The ideologization of religion that contemporary analysts have witnessed, and the subsequent framing of religious manifestations in an almost exclusively geopolitical context, does not bode well in terms of reaching the plane of the "inner Islam" that Massignon, Guénon, Corbin, and Schuon had in view. In point of fact, however, for that very reason this inner Islam is all the more needed, as an important complement to, or correction of, the popular, ideological and mediatic images and concepts of Islam that circulate in the communicative frenzy of our information age. The primary commonality of all the contributions that we have studied lies in their stessing the primacy of inwardness for any transmission, permanence, confirmation, or "restoration" of the outward structures and realities of Islam. Instead of making use of Islam as the primary ideological component of a collective affirmation of identity in reaction to the perceived, or real, infringements of the modern West, our authors' contributions bear witness to the existence, validity, and effectiveness of a spiritual assimilation of the substantive marrow of the tradition as a necessary precondition and informing principle for any serious "rebuilding" of Islam in the modern world. Meditating these works cannot but make one sensitive to the ways in which the inner, far from being reducible to the ethical product of outer structures, is in fact the prerequisite for any integrative understanding and effectual treatment of the latter.

One of the main challenges of Islam today lies in its ability, or lack thereof, to remain faithful to the absoluteness of its message, while being able to negotiate the terms of its survival in a world that has, by and large, abandoned traditional benchmarks and normative, sacred institutions. Those who claim to fight for a restoration of outer forms and structures do so in a way that is almost invariably predicated on a literal, exterior, understanding of these forms, manifesting thereby no or little understanding of the *ihsānī* and *'irfānī* foundations of tradition.[40] Such a counter-traditional way of understanding the task of revitalizing and reasserting the message of Islam cannot but bear at least ambiguous, if not utterly poisonous, fruits in a context in which the intellectual principles and living examplars of the tradition are far from being readily available. It bears repeating that Islam, or any other religion for that matter, is not an ideological recipe for success in the modern world, but a sacred means of realizing the human vocation in the world by transcending the latter inwardly.

Away from any sense of political vying for power and confrontation, the perspective of inner Islam opens the way to a greater, deeper understanding of both the diversity and the essential convergence of world religions. Assimilating the spiritual keys it provides amounts to moving away from the external exclusiveness of formalism, and cultivating a concentration on inner modification and purification. Thanks to such a subjective assimilation, a greater understanding of, and receptivity to, other faiths becomes possible. Objectively speaking, this approach also has the merit of looking at Islamic forms in a way that emphasizes their intention, their finality, rather than their formal status *qua* forms. Such an understanding and assimilation of Islam may enable one to reach a degree of intuition of the meaning of other forms. While it allows one to reach a more central, primordial zone of Islam, thereby asserting the essential specificity of this religion, it does so in a way that fathoms the depth of this formal specificity while perceiving it in the universal light that shines through it, as it were.

There is no question that inner Islam cannot be externalized as such on the collective level. However, it can and must be the sap of Islam as a whole. In the history of Islam, Islamic spirituality and mysticism, primarily in the forms of this manifold and multilayered phenomenon called Sufism, have played an integrative and vivifying function in the permanence and development of the religion, including its more external dimensions. An increased receptivity to the message of inner Islam, and a wider attempt at making it a living reality, would contribute in not a small degree to re-centering the focus of the Islamic community and providing it with authentic means of engaging and understanding other faiths.

NOTES

CHAPTER ONE. INTRODUCTION

1. "Les ambassadeurs mystiques de l'islam," in Numéro spécial sur les religions, *Le Nouvel Observateur*, 1998.

2. "People often speak of 'conversions' very inappropriately and in cases where this word (. . .) could never be applied, that is, the case of those who, for reasons of an esoteric and initiatic order, adopt a traditional form different from that to which they would have seem[ed] to be linked by their origin. This could be either because their native tradition furnished them with no possibility of an esoteric order, or simply because their chosen tradition, even in its exoteric form, gives them a foundation that is more appropriate to their nature, and consequently more favorable to their spiritual work. Whoever places himself at the esoteric point of view has this absolute right, against which all the arguments of the exoterists are of no avail, since by very definition this matter lies completely outside their competence. Contrary to what takes place in 'conversion', nothing here implies the attribution of the superiority of one traditional form over another. It is merely a question of what one might call reasons of spiritual expediency, which is altogether different from simple individual 'preference', and for which exterior considerations are completely insignificant. Moreover, it is of course understood that one who can legitimately act in this way must, since he is truly capable of placing himself at the esoteric point of view, be conscious, at least by virtue of a theoretical if not an effectively realized knowledge, of the essential unity of all traditions. This alone is sufficient to show that when the word 'conversion' is applied to such cases, it is meaningless and truly inconceivable." René Guénon, *Initiation and Spiritual Realization* (Hillsdale, NY: Sophia Perennis, 2001), 62–63.

3. With the exception of Jacques Berque, whose sociological outlook was not particularly conducive to emphasizing the mystical dimension of Islam.

4. This in spite of the fact that the small publisher Sophia Perennis (Hillsdale, New York) has played an active and courageous role in the translation and dissemination of Guénon's works.

5. *Massignon intérieur* (Paris-Lausanne: L'Age d'Homme, 2001) and, in collaboration with Jean-Baptiste Aymard, *Frithjof Schuon, Life and Teachings* (Albany, SUNY Press, 2004).

6. Frithjof Schuon, *Light on the Ancient Worlds* (Bloomington, IN: World Wisdom, 2006), 103.

7. "If you wish your path to be shortened in order to attain realization swiftly, hold fast to what is ordained (in the *Qur'ān*) and to what is particularly recommended concerning voluntary observances; learn outer knowledge as is indispensable for worshiping God, but do not linger on it, since you are not required to study this deeply." *Letters of a Sufi Master The Shaykh al-'Arabī ad-Darqāwī* (Louisville, KY, Fons Viatae, 1998), 15.

8. Michel Chodkiewicz, *An Ocean Without Shore: Ibn Arabi, The Book, and the Law* (Albany, NY: SUNY Press, 1993), 106.

9. cf. Muhammad ibn al-Husayn al-Sulamī, *La lucidité implacable*, ed. Roger Deladrière (Paris: Arléa, 1999), 29.

10. Seyyed Hossein Nasr, *Traditional Islam in the Modern World* (London & New York: KPI, 1987), 148.

11. On the other hand, it must be acknowledged that the a priori status of "outsider" can be a double-edged sword, when considering the ways in which not a few "converts" to Islam can espouse the exclusivist litterality of the creed to champion zealously their new religion by contrast with what they consider to be the errors and deficiencies of their original confession.

12. cf. Latifa Ben Mansour, *Les mensonges des intégristes* (Monaco: Le Serpent à Plumes, 2004), 72.

13. Shayegan is an implacable analyst of the effects of such a distortion on the newer generations: "This produces an ambivalent attitude in the children, who learn double standards (and the double language which goes with them) in the hedge-school of hypocrisy. Their private world is inspired by the heroes of video clips. Michael Jackson, Prince and Madonna are more real to them than martyred Imam; break-dancing is more familiar than the pettifogging of interminable prayer. They may submit to the imperious commands of the religious authorities, but deep inside they are living a secret life in a completely different dimension. This is producing a whole schizophrenic generation even more neurotic than the last one." *Cultural Schizophrenia: Islamic Societies Confronting the West* (Syracuse University Press, 1997), 96.

14. *The Philosophy of Seyyed Hossein Nasr*, The Library of Living Philosophers, vol. XXVIII, ed. Lewis Edwin Hahn, Randall E. Auxier, and Lucian W. Stone, Jr. (Chicago and La Salle, Open Court, 2001), 29.

15. Ibid., 29–30. Schuon's influence on Nasr was also determining: "The traditional writings of Schuon, with their singular emphasis on the need for the practice of a spiritual discipline as well as theoretical knowledge, were especially instrumental in determining the course of Nasr's intellectual and spiritual life from that time onward." Zailan Moris, "The Biography of Seyyed Hossein Nasr," in *Knowledge is Light*, ed. Zailan Moris (Chicago: ABD International Group, 1999), 14.

16. Cyril Glassé, *The New Encyclopedia of Islam* (Lanham, MD: Rowman Altamira, 2001), 128. This is true a fortiori for Western intellectuals who have been brought to Islam. Such is the case for one of the most prominent American Muslims, Hamza Yusuf, who was brought to Islam by the reading of Martin Lings' *The Book of Certainty*: "I read as much of the book as I could but recall not understanding very much. It quoted extensively from the Quran and offered highly esoteric commentaries in a language quite foreign to me. I set it aside, but my curiosity had been piqued and shortly thereafter, in a life-altering transaction, I purchased a Quran and began to read a very personal revelation that would compel me to convert to the religion of

Islam." Martin Lings, *A Return to the Spirit* (Louisville: Fons Vitae, 2005). In Memoriam section: "A Gentle Soul" by H.Yusuf, 112–113.

17. Here is the version of these events provided by Massignon himself in a lecture given in Toumlinine in 1956, the text of which was transcribed by Jacques Keryell: "Etant dénoncé comme espion, on m'a tendu un piège et j'ai été arrêté. (. . .) Alors j'ai été sauvé. J'ai été sauvé par des amis avec qui, d'ailleurs, j'avais eu bien des histoires! Parce que j'avais eu le pacte de l'hospitalité. Alors quand on leur a dit que j'allais être fusillé, ils ont été très embêtés; j' étais tout de même leur hôte. (. . .) Alors ils ont dit: 'Si l'on tue M. Massignon, c'est pire que si l'on tuait notre fils aîné. Nous ne savons pas si c'est un espion, ça ne nous intéresse pas. Il est notre hôte, il est sacré . . . ' ('If Mr. Massignon is killed, it is worse than our eldest son being killed. We do not know whether he was a spy, that does not interest us. He was our guest, he is sacred.')" in Jacques Keryell, *Louis Massignon, de Bagdad au Jardin d'une Parole extasiée*, Angers, 2008, 101.

18. This is symbolically and anecdotally attested to by the existence of a "Henry Corbin street" in Tehran.

19. The name of René Guénon, Shaykh 'Abd al-Wāhid Yahyā, can be occasionally pronounced in a *khutba* in traditional mosques such as Sultan Hassan in Cairo. Some of his works are also studied at Al-Azhar. However, the number of Egyptian and Arab scholars who have been profoundly influenced by his works is relatively limited.

20. cf. Xavier Accart, *L'ermite de Duqqi. René Guénon en marge des milieu franco-phones* (Milano: Archè-Edidit, 2001).

21. 'Abd-al-Halīm Mahmūd, *Un soufi d'Occident: René Guénon*, trans. Jean Abd-al-Wadoud Gouraud (Cairo-Beirut: Gebo and Albouraq, 2007), 14. "One may cite in this regard the high regard in which the late and much revered Shaykh of Al-Azhar, 'Abd al-Halīm Mahmūd, held the person and the writings of René Guénon, one of the founders of the school of *sophia perennis*, to which Nasr belongs. This paragon of Muslim 'orthodoxy' went so far as to say that Guénon was one of those personalities who have rightfully taken up their place in history, and that 'Muslims place him close to al-Ghazālī and his like'. It is interesting to note also that Frithjof Schuon is mentioned by Shaykh 'Abd-al-Halīm as a 'formidable scholar; and refers on also to Schuon's important exposition of the sophia perennis entitled *L'Oeil du Coeur.*" Reza Shah-Kazemi, *The Other in the Light of the One—The Universality of the Qur'an and Interfaith Dialogue* (Cambridge: The Islamic Texts Society, 2006), 264–265.

22. René Guénon, *The Symbolism of the Cross* (Hillsdale, New York: Sophia Perennis, 1996).

23. "A short time after his arrival (in Mostaghanem) at the end of November 1932, Schuon received a letter from René Guénon which Lucy von Dechend had forwarded: '(. . .) I would advise you to go to Mostaghanem and see Shaykh Ahmad ibn 'Aliwa, toi whom you can introduce yourself from me." Jean-Baptiste Aymard and Patrick Laude, *Frithjof Schuon: Life and Teachings* (Albany, New York: SUNY Press, 2004),18.

24. "Schuon stayed nearly four months in the Shaykh al-'Alāwī proximity and became affiliated at the end of January 1933 by the old Shaykh himself in the presence of Adda Ben Tounes, who was then *muqaddam*" (ibid.).

25. "When speaking of Shi'ism, he usually spoke of 'us' and considered himself to be identified with Shi'ism in spirit as well as in mind." Nasr, *Traditional Islam*, 280.

26. In the preface of *Understanding Islam*, Schuon thus writes: "As may be inferred from its title the purpose of this book is not so much to give a description of Islam as to

explain why Moslems believe in it, if we may express it thus (. . .)." (Bloomington, IN: World Wisdom, 1998), viii.

27. The Melkite church originated when bishops from the oriental churches, who were excommunicated in the wake of the Council of Chalcedon in 451, took sides with Marcian, the Roman Emperor of the East. Following the reaffirmation of the union of the church with Rome in 1724 and the consequent division of the Melkite church into two branches, the "Melkite Catholic patriarch of Antioch and of All the East" was established.

28. This is told by Massignon himself in the brief notes he wrote the very evening of his audience with the Pope. In addition, the Pope asked Massignon how long he had been a Muslim, to which Massignon responded, in a characteristic fashion: "I was merely a sympathizer, after having become an unbeliever; I did not say the shahadah (the testimony of Islamic faith)." Cf. "Annexe D" in Louis Massignon, *Les trois prières d'Abraham* (Paris: Le Cerf, 1997), 192.

29. The latter refer particularly to the Alusi family, who hosted him in Baghdad at the time of his crisis, while the former include Joris-Karl Huysmans and Charles de Foucauld.

30. Corbin tells the story, which took place in 1927–28, in the following terms: "I spoke to him of the reasons that had led me, as a philosopher, to undertake the study of Arabic. (. . . .) Then Massignon had an inspiration from Heaven. He had brought back from a trip to Iran a lithographed edition of Suhravardī's major work, Hikmat al-Ishrāq. (. . .)—Take it, he says, I believe there is something for you in this book." Cf. Henry Corbin, *L'Imām caché* (Paris: L'Herne, 2003), 219–220.

31. "[The Metaphysical Reality of Prophecy] includes an exoteric dimension or a dimension ad extra, that is a manifestation of the person of the prophet, and an esoteric dimension manifested in the person of each of the Twelve Imāms who, as a whole, constitute a single and same essence (. . .)." Ibid, 31.

32. Guénon was adamantly opposed to the academic establishment, which he considered as utterly incompetent in spiritual matters, by virtue of the incompatibility that he perceived between the "critical" approach and the inner work of spiritual assimilation. Much more nuanced in his appreciation of academia, Schuon was far from neglectful of the contributions of institutional scholars, and he counted in fact not a few university-affiliated scholars among his associates and disciples, not the least of whom was Seyyed Hossein Nasr.

33. For a biographical account of Guénon's life in Egypt, one will greatly benefit from reading Xavier Accart's book, *L'ermite de Duqqi. René Guénon en marge des milieu francophones* (Milano: Archè-Edidit, 2001).

34. Schuon was the founder of the *Tarīqah Maryamiyyah*, a branch of the *Shādhiliyyah ʿAlāwiyyah*. He exercised his spiritual function within the framework of Islam and required from his disciples that they fulfill all the basic formal duties of Muslim life. By virtue of his purely esoteric and universalist outlook, he also directed a smaller number of spiritual seekers from other religions, mostly Orthodox and Catholic Christians. In this regard, it must be stressed that Schuon impressed upon his Christian disciples the fundamental principle that "Christ is your master." He considered his Christian followers as initiated into spiritual life by the graces of baptism, the latter being confirmed by a vow of perpetual invocation.

35. "So set thy purpose (O Muhammad) for religion as a man by nature upright— the nature (framed) of Allah, in which He hath created man. There is no altering (the

laws of) Allah's creation. That is the right religion, but most men know not–," trans. Marmaduke William Pickthall. (*Qur'an* 30:30).

36. Frithjof Schuon, *Sufism: Veil and Quintessence* (Bloomington, IN: World Wisdom, 2006), 30.

37. " (. . .) The plan of salvation also includes those who acknowledge the Creator. In the first place amongst these there are the Mohamedans, who, professing to hold the faith of Abraham, along with us adore the one and merciful God, who on the last day will judge mankind." *Dogmatic Constitution on the Church—Lumen Gentium*, November 21, 1964.

38. " The Church regards with esteem also the Moslems. They adore the one God, living and subsisting in Himself; merciful and all-powerful, the Creator of heaven and earth, who has spoken to men; they take pains to submit wholeheartedly to even His inscrutable decrees, just as Abraham, with whom the faith of Islam takes pleasure in linking itself, submitted to God. Though they do not acknowledge Jesus as God, they revere Him as a prophet. They also honor Mary, His virgin Mother; at times they even call on her with devotion. In addition, they await the day of judgment when God will render their deserts to all those who have been raised up from the dead. Finally, they value the moral life and worship God especially through prayer, almsgiving and fasting." "Declaration on the Relation of the Church to Non-Christian Religions, *Nostra Aetate,*" October 28, 1965.

39. In his preface to this volume, Antoine Compagnon encapsulates the influence of Guénon on his time in a suggestive way: "Guénon s'avère dans ce livre une figure fascinante, toujours et partout présente à l'arrière-plan de l'époque, un peu comme le Zelig de Woody Allen." [In this book Guénon is revealed as a fascinating figure, ever and everywhere present in the background of our time, somewhat in the way of Woody Allen's Zelig.] Xavier Accart, *Guénon ou le renversement des clartés: Influence d'un métaphysicien sur la vie littéraire et intellectuelle française (1920–1970)* (Paris, Edidit, Milano: Archè, 2005), 16.

40. Dumont has acknowledged that his reading the *Introduction générale à l'étude des doctrines hindoues* was a determining factor in his decision to focus upon India. Cf. ibid., 198.

41. This character, which distinguishes Guénon's opus from Schuon's, probably stems from the purely doctrinal nature of his works, in contrast with Schuon's more directly spiritual and moral implications.

42. In the preface to his magnum opus *Knowledge and the Sacred*, Nasr clearly acknowledges his intellectual and spiritual debt toward Schuon: "We wish to express our gratitude especially to Frithjof Schuon whose unparalleled exposition of traditional teachings is reflected, albeit imperfectly, upon many of the pages which follow." (Albany, NY: SUNY Press, 1989), ix.

43. *Essai sur les origines du lexique technique de la mystique musulmane* was first published in Paris (Geuthner) in 1922. The most recent edition of this essay is the 1999 Cerf edition.

44. As Henry Corbin informs or reminds his readers, "this term *tasawwuf* is the verbal noun of the fifth form derived from the root swf; it means to 'profess faith in Sufism', and it is used to refer to Sufism as such (compare with the words *tashayyu'*, to profess faith in Shī'ism; *tasannun*, to profess faith in Sunnism, etc.)." Cf. *Histoire de la philosophie islamique* (Paris: Gallimard, 1964), 262. Note that *tasawwuf* is sometimes used generically today in the Arab world as referring to "mysticism."

45. William Chittick has humorously staged this kind of appraisal: "Even specialists in fields like Religious Studies or Islamic Studies will sometimes remark, 'Oh, but he's a Sufi,' meaning, 'You know, you do not have to take him seriously, because he's a mystic,' or, 'Sufism really has nothing to do with Islam, so don't pay attention to him.'" *Science of the Cosmos, Science of the Soul* (Oxford: Oneworld, 2007), 80.

46. "The real is encountered only at that station of no station and at that point where the Sufi encounters and becomes one with the eternal deity in each of the constantly changing forms of its manifestation, in each moment, in each breath." Michael A. Sells, "The Station of No Station," in *Mystical Languages of Unsaying* (Chicago: University of Chicago Press, 1994), 105.

47. This is expressed symbolically by a famous passage of the *Sūrah al-Kahf* concerning the Seven Sleepers: "Thou wouldst have deemed them awake, whilst they were asleep, and We turned them on their right and on their left sides: their dog stretching forth his two fore-legs on the threshold: if thou hadst come up on to them, thou wouldst have certainly turned back from them in flight, and wouldst certainly have been filled with terror of them." (Qur'an 18:18).

48. There is little doubt that a classical authority as universally recognized in Islam as Abu Hamīd al-Ghazālī would have considered Salafism as a heterodoxy, precisely because of—among other factors—its exclusion of the inner dimension of Islam. T.J. Winter judiciously noted that when the *da'wa* (preaching) of Ibn 'Abd al-Wahhāb, the eighteenth-century inspirer of the Reformist movement that spread from Najd, and whose principles constitute the ideological backbone of Salafi and Wahhābi contemporary discourse, became the official version of Islam in some parts of Arabia and a most influential force in most other Muslim countries, "the scholars and muftīs (judges) of the day applied to it the famous hadīth of Najd: 'Ibn Umar reported the Prophet (upon whom be blessings and peace) as saying: 'Oh God, bless us in our Syria; O God, bless us in our Yemen.' Those present said: 'And in our Najd, O Messenger of God!' but he said, 'O God, bless us in our Syria; O God, bless us in our Yemen.' Those present said, 'And in our Najd, O Messenger of God!' 'Ibn Umar said that he thought that he said on the third occasion: 'Earthquakes and dissensions (fitna) are there, and there shall arise the horn of the devil'." *Islam, Fundamentalism, and the Betrayal of Tradition*, ed. Joseph Lumbard (Bloomington, IN, World Wisdom, 2004), 293.

49. Daryush Shayegan, *Cultural Schizophrenia. Islamic Societies Confronting the West* (New York: University of Syracuse Press, 1992), 74.

50. Mohammad Arkoun, book review of Frithjof Schuon's *De l'unité transcendante des religions* (Paris: Le Seuil, 1979), in Mohammad Arkoun, *Archives des sciences sociales des religions* 48, no. 2 (1979): 349.

51. Tariq Ramadan, *Western Muslims and the Future of Islam* (Oxford: Oxford University Press, 2004), 32.

52. This was already suggested by Muhammad Asad in his *Road to Mecca*, first published in 1954: "Nothing could be more erroneous than to measure the potentialities of Muhammad's message by the yardstick of present-day Muslim life and thought." *The Road to Mecca* (Louisville, KY: Fons Vitae, 2005).

53. Henry Corbin, *The Voyage and the Messenger: Iran and Philosophy* (Berkeley, CA: North Atlantic), 97.

54. Salih bin Abdul Aziz Aali Shaikh, *The Destination of the Seeker of Truth* (Darussalam, 2003). This primacy of *tawhīd* is also clearly indicated by the oft-quoted *hadīth* of Jibrail (Gabriel): "One day while we were sitting with the Messenger of

Allah (. . .) there appeared before us a man whose clothes were exceedingly white and whose hair was exceedingly black; no signs of journeying were to be seen on him and none of us knew him. He walked up and sat down by the Prophet (. . .). Resting his knees against his and placing the palms of his hands on his thighs, he said: O Muhammad, tell me about Islam. The Messenger of Allah (. . .) said: Islam is to testify that there is no god but Allah and Muhammad is the Messenger of Allah, to perform the prayers, to pay the zakāt, to fast in Ramadān and to make the pilgrimage to the House if you are able to do so. He said: You have spoken rightly, and we were amazed at him asking him and saying that he had spoken rightly. He said: Then tell me about īmān. He said: It is to believe in Allah, His angels, His books, His messengers, and the Last Day, and to believe in divine destiny, both the good and the evil thereof. He said: You have spoken rightly. He said: Then tell me about ihsān. He said: It is to worship Allah as though you are seeing Him, and while you see Him not yet truly He sees you. "*An-Nawawī's Forty Hadīth*, trans. Ezzeddin Ibrahim and Denys Johnson-Davies, Cambridge, England: The Islamic Texts Society, 2007), 28–30.

55. Geoffroy illustrates the first of these attitudes by Rashīd Ridā's paradoxically passeist and progressive Salafism, and the second by the "deconstructionists" of Islam and their "*rationalisme complexé de l'ex-colonisé.*" *L'islam sera spirituel ou ne sera pas,* Paris: Le Seuil, 2009, 75. Now it must be acknowledged that the contrast between the two approaches that we have just sketched is in some ways a pedagogical simplification. Historically, the two ways have been sometimes joined, or been parallel. The Sanusi movement of Lybia was, for example, a Salafi inspired movement that was also nourished by Sufi concepts and practices. Conversely Sufi masters such as the Algerian Amir 'Abd al-Qādir in the nineteenth century, or Shaykh Ahmad al-'Alāwī in the twentieth century, while being rooted in the pure metaphysics of *tawhīd* and spiritual science of *dhikr* and virtues, have had also an important external, social, and, for the former, political presence and impact. This shows that our distinction points to an emphasis rather than to an exclusive focus. It remains nevertheless true that phenomena such as Wahhabism in Arabia, *al-Ikhwān al-Muslimīn* in Egypt, or *Jamā'at-i-Islami* in Pakistan have been primarily propagating an external agenda of Islamicization of society, while Sufi brotherhoods have tended to place the emphasis on inner reformation and remembrance of God.

56. The main reason for this restriction lies in the interpretation of Shī'ism as the inner dimension of Islam, an interpretation that will be critically addressed in some of the following chapters.

57. Jean-Louis Michon notes that this form is the passive participle of *sāfā*, to be sincere, faithful. *Le soufi marocain Ahmad Ibn 'Ajība et son Mi'rāj* (Paris:Vrin, 1973), 181.

58. "People whom neither [worldly] commerce nor striving after gain can divert from the remembrance of God, and from constancy in prayer, and from charity:" Qur'ān, 24:37.

59. Massignon, *Essai sur les origines du lexique technique de la mystique musulmane* (Paris: Cerf, 1999), 156.

60. A lecture delivered at the David M. Kennedy Center for International Studies, Brigham Young University, May 2003. © 2003 William C. Chittick.

61. "Sufism is a touchstone, an implacable criterion which reduces everything else, except its own equivalents, to a flat surface of two dimensions only, being itself the real dimension of height and depth." Martin Lings, *What is Sufism?* (Cambridge, UK: The Islamic Texts Society, 2006), 8.

62. Cf. *Ecrits spirituels*, ed Michel Chodkiewicz (Paris: Le Seuil, 1982), 133.

63. In Ahmad b. Hanbal. Cf. Tayeb Chouiref, *Les enseignements spirituels du Prophète*, volume I, (Wattrelos, France: Tasnîm, 2008), 236.

CHAPTER TWO. SUFISM, SHĪ'ISM, AND THE DEFINITION OF INNER ISLAM

1. "In my own writings, I have always avoided the word 'mysticism,' partly because of its strong negative connotations. I prefer instead the word 'Sufism,' which has the advantage of deriving from Arabic and pertaining specifically to Islam. Nowadays, this word is rather well known in the West. In the United States, Rumi has recently been the best-selling poet, and every introduction to his poems points out his affiliation to the Sufi tradition. Health clubs and New Age centers teach 'Sufi dancing' along with yoga and Zen meditation. At least the name is no longer strange in English, even if, in contrast to 'mysticism,' few people have any real idea as to what it might mean." William Chittick, lecture delivered at the David M. Kennedy Center for International Studies, Brigham Young University, May 2003. © 2003 William C. Chittick.

2. "(. . .) Sufism is a kind of mysticism (. . .)." Martin Lings, *What is Sufism* (Cambridge, UK: Islamic Texts Society, 1995), 12.

3. This course of events has been documented by Jacques Keryell in his *L'Hospitalité sacrée* (Paris: Nouvelle Cité, 1987), 40–54, and by Christian Destremau and Jean Moncelon in their biography of Massignon. *Massignon* (Paris: Omibus, 1994).

4. Keryell, *L'Hospitalité sacrée,* 41–42.

5. This secret is the ultimate meaning of *tawhīd*, or unity, according to Islam.

5. Cf. Louis Massignon, *La Guerre Sainte suprême de l'Islam arabe* (Paris: Fata Morgana, 1998), 44.

7. *Sufi Poems. A Mediaeval Anthology.* Compiled and translated by Martin Lings (Cambridge UK: Islamic Texts Society, 2004), 38.

8. For Massignon, the "truth" of a great spiritual figure is better approached by means of a sympathetic study of folkloric and hagiographic accounts, in the spiritual and collective traces that he has left in the collective consciousness, rather than by the fastidious historical and juridical accounts archived by scholars.

9. As a noun, the French word *gauche* refers to the left, the side of the heart, while as an adjective it conveys the idea of awkwardness.

10. Recent scholarship has tended to deflect the opposition between *wahdāt al-wujūd* and *wahdāt ash-shuhūd* while acknowledging a definite difference in emphasis, as exemplified, for example, in the gradual decline of Ibn 'Arabī's influence in *turuq* such as the *Naqshbandiyyah*. Cf. William Chittick, *The Sufi Path of Knowledge* (Albany, NY: SUNY Press, 1989), 227, and also Hamid Algar, "Reflections of Ibn 'Arabi in Early Naqshbandī Tradition," *Journal of the Muhyiddin Ibn 'Arabi Society*, Vol. 10 (1991).

11. The two Sufi schools of *wahdāt al-wujūd* and *wahdāt ash-shuhūd* have occasionally been compared with the Hindu schools of *Ādvaita* and *Viśishtādvaita Vedānta*. The qualified nondualism of the latter is not without affinity with the *wahdāt ash-shuhūd* as taught by Sufis such as Ahmad Sirhindī in that it may be interpreted as an attempt at preserving the relative reality of multiplicity in fear of a possible "monistic" confusion.

12. Chittick, *The Sufi Path of Knowledge*, 94.

13. Massignon. "Grâce à Ibn'Arabī, le vocabulaire syncrétiste hellénistique domine désormais, et le souci théorique de rester d'accord avec lui l'emporte sur l'analyse

expérimentale et l'introspection de la pratique cultuelle." *Essai sur les origines du lexique technique de la mystique musulmane* (Paris: Cerf, 1999), 80.

14. Ibid.

15. "'In 30 years of living in Algeria,' an apologist who believed himself a Christian once objected to me, 'I've never met one Muslim *qadi* (religious judge) who was sincere, impartial, and a truly honest man (an *afifi*).' 'On earth we find in people only that which we are looking for,' I answered him. 'If you had been looking for the goodness of God in the first *qadi* who came to you, you would have heard speaking the truth for you, you would have understood him in the sense of his canonical mandate and willy-nilly he would have answered you in the name of the God of Abraham.'" Quoted in Giulio Basetti-Sani, OFM, *Louis Massignon: Christian Ecumenist* (Chicago: Franciscan Herald Press, 1974), 58.

16. Michel Chodkiewicz, *An Ocean Without Shore: Ibn 'Arabī, the Book and the Law* (Albany, NY: SUNY Press, 1993), 23.

17. "I have never been able to understand the obscure reasons for his exclusion of certain individuals and spiritual schools of Islam from the light of his intuitive understanding." Corbin, *The Voyage and the Messenger:Iran and Philosophy* (Berkeley, CA: North Atlantic Books, 1998), 96.

18. Ibid., 16–17

19. Henry Corbin, *En Islam Iranien*, vol. 3 (Paris: Gallimard, 1972), 153.

20. Ibid., 180.

21. Henry Corbin, *Swedenborg and Esoteric Islam* (West Chester, PA: Swedenborg Foundation, 1993), 114.

22. "Precisely, it seems that it is first of all the congregational organization of Sufism that is targeted by Shī'ite critics: the *khānqāh* (convent), the 'monacal' garb, the role of the shaykh who tends to be substituted to the Imām, namely the hidden Imām, inner master and guide, since he is invisible." Our translation, Cf. Henry Corbin, *Histoire de la philosophie islamique*, 266.

23. "(. . .) Many Sufi chains of authority (*silsilah*, pl. *salāsil*) include the first eight Imāmī Shi'ite Imāms (the last of whom died in the early third century) and consider all eight to have been important or even axial links in their spiritual genealogies." Maria Massi Dakake, *The Charismatic Community, Shi'ite Identity in Early Islam* (Albany, NY: SUNY Press, 2007), 24.

24. 'Uways al-Qarnī is the "patron" of Sufis who have no living master: "The Sufi tradition has distinguished a special group of seekers: those whose *sole* link with the teaching is through Khidr himself. There are those rare Sufis who do not have a teacher in the flesh. (. . .) They have been given a special name: *uwaysiyyūn*." Sara Sviri, *The Taste of Hidden Things* (Inverness, CA: The Golden Sufi Center, 1997), 98.

25. "The dominant fact (of this Reformation) was the initiative taken by Imām Hassan (1126–1166) who proclaimed the Great Resurrection (*Qiyāmat al-Qiyamāt*) before all of the adepts gathered on the high terrace of the fortress of Alamūt. (. . .) What this proclamation implied was nothing less than the advent of a pure spiritual Islam, freed from all legalitarian spirit, from all servitude to the law, a personal religion of the Resurrection which is a spiritual birth, because it leads one to discover and live the spiritual meaning of Prophetic revelations." Cf. Corbin, *Histoire de la philosophie islamique*, 139.

26. Henry Corbin, *Avicenna and the Visionary Recital* , trans. Willard Trask (Princeton, New Jersey: Princeton University Press, 1960), 20.

27. Corbin, *The Voyage and the Messenger: Iran and Philosophy*, 23.

28. Cf. Henry Corbin, *L'homme et son ange* (Paris: Fayard, 1983), 48.

29. Corbin forged the neologism "imaginal" in order to avoid the negative connotations attached to the adjective "imaginary," which implies de facto a notion of unreality on the part of the domain encompassed by imagination: "Regardless of our efforts (. . .) we cannot prevent the term *imaginary*, in current usage that is not deliberate, from being equivalent to signifying *unreal*, something that is and remains outside of being and existence—in brief, something *utopian*. I was absolutely obliged to find another term because, for many years, I have been by vocation and profession an interpreter of Arabic and Persian texts, the purposes of which I would certainly have betrayed if I had been entirely and simply content—even with every possible precaution—with the term *imaginary*. I was absolutely obliged to find another term if I did not want to mislead the Western reader that it is a matter of uprooting long-established habits of thought, in order to awaken him to an order of things (. . .)." Corbin, *Swedenborg and Esoteric Islam*, 2.

30. Corbin, *Swedenborg and Esoteric Islam,* 11.

31. Ibid., 12. See also Tom Cheetham, *The World Turned Inside Out: Henry Corbin and Islamic Mysticism.* Woodstock, Connecticut: Spring Journal Books, 2003.

32. When Haydar Āmulī quotes Ibn 'Arabī, Corbin reads in this quote the "symbol of the integration of Ibn 'Arabī into Shī'ite gnosis." *En islam iranien*, vol 3, 190.

33. Henry Corbin, *L'Homme et son Ange, Initiation et chevalerie spirituelle* (Paris: Fayard, 1983), 251.

34. Many of the European and American scholars whose intelligence has been reoriented by reading Guénon have become proficient in Islamic studies, at least in the domain of *tasawwuf*, and a significant number of so-called Guénonians, broadly defined as people who have been deeply marked by his work, have entered Islam and affiliated themselves to Sufism. A large section of the scholarly work of translation and commentary of classics of *tasawwuf* in French has come from scholars who have been touched by Guénon and have entered Islam in his wake, such as Jean-Louis Michon, Jean Canteins, Roger Deladrière, Michel Vâlsan, Michel Chodkiewicz, Denis Gril, Eric Geoffroy, Claude Addas, Maurice Gloton, and Charles-André Gilis, to name just a few.

35. It is not without importance to specify that Guénon sharply distinguishes between the "general" and the "universal." The former is nothing but an extension of the individual, as the genre is an extension of the individual. By contrast, the universal transcends the individual modality, which means that there is no "metaphysical common measure" between the two. The individual as such cannot access the universal, although the universal may be realized from the departing point of individuality. This important distinction implies that the spiritual path involves a kind of metaphysical inversion of perspectives. This inversion has been identified by some Sufis as the "confluence of the two seas" (*majma' al-bahrayn*) mentioned in the *Sūrah al-Kahf*. Significantly, this is the juncture where the paths of Moses (prophet of the law) and al-Khidr, the prophet of esoterism ('*ilm min ladunni*), part.

36. He was initiated into *tasawwuf* by the Swedish painter Ivan Agueli, whose Islamic name was 'Abd-ul-Hadi. As developed below, Guénon does not seem to have been bound by the outer requirements of the *sharī'ah* during the years he was already initiated into Sufism in France. This is undoubtedly indicative of some aspects of his conception of the relationship between the esoteric path and the exoteric framework.

37. In Xavier Accart, *L'Ermite de Duqqi. René Guénon en marge des milieu francophones égyptiens* (Milano: Archè, 2001), 268.

38. Ibid., 269.

39. Guénon lived in a villa of the neighborhood of Duqqi. He married an Egyptian *sharifah*, from whom he had four children, two girls and two boys, Khadija, Layla, Ahmad, and Muhammad, the latter born a few months following his father's death in January 1951. Cf. Jean-Louis Michon, "Dans l'intimité du Cheikh Abd al-Wahid—René Guénon—au Caire, 1947–1949" in Accart, *L'Ermite de Duqqi*, 252–259.

40. René Guénon, "The Shell and the Kernel," *Insights into Islamic Esoterism & Taoism* (Hillsdale, NY: Sophia Perennis, 2004), 11.

41. Guénon, *Insights into Islamic Esoterism & Taoism*, 1.

42. Ibid., 12.

43. Guénon, *Initiation and Spiritual Realization* (Hillsdale, NY: Sophia Perennis, 2004), 144.

44. Guénon, *Insights in Islamic Esoterism and Taoism*, 10.

45. "(. . .) when the inner is understood in its full plenitude it will be realized that that which allows access to it—namely the outer—itself contains everything, for the *haqīqah* is the *sharī'ah*, and the *sharī'ah* is the *haqīqah*." Mohammed Rustom, Review of Michel Chodkiewicz, *An Ocean without Shore: Ibn 'Arabi, the Book and the Law*, trans. David Streight (Cambridge, UK: Islamic Texts Society), 1993.

46. Guénon, *Insights into Islamic Esoterism & Taoism*, 14.

47. Ibid., 20.

48. Ibid., 17.

49. The solar symbolism that is brought into play is all the more adequate in that the sun itself allows for the visibility of phenomena, whereas its intensity causes the latter to disappear from sight, as it were. This is an image of the productive and reductive functions of the Principle. The sun as source of light is identifiable with the Principle as Infinite, whereas its intensity is identifiable with its dimension of absoluteness.

50. "The question has been asked why Guénon 'chose the Islamic path' and not another; the 'material' reply is that he really had no choice, given that he did not admit the initiatory nature of the Christian sacraments and that Hindu initiation was closed to him because of the caste system; given also that at that period Buddhism appeared to him to be a heterodoxy. The key to the problem is that Guénon was seeking an initiation and nothing else; Islam offered this to him, with all the essential and secondary elements that must normally accompany it." Frithjof Schuon, "A Note on René Guénon."

51. "The modes of participation in Guénon's work are necessarily diverse: some readers have been influenced by it in a more or less partial or superficial manner, whereas others have been convinced by the very essence of the work; some have been 'converted' from the current errors of our time; *others still, not in need of 'conversion', have found in Guénon what they already thought themselves, except for metaphysics which no one can draw forth from himself, and which they received from Guénon* (. . .)." Frithjof Schuon, "René Guénon: Definitions."

52. Schuon, *Sufism: Veil and Quintessence*, 103.

53. "(. . .) The sharp dichotomy between Sufism and legalism commonly postulated reflects modern anti-Sufi polemic more than it does historical Sufi practices." Frederick S. Colby in *The Subtleties of the Ascension* (Louisville, KY: Fons Vitae, 2006), 12.

54. The last portion of this Quranic passage is stated as "*wa la-dhikru Allāhi akbar.*" The translation of *wa* as "but," which Pickthall and some other translators have favored,

emphasizes the difference in degree, as it were, between *salāt* and *dhikr,* whereas a more literal translation as "and" would imply both that *salāt* is a form of *dhikr, dhikr* itself—as methodical invocation of the Name of God—being the quintessence of all prayers.

55. "The esoterism of these practices is not only in their obvious initiatory symbolism but in the fact that our practices are esoteric to the extent we ourselves are, first by our understanding of the Doctrine and then by our assimilation of the Method, these two elements being contained in the twofold Testimony precisely." Schuon, *Sufism: Veil and Quintessence,* 116.

56. It is significant that, in his classic *Understanding Islam,* Schuon devotes a final chapter to Sufism under the title "The Path," without making use of the term Sufism, which one might have expected him to choose as his title. This is not unconnected to what we have just written, and is moreover confirmed by his statement: "In this section our aim is not so much to treat of Sufism exhaustively or in detail—other writers have had the merit of doing so with varying degrees of success—but rather to envisage the "path" (*tarīqah*) in its general aspects or in its universal reality." Schuon, *Understanding Islam,* 127.

57. "Sufism seems to derive its originality, both positive and problematical, from the fact that it mixes—metaphorically speaking—the spirit of the Psalms with that of the *Upanishads:* as if David had sung the *Brahmasutra,* or as if Badarayana had implored the God of Israël." Schuon, *Sufism: Veil and Quintessence,* 19.

58. "Let us note here—since we are on the topic of Sufism—that it is aberrant to have the esoterism of Islam coincide with Shiite 'imamology' and 'gnoseology', as Corbin would have it; then to reduce metaphysics to an inspirationist exegesis, as if intellection—which is also supra-rational—did not exist or had no role to play. Authentic esoterism stems from the nature of things and not from a dynastic institution; its seeds are everywhere present, sparks can flash from every flint; to make esoterism result from a religious program and a theological argument is a contradiction in terms. Of course, fundamental truths were expressed initially by those whom the Shiites consider to be imams; however, Sunnite Sufism refers to these sages, not insofar as they are supposed to be imams in the theological sense of Shiism, but insofar as they are 'poles' (*qutb,* pl. *aqtāb*) of Islam as such, outside all confessional interpretation or annexation; *Spiritus autem ubi vult spirat.*" "Diversity of Paths," *In the Face of the Absolute* (Bloomington, IN: World Wisdom, 1989), 174.

59. Muhammad ibn 'Abd al-Jabbar ibn al-Hasan an-Niffarī is a relatively obscure tenth-century mystic from Iraq who wrote the *Mawāqif* and the *Mukhātabat.* Cf. A.J. Arberry, *The Mawāqif and Mukhātabāt of Muhammad Ibn 'Abdi'l-Jabbār Al-Niffarī with other fragments* (London: Luzac, 1935).

60. Cf. Michel Chodkiewicz, *Le Sceau des saints* (Paris: Gallimard, 1986), 103.

61. *René Guénon et l'Actualité de la Pensée Traditionnelle,* René Alleau and Marina Scriabine, edit. (Braine-le-Comte, Belgium : Editions du Baucens, 1977), 54.

CHAPTER THREE. THE *QUR'ĀN*

1. Schuon wrote in French and lived part of his early life in France, while his cultural background and sensibility was primarily Germanic.

2. Louis Massignon, "Valeur de la parole humaine en tant que témoignage," 1951, in *Sur l'islam,* (Paris: Editions de l'Herne, 1995), 77.

3. Massignon, *Sur l'islam,* 56.

4. "One can only think a human 'history'—since the duration in which we live is oriented, by postulating a finalist structural continuity (against a fortuitous discontinuity); one can only write such a history by explaining linguistic facts phonologically (and not phonetically), and explaining psychic facts by means of a 'psychology of form' (against associationist empiricism). Historical finality must become 'inwardly' intelligible, for it concerns the person who extracts by herself the meaning of the common trial (and not the individual, i.e. a differentiated element who depends on the social group which remains its natural end.)" Massignon, *Sur l'islam,* 55.

5. Ibid.

6. Ibid.,12.

7. In grammar, the "communicative meaning (. . .) of *tadmīn* is to allow one word to indicate, or to convey, the import or meaning of two words. . . ." Adrian Gully, *Grammar and Semantics in Medieval Arabic* (UK: Routledge, 1995), 43.

8. Louis Massignon, *Testimonies and Reflections,* selected and introduced by Herbert Mason (Notre Dame, IN:University of Notre Dame Press, 1989), 70.

9. Massignon, *Sur l'islam,* 12.

10. Louis Massignon, *Les trois prières d'Abraham* (Paris: Le Cerf, 1997), 85.

11. This anagogic meaning, one of the four meanings assigned to the Bible in Christian hermeneutics, is both evidence of the divine origin of the Book and the seed of Islamic mysticism.

12. Massignon, *Les trois prières d'Abraham,* 89.

13. Henry Corbin, *History of Islamic Philosophy,* trans. L. Sherrard (London and New York: Kegan Paul International, 1993), 1. *Histoire de la philosophie islamique* (Paris: Gallimard, 1964), 14.

14. Ibid.

15. "La situation vécue est essentiellement une *situation herméneutique,* c'est-à-dire la situation où pour le croyant éclôt le *sens vrai,* lequel du même coup rend son existence vraie. Cette vérité du sens, corrélative de la vérité de l'être, vérité qui est réelle, réalité qui est vraie, c'est tout cela qui s'exprime dans un des termes-clefs du vocabulaire philosophique: le mot *haqīqat.* " Ibid.

16. "(The literal sense) is the containant, the basis, and the protection to such a degree that in the absence of this natural literal sense, the celestial sense and the spiritual sense would not be the Word, but would be like spirit and life without body, or like a temple with many sanctuaries and a Holy of Holies at its center, but lacking a roof and walls, so that the temple would be exposed to the depredations of thieves and wild beasts." Henry Corbin, *Swedenborg and Esoteric Islam* (West Chester, PA: Swedenborg Foundation, 1995), 61.

17. " . . . l'ésotérique (*bātin*), la profondeur cachée du Qorān, est cette Vraie Réalité, le Verbe divin, qui subsiste éternellement avec et par l'Ipséité divine, et qui se manifeste dans le corps de la lettre et du sens littéral, comme l'image dans un miroir." Corbin, *En islam iranien,* vol. 3. (Paris: Gallimard, 1972), 225.

18. Ibid., 231.

19. Henry Corbin, *Creative Imagination in the Sūfism of Ibn ʿArabī,* translated from the French by Ralph Manheim (Princeton, NJ: Princeton University Press, 1969), 211.

20. This is linked by Corbin to the anathema against Montanus and his followers. The Montanists were an ecstatic Christian movement of the second century, first known as Phrygians. The movement was founded by Montanus himself and two

prophetesses, Maximilla and Priscilla. Tertullian was the most famous Montanist. The ecstatic and prophetic nature of Montanism represented a challenge to the fledgling *magisterium* of the Church, whence the final excommunication of Montanus and his followers.

21. Henry Corbin, *History of Islamic Philosophy* (London and New York: Kegan Paul, 1993), 11.

22. Corbin, *Histoire*, 17.

23. Cf. F. E. Peters, *Islam: A Guide for Jews and Christians* (Princeton, NJ: Princeton University Press, 2003), 123.

24. "(. . .) the uncreated *Qur'ān*—the Logos—is the Divine Intellect, which crystallizes in the form of the earthly *Qur'ān* and answers objectively to that other immanent and subjective revelation which is the human intellect." Schuon, *Understanding Islam*, 57.

25. "God's revelation in the *Qur'ān* distinguishes (*faraqa*) right from wrong and also differentiates (*faraqa*) the Muslims from the unscriptured and from the recipients of earlier revelations." Daniel Madigan, *Qur'an's Self-Image*, (Princeton, NJ: Princeton University Press, 2001), 127.

26. This is particularly the case in *Sufism: Veil and Quintessence*, in which he debunks the confessional exaggerations and abuses of Islamic exegesis.

27. "When approaching Scripture, one should always pay the greatest attention to rabbinical and cabalistic commentaries and—in Christianity—to the patristic and mystical commentaries; then will it be seen how the word-for-word meaning practically never suffices by itself and how apparent naiveties, inconsistencies, and contradictions resolve themselves in a dimension of profundity for which one must possess the key." Schuon, *Light on the Ancient Worlds*, 115.

28. Schuon, *Understanding Islam*, 48.

29. In Kabbalah, the Torah is considered to be the first creation of God and, as such, the intelligible design of the whole cosmos. The Divine Name which is with God encapsulates its whole reality. The essence of the Torah is the Name. "To say that the Torah was in essence nothing but the great Name of God was assuredly a daring statement that calls for an explanation. Here the Torah is interpreted as a mystical unity, whose primary purpose is not to convey a specific meaning but rather to express the immensity of God's power, which is consentrated in His 'Name'." Gershom Scholem, *On the Kabbalah and its Symbolism* (New York: Schocken Books, 1996), 40.

CHAPTER FOUR. THE PROPHET

1. "Il (Muhammad) n'entra pas dans l'enceinte de l'Union." ["He did not enter the surrounding walls of Union"] Massignon, "L'Hégire d'Ismael," *Les trois prières d'Abraham*, 70.

2. In his introduction to the recent publication of this text in the volume entitled *Les trois prières d'Abraham* (Paris: Cerf, 1997), Daniel Massignon, son of the Islamicist, explains that the first draft of "l' Exil d' Ismaël" was sketched between 1912 and 1917. A 15-page long "Hégire d' Ismaël" was then composed between 1925 and 1927. A 66-page version of the text was published in 1935. This version of the text was modified and expanded through marginal annotations or the addition of new pages on Massignon's personal copies until his death in 1962. The edition of 1997 reflects the state of the text as it was published in 1935.

3. *The Glorious Qur'ān* , bilingual edition with English translation by Marmaduke Pickthall (New York:Knopf 1930).

4. A famous twelfth-century Iranian Mu'tazilite scholar of the *Qur'ān*.

5. "Le texte très elliptique de la sourate al-Najm (LIII) sur cette extase montre Mohammed enelevé par-delà 'l'horizon suprême', jusque par-devant un Buisson, 'l'ultime jujubier', haie d'épine derrière laquelle Dieu se cache, 'à une distance de deux portées d'arc ou un peu moins." Massignon, *Les trois prières d'Abraham*, 69.

6. "L'allusion aux *gharānīq*, sortes d'anges planétaires adorés à la Mekke, indique que Mohammad, tenté un moment d'adorer Dieu à travers leur nature angélique, s'y serait refusé, comme l'Abraham coranique." Massignon, *Les trois prières d'Abraham*, 69.

7. Cf. Massignon, *Les trois prières d'Abraham*, 70.

8. Ibid., 69.

9. This is clearly illustrated in several of the mystical sayings compiled by Sulamī and translated by Frederick S. Colby in *The Subtheties of the Ascension* (Lexington KY: Fons Viate, 2006). We read, for example, in Wāsitī's comments on the Mi'rāj: "Were it not for what adorned him, the alighting of the description upon him and the clothing of select lights, he would have been burned by the lights of that station." (*Subtleties*, 66) This is akin to a transfiguration in and by light that calls to mind the deification of Eastern Christian mysticism.

10. " (. . .) la nature angélique toute nue qu'assumait son guide ne saurait en effet normalement présenter le type de cette union, réalisée avec la nature humaine dans les saints, grâce à une femme, une seule, Marie." Massignon, *Les trois prières d'Abraham*, 70.

11. " Mais il faut constater que, demeuré sur le seuil, ébloui, il ne tente pas de s'avancer dans l'incendie divin; et, par cela même, il s'exclue de comprendre *ab intra* la vie personnelle de Dieu qui l'aurait sanctifié." Massignon, *Les trois prières d'Abraham*, 70.

12. Massignon, *Les trois prières d'Abraham*, 70–71.

13. Massignon's first discovery of Hallāj goes back to March 24, 1907 when he first read a distich of the Sufi mystic in the *Tadhkirat al-Awliya* (*Memorial of the Saints*) of Farid ud-Din 'Attar. Upon reading these two verses, "Two series of prostrations suffice in love, but the preceding ablution must be performed with blood," he decided to write his doctoral thesis on Hallāj. His masterpiece, and only book partially translated into English (in addition to articles excerpted from the *Opera minora*, collected and translated by Herbert Mason and published under the title *Testimonies and Reflections* at the University of Notre Dame Press in 1989), *The Passion of al-Hallaj, Mystic and Martyr of Islam*, constitutes a comprehensive study of Hallāj's life, his reception, the influences on his development, his spiritual heritage in the Muslim world, and a host of psychosociological issues pertaining to his place in the Muslim collective consciousness.

14. "(The Prophetic human being) does not mean someone who 'predicts the future', but someone of more than human inspiration, who brings a divine message which ordinary people would be incapable of attaining themselves." Henry Corbin, *The Voyage and the Messenger: Iran and Philosophy*, 209.

15. Quoted in Corbin, *Histoire de la philosophie islamique*, 65.

16. We write "to some extent" because Corbin·makes it plain that the infinitive forms of Indo-European languages fall short of suggesting in a fully satisfactory manner the very notion of the "act" of being.

17. Corbin, *The Voyage and the Messenger: Iran and Philosophy*, 214.

18. The term Pleroma refers to the fullness of the Divine. It therefore comprehends all the dimensions, levels, and aspects of the Divine Reality.

19. The term "associationism" is often used by Islamicists to refer to the key concept of *shirk*, which consists in falsely or abusively "associating" any reality to the One Reality. This is best expressed by the recurrent Quranic phrase *lā sharika lahu*, meaning "(there is) no associate to Him."

20. This *hadīth* alludes to the terms *Ahad* (Ah-*m*-ad) and *Rabb* ('*A*-Rab), two Names of God in Islam.

21. Corbin, *The Voyage and the Messenger: Iran and Philosophy*, 119.

22. For the analogy with the three concentric circles, cf. Corbin, *Histoire de la philosophie islamique*, 69. Concerning the two "faces" of the Prophet, see Corbin, *En islam iranien,* vol. 3, 267. The analogy between *walāyah* and *nubuwwah* and *nubuwwah* and *tawḥīd* is developed in *En islam iranien* 1, 102.

23. Corbin, *The Voyage and the Messenger: Iran and Philosophy*, 118 and 122.

24. Corbin, *En islam iranien,* vol. 3, 279–280.

25. René Guénon, *La métaphysique orientale* (Paris: Editions traditionnelles, 1976), 10–11. Guénon envisages the supreme Principle as Non-Being. Here is a passage from *The Multiples States of Being* in which he delves into this concept: "(. . .) Being as the principle of manifestation, although it does indeed comprise all the possibilities of manifestation, does so only insofar as they are actually manifested. Outside of Being, therefore, are all the rest, that is, all the possibilities of non-manifestation, as well as the possibilities of manifestation themselves insofar as they are in the unmanifested state; and included among these is Being itself, which cannot belong to manifestation since it is the principle thereof, and in consequence is itself unmanifested. For want of any other term, we are obliged to designate all that is thus outside and beyond Being as 'Non-Being', but for us this negative term is in no way a synonym for 'nothingness', as seems to be the case in the language of certain philosophers; besides being directly inspired by the terminology of the metaphysical doctrine of the Far East, it is sufficiently justified by the need to use some kind of terminology in order for one to speak of these things at all; moreover (. . .), the most universal ideas, being the most indeterminate, can only be expressed—to the degree that they are expressible at all—by terms that are in effect negative in form, as we have seen in connection with the Infinite." Translated by Henry D. Fohr (Hillsdale, NY: Sophia Perennis, 2001), 20–21.

26. René Guénon, *The Symbolism of the Cross*, translator Angus Macnab (Hillsdale, NY: Sophia Perennis, 1996).

27. Ibid., 16.

28. Ibid., 17.

29. Ibid., note 2, 17.

30. Massignon's study of the career of the Prophet is steeped in an extensive examination of the historical and sociological ambience in which his "advent" took place. This is in conformity with Massignon's method—as best exemplified in his *The Passion of Hallāj*—which consists in apprehending a spiritual phenomenon within the network of the influences, contacts, and interactions, whether theological or psychosocial, which shaped its unfolding, and also in relation with its spiritual posterity, not only in intellectual and religious history, but also, and perhaps above all, in the "mythological" and "folkloric" traces left by such figures in the collective psyche of the faithful. The limits of our work have not allowed us to delve into this aspect of

Massignon's approach to the Prophet. Let us say, very generally, that in this respect Massignon's contribution is highly sensitive to the specificities of the Bedouin culture, and to the relationships of Muhammad with the Christian presence in Arabia at his time. This is in conformity with Massignon's double emphasis upon the Ishmaelite—and thereby Abrahamic—identity of the Prophet, and his withdrawal from what Massignon considers to be the full fruition of this heritage, which is for him inseparable from a full recognition of the Incarnation.

31. "Let us specify that the idea of the Logos is polyvalent: if God is 'Beyond-Being'—which He never is in ordinary theology—the Logos will be creating or conceiving Being; if God is Being, the Logos will be His creating or efficient Word; if this Word is God, the Logos will be the reflection of God in the cosmos, namely the universal Intellect, the Koranic *Rūh*, whose fundamental functions are manifested by the Archangels. Beyond-Being, Being, Existence." Cf. Frithjof Schuon, *Christianisme/Islam: Visions d'Oecuménisme ésotérique* (Milan: Archè, 1981), 115, note 8.

32. Schuon illustrates this spiritual reality of the Virgin in Islam by quoting the Quranic passage concerning Maryam: "And make mention of Mary in the Scripture, when she had withdrawn from her people to a chamber looking East, and had chosen seclusion from them." (*Qur'an* 19, 16–17)

33. Cf. Schuon, *Christianisme/Islam*, 83.

34. Schuon, *Understanding Islam*, 103.

35. Ibid., 103.

36. Ibid., 104, note 2.

37. Ibid., 110.

38. "And this is important: an outward attitude, whatever may be its usefulness, always remains an approximation, not a totality; it has the value of a symbol and a key, not that of a rigorous adequation, otherwise hypocrisy would not be a possibility: any more than in the case of scriptural symbolism must moral exteriorizations be taken literally, for here too 'the letter killeth, but the spirit giveth life.'" Frithjof Schuon, *Treasures of Buddhism* (Bloomington, IN: World Wisdom, 1993), 101.

39. Schuon does not explicitly consider this duality in *Understanding Islam*, but it clearly stems from his mention of the *walī* in the context of a discussion on the Prophet's piety as the "apex" of his personality: "There is no saint (*walī*, 'representative', thus 'participant') who is not a 'knower through God' (*'ārif bi'l-Llāh*). This explains why in Islam piety, and *a fortiori* the sanctity which is its flower, has an air of serenity; it is a piety whose essence is that it opens onto contemplation and gnosis." Schuon, *Understanding Islam*, 112.

40. "To say Judeo-Islamic morals—or Abrahamic morals if one prefers—is to say 'equilibrium in view of ascension', or 'the horizontal in view of the vertical'; not equilibrium for its own sake, nor the horizontal for its own sake." Cf. Schuon, *Christianisme/Islam*, 76. The reference to "Judeo-Islamic morals" is to be understood in contradistinction with Christianity, the spiritual perspective of which could almost be paraphrased as "a holy disequilibrium in view of ascension."

41. This spiritual synthesis is included in the chapter "The Mystery of the Prophetic Substance," which was initially published in French in *Approches du phénomène religieux* (Paris: Courrier du Livre, 1984), and later in English in Schuon, Frithjof, *In the Face of the Absolute* (Bloomington, IN: World Wisdom, 1989).

42. The "Stations of Wisdom" includes two other perfections, i.e., discernment and union, that pertain to a more directly intellective perspective than do the four primary ones.

43. Schuon, *Understanding Islam*, 109.

44. The term "esoterism" has been for the most part understood in this sense by the various representatives of the "Perennialist" school, like Coomarawamy, Huston Smith, or Seyyed Hossein Nasr. One must note, however, William Chittick's reservations about the use of this term: "Nasr has not necessarily helped his case by describing Sufism as 'Islamic esoterism.' In this he is presumably following Schuon (and to a lesser degree, Henry Corbin). Schuon has written voluminously, employing the esoteric/ exoteric dichotomy as a key conceptual tool for understanding religion. However, not many English-speaking scholars have followed this practice, partly because few specialists have found it helpful in dealing with the actual texts." William C. Chittick, *Science of the Cosmos, Science of the Soul: The Pertinence of Islamic Cosmology in the Modern World* (Oxford: Oneworld, 2007), 81.

45. Schuon, *Understanding Islam*, viii.

46. Ibid., 96.

47. Ibid., 125.

48. Schuon, *Sufism: Veil and Quintessence*, 115.

49. In this respect, Schuon reminds his readers that "in principle or in themselves the intrinsic qualities are independent of outward comportment, whereas the latter's entire reason for being lies in the former." *In the Face of the Absolute*, 210.

50. Author's translation of Louis Massignon, *Les trois prières d'Abraham*, 110.

CHAPTER FIVE. THE FEMININE

1. Cf. Louis Massignon, "Un voeu et un destin: Marie-Antoinette," *Opéra minora*, vol. 3, (Paris: Presses Universitaires de France, 1969), 654.

2. Louis Massignon, "L'oratoire de Marie à l'Aqça," *Opera minora,* vol.1 (Paris: Presses Universitaires de France, 1969), 596. Massignon takes side with the Shī'ites by opining that Fātima was in fact whipped by 'Umar, "the true founder of the Muslim theocratic state." This is the most spectacular and symbolic opposition between two "archetypes" of Islam.

3. Massignon, "La notion du voeu et la dévotion musulmane à Fatima," *Opera minora*, vol. 1, 572.

4. Ibid.

5. Massignon, "Gandhi et les femmes de l'Inde," *Opera minora,* vol. 3, 385.

6. This rite of ordeal was finally renounced by the group of Christians from Najrān whom the Prophet had challenged. This event took place in the year 10 of the hegira.

7. "And as for Fatima, the blessings of Allah and His peace be on her, our belief is that she is the leader of the women of the world, both the earlier and the later ones. And verily Allah the Mighty and Glorious is wroth with him who evokes her anger, and is well-pleased with him who pleases her, for He has weaned her and those who revere her from the Fire. And she left the world displeased with those who had wronged her and usurped her rights, and denied her the inheritance left by her father. The Prophet said: Verily, Fatima is a part of myself; he who angers her

has angered me, and he who gladdens her has gladdened me. And the Prophet said: Verily Fatima is a part of myself, and she is my spirit (*ruh*) which is between my two flanks. What displeases her displeases me, and what gladdens her gladdens me." *A Shiite Creed*, a translation of *I'tiqadatu 'l-Imamiyyah* (*The Beliefs of the Imamiyyah*) of Abu Ja'far, Muhammad ibn 'Ali ibn al-Husayn, Ibn Babawayh al-Qummi known as ash-Shaykh as-Saduq (306/919–381/991), trans. Asaf A. A. Fyzee (Tehran: Wofis, 1999), 135.

8. Cf. Massignon, "La rawda de Médine," in *Opera minora* III, 297.

9. Louis Massignon, "The Temptation of the Ascetic Çuka," *Testimonies and Reflections, Essays of Louis Massignon* (Notre Dame, IN: University of Notre Dame Press, 1989), 174.

10. "Transmigration is generally not accepted by Muslims. It is however sometimes asserted that a form of transmigration is accepted by Isma'ilis, Affifi 90 (citing Shahrastani); *EI, iv.* 648. It is not easy to say how far this is correct; it may be that while authoritative works always rejected this doctrine, some popular beliefs lend color to this common fallacy." *A Shiite Creed*, note 163,174.

11. Massignon, "The Temptation of the Ascetic Çuka," *Testimonies and Reflections, Essays of Louis Massignon,* 175. "Nicodemus said to him, 'How can a person once grown old be born again? Surely he cannot reenter his mother's womb and be born again, can he?' Jesus answered, 'Amen, amen, I say to you, no one can enter the kingdom of God without being born of water and Spirit. What is born of flesh is flesh and what is born of spirit is spirit." (John, 3, 4–7).

12. Massignon notes that a nineteenth-century Indonesian catechism goes so far as to replace the name Muhammad by Fātima's in the second *shahādah*. "L'oratoire de Marie à l'Aqça," *Opera minora* I, 612.

13. Massignon, "La rawda de Médine," *Opera minora* III, 300. Al-Qarāmita were Ismailis who refused to recognize the Fatimid Ubayd Allāh al-Mahdī as *imam*. They spread in Iraq and Syria, and founded a state in Bahrein and Oman in the tenth and eleventh centuries.

14. Massignon, "L'expérience musulmane de la compassion ordonnée à l'universel", *Opera minora* III, 651.

15. "And all faithful souls, in their passivity toward Grace, are, in the innermost secret of their hearts, 'one single Virgin', in the profound words of Hallāj." Ibid., 651.

16. "Whereas the '*kūn*' ('*fiat*') with Maryam is the Annunciation by an Angel of a Birth in time (for the Christians: Incarnation). The *kūn* with Fātima is the Reminder, by the Rūh-al-Amr (spirit of God in the Night of Destiny) of a Destiny in pre-eternity, the mark of creation, Fitra, predestining the Elected to the Paternal Pity." Massignon, "La Mubāhala," *Opera minora,* vol. 1, 567.

17. Ibid.

18. Massignon, "L'expérience musulmane de la compassion," 649.

19. Ibid., 647.

20. This awareness transpires in his question: "Does Fātima thereby renounce (through her humiliated anger and revolt) the pure Sita-like non-violence that her sacralization imposes upon every woman as her line of conduct?" Massignon, *Opera minora,* vol. 3, 650.

21. Massignon, "La cité des morts au Caire," *Opera minora,* vol. 3, 280.

22. Ibid., 263.

23. Muhammad An-Nafs Az-Zakiyya was a descendant of the Prophet through his daughter Fatimah. He led a rebellion in Medina against the second Abbasid Caliph in 762.

24. I am indebted to the generous friendship of Jacque Keryell for being able to quote in the following pages from some excerpts of a typographic transcript of this lecture.

25. Roneotyped script of a lecture given by Louis Massignon at the Benedictine monastery of Toumlinine, Morocco, in 1957, 3.

26. Ibid., 9.

27. *The Ringstones of Wisdom (Fusūs al-hikam)*, translated by Caner K. Dagli (Chicago: Kazi, 2004), 282.

28. Massignon, "La cité des morts au Caire," *Opera minora* III, 270.

29. *Kitāb-e 'Abhar al-'āshiqīn, Le Jasmin des Fidèles d'Amour*, translation by Henry Corbin (Paris: Verdier, 1991). .

30. *The Ringstones of Wisdom*, 282.

31. "(. . .) The Feminine is not opposed to the Masculine as the *patiens* to the *agens*, but encompasses and combines the two aspects, receptive and active, whereas the Masculine possesses only one of the two." Henry Corbin, *Alone with the Alone: Creative Imagination in the Sūfism of Ibn 'Arabī* (Princeton, NJ: Princeton University Press, 1997), 160.

32. Ibid., 113.

33. Ibid., 162.

34. "On the one hand, the Sigh of Divine Compassion expresses here the divine *pathos*, delivers the divine Names, that is to say, emancipates beings from the virtuality in which, anguished over their latent existentiating energy, they were confined, and they in turn deliver the God whose Names they are from the solitude of His unknownness." Ibid., 115–6.

35. Corbin, *En Islam Iranien* 3, 66–67.

36. This term refers to a group of Italian poets of Neoplatonic leaning, who considered the experience of human love and beauty as a set of six contemplative steps leading to the contemplation of the Divine. Guido Cavalcanti (1250–1300) is the most famous of these. Their philosophy is in a sense encapsulated in Dante's verse, *"Amor e'l cuor gentil sono une cosa"* (Love and the noble heart are one and the same thing).

37. *Kitāb-e 'Abhar al-'āshiqīn, Le Jasmin des Fidèles d'Amour*, 45–46.

38. Ibid., 47.

39. Ibid., 48.

40. Ibid., 48.

41. Ibid., 49.

42. Ibid., 50.

43. Corbin, *En Islam iranien* 3, 71–72.

44. "She became in her turn his disciple, as Rūzbehān had been hers, since the contemplation of her beauty had led him to the term where the attachment to the outer form comes, for the mystic, to an end." Corbin, *En Islam iranien* 3, 70.

45. Corbin, *En Islam iranien* 3, 70.

46. Kitab-e 'Abhar, Le Jasmin, 109

47. "And when We said unto the angels: Prostrate yourselves before Adam, they fell prostrate, all save Iblis. He demurred through pride, and so became a disbeliever." (2:34)

48. Corbin, *Swedenborg and Esoteric Islam*, 105.

49. Ibid., 104.

50. Plato, *Republic* 509b. Cf. Plato, *The Republic*, G.R.F. Ferrari, edit., Cambridge, UK: Cambridge University Press, 2000.

51. (Pickthall 19, 16).

52. "Whenever Zachariah went into the sanctuary where she was, he found that she had food. He said: O Mary! Whence cometh unto thee this (food)? She answered: It is from Allah. Allah giveth without stint to whom He will." (Pickthall 3, 37),

53. (Pickthall 19, 25).

54. This *sūrah* juxtaposes in fact four names of the Essence in stating, "*Qul Huwa Allāhu Ahād Allāhu as-Samād*."

55. Schuon, *Roots of the Human Condition* (Bloomington, IN: World Wisdom, 2002), 40.

56. Ibid., 40

57. "Hypostatic and Cosmic Numbers," in *The Essential Frithjof Schuon*, ed. Seyyed Hossein Nasr (Bloomington, IN: World Wisdom, 2005), 351–2. In addition to the aforementioned references, our considerations on Divine Femininity are primarily based on the following passages from Schuon's works: "The Onto-Cosmological Chain," in *Survey of Metaphysics and Esoterism* (Bloomington, IN: World Wisdom, 2000), 61–62; "The Problem of Sexuality," in *The Essential Frithjof Schuon*, 414–415. Cf. also the very penetrating essay by James Cutsinger, "The Virgin," in *Sophia: Journal of Traditional Studies* 6, no. 2 (2000).

58. Schuon, *Roots of the Human Condition*, 29.

59. "The Blessed Virgin (. . .) personifies this merciful Wisdom which descends towards us and which we too, whether we know it or not, bear in our very essence." Schuon, "Sedes Sapientiae," in *In the Face of the Absolute*, 144.

60. Ibid., 80.

61. Frithjof Schuon, *Spiritual Perspectives and Human Facts* (London: Faber, 1954), chap. 6, 283.

62. It bears stressing that this Quranic phrase is situated in the context of a discussion on the social definition and limitations of women, as if pointing thus to the way of transcending them, from within the very spirit of the religion.

CHAPTER SIX. THE UNIVERSAL HORIZON OF ISLAM

1. "Every unbaptized human being can, as soon as he reaches a sufficient command of his moral conscience, adhere as much as needed, by an act of supernatural faith, to the truths of faith that are indispensable to produce the act of charity." George Anawati, "Christianisme et Islam: Point de vue chrétien," *Présence de Louis Massignon* (Paris, Maisonneuve et Larose, 1987), 88.

2. Dara Shikoh was a disciple of Lahore's Sufi saint Mian Mir. His efforts toward unveiling mystical commonalities between Islam and Hinduism resulted in the Persian translation of the Upanishads from its original Sanskrit.

3. "My heart has become capable of every form: it is a pasture for gazelles and a convent for Christian monks, and a temple for idols, and the pilgrim's Ka'ba and the tables of the Tora and the book of the Koran. I follow the religion of Love (*adīnu bi-d-dīni al-hubb*): whatever way Love's camel take, that is my religion and my faith." Ibn 'Arabī, *Tarjumān al-'Ashwāq*, trans. Reynold Nicholson (London: Theosophical

Publishing House, 1978), 67. "What shall I do, Muslims? I do not recognize myself . . . I am neither Christian nor Jew, nor Magian, nor Muslim. I am not of the East, nor the West, not of the land, nor the sea. (. . .) I have put duality away and seen the two worlds as one. One I seek, One I know. One I see, One I call. He is the First, He is the Last. He is the Outward, He is the Inward. I know of nothing but *Hu*, none but Him." *Love is a stranger: selected lyric poetry of Jelaluddin Rumi,* translated by Kabir Edmunch Helminski (Boston: Shambhala, 2000), 56.

4. Louis Massignon, Letter of January 16, 1955 to Mary Kahil, trans. Dorothy Buck, in *L'Hospitalité Sacrée,* ed. Jacques Keryell (Paris: Nouvelle Cité, 1987), 293.

5. Schuon has underlined the characteristically problematic aspect of this distinction between "natural" and "supernatural" mysticism, which is often no more than a petition of principle: "The concept of a 'natural mysticism' is a *petitio principii* which enables one to assign to a class, as if once and for all, forms of spirituality not entering into the framework of a given religion, which is held to be the sole true and supernatural religion: it is then maintained that even a spirituality which may seem to be on the highest level, but which is situated outside this framework, remains in fact enclosed within the created; it may perhaps attain the center or the summit of this, but could not in any way transcend it, since man can do nothing without God and since, so it is argued, God intervenes directly only in the one supernatural religion that exists, and not outside it. It will readily be admitted that supernatural graces could be bestowed on some non-Christian saint, but these graces will be held to have an 'irregular', seemingly accidental character, and to be produced not by virtue of this saint's religion, but despite it."

6. " My feeling—and it is by the way an opinion that has been shared by several among the most rigid Catholic theologians—is that the Muslims' faith is not simply a natural faith, but a theological faith, it does not suffice for salvation according to Christian doctrine but it is still faith that is the root of justification, and from a Christian point of view, we are obliged toward them to manifest this respect of friendship that discovers a profoundly common point at the foundation of a common meditation, liturgical meditation for the Muslim as for the Christian." Louis Massignon, "Réponse à un ami musulman," *Question de,* no. 90 (Paris: Albin Michel, 1992), 196.

7. Ibid., 190.

8. The term "theosophy" has, in itself, nothing pejorative, since it simply connotes a "God-wisdom." However the term has been too closely associated with the nineteenth- century Theosophical Society founded by Helena Blavatsky, whose strong interest in mediumistic phenomena and somewhat syncretistic tendencies have colored the term since then. It may very well be that Massignon's use of this term is already an indication of his dismissal of the idea of a perennial wisdom.

9. "I consider even the theosophic point of view as being incompatible with the group to which we belong, because it means placing oneself above all religious ideas, considering that religions are nothing but interchangeable laws, and, at the same time, it means not giving enough importance to devotion, this devotion that each religion has toward human beings the existence of whom is often little known." Massignon, "Réponse à un ami musulman," *Question de,* 199.

10. Cf. *supra page 192,* Note 25, Toumlinine lecture, 1957, 18.

11. Massignon, *Les trois prières d'Abraham,* 112.

12. Ibid., 114.

13. Ibid., 111.

14. Guénon, *The Reign of Quantity and the Signs of the Times* (New Delhi: Munshiram Manoharlal, 2000), 67.

15. René Guénon, *Insights into Islamic Esoterism & Taoism* (Hillsdale, NY: Sophia Perennis, 2003), 15.

16. It bears mentioning that Guénon perceives an eschatological meaning in the encounter of Hinduism and Islam on the soil of India. The contradictory effects of this encounter, that is, spiritual interactions, or even merging—through figures like Kabir and Sai Baba of Shirdi—among mystics, and oppositions and wars among exoteric zealots, testify to Guénon's point about the incompatibility between the metaphysical and religious points of view.

17. "Whoever is aware of the essential unity of all traditions can, according to the case, use different traditional forms to expound and interpret doctrine, if there happens to be some advantage in doing so, but this will never even remotely resemble any sort of syncretism or the 'comparative method' of scholars." René Guénon, *Perspectives on Initiation* (Hillsdale, NY: Sophia Perennis, 2004), 41.

18. René Guénon, *La métaphysique orientale* (Paris: Editions Traditionnelles, 1976), 9.

19. Ibid., 6. "(. . .) The equivalent of Hindu metaphysics is to be found, in China, in Taoism; it is also to be found, on the other hand, in some esoteric schools of Islam."

20. Ibid., 5.

21. René Guénon, *The Multiple States of the Being* (Hillsdale, NY: Sophia Perennis, 2001).

22. René Guénon, *Man and His Becoming According to the Vedānta* (Hillsdale, NY: Sophia Perennis, 2001)

23. June 5th, 1931, quoted in *Frithjof Schuon,* ed. Patrick Laude and Jean-Baptiste Aymard (Paris-Lausanne: L'Age d'Homme, 2002), 460.

24. Guénon, *Initiation and Spiritual Realization*, 63.

25. *Frithjof Schuon*, ed. Laude and Aymard, 461.

26. Corbin, *The Voyage and the Messenger: Iran and Philosophy*, 19.

27. Henry Corbin, "Le tragique et l'Occident à la lumière du non-dualisme Asiatique," *Revue Philosophique*, Juillet-Septembre 1975, 275–288.

28. "What seems to us to constitute the permanent ideology of Western mankind is the belief in the *reality of the individual* or the identification of reality and individuality, by opposition to *the fundamental ideology* of traditional Asia, such as it appears in the doctrines of non-dualistic Vedānta, Taoism or Buddhism of the Great Vehicle." Ibid., 276.

29. Henry Corbin, *Le paradoxe du monothéisme* (Paris: L'Herne, 1981), 184.

30. Cf. *Sufi Poems*, translated and edited by Martin Lings, 1.

31. *Le paradoxe du monothéisme*, 185.

32. Ibid., 186.

33. Ibid., 184.

34. Cf. Al-Balabanī, *Le Traité de l'Unité* (Paris: Editions Orientales, 1977), 25.

35. "(. . .) How can (the mental) process be employed as a criterion for the making of distinctions between 'orders of being'? The advaitic answer to this is embodied in the Sanskrit term *bādha*—which means 'contradiction' and, in the context of Advaita ontology, is often translated as 'cancellation' or 'sublation'. For purposes of clarity and for drawing out its meaning more fully, this concept may be

reconstructed as *subration*." Eliot Deutsch, *Advaita Vedānta* (Honolulu: University of Hawaii, 1971), 15.

36. Ibid., 15.

37. Sda Vārtikka, in N.K. Devaraja, *An Introduction to Sankara's Theory of Knowledge* (Delhi: Motilal Banarsidas, 1972), 16.

38. Cf. Al-Balabanī, *Le Traité de l'Unité*, 47.

39. It must be added, though, that an attestation of Unity not fully *realized* has still a theoretical and symbolic validity inasmuch as it is a prefiguration of, or a pointer to, the Reality as such. Schuon makes this point in the following passage: "To pretend, as some do, that it is necessary to have realized the Self in order to expound and comment on the sacred doctrine, amounts to saying that there is no place for a relative comprehension; this is to pretend that there is only absolute comprehension on the one hand and absolute incomprehension on the other. In point of fact, however, there is no possible contact between the absolute and the nothing. If there is only absolute knowledge, it is useless to speak of it; to whom would one speak about it?" "Self-knowledge and the Western Seeker," *Language of the Self* (Madras: Ganesh, 1959), Chapter 3.

40. Frithjof Schuon, *Logic and Transcendence* (London: Perennial Books, 1975), 212.

41. The preposition "before" is provisional, and in fact strictly speaking inadequate, since there is no "before" the *Absconditum*, which bears no relationship whatsoever with human reality.

42. Frithjof Schuon, *Gnosis: Divine Wisdom* (Bloomington, IN: World Wisdom, 2006), 18.

43. Frithjof Schuon, *Form and Substance in the Religions* (Bloomington, IN: World Wisdom, 2002), 14.

44. Ibid., 15.

45. Schuon, *Roots of the Human Condition*, 81.

46. Schuon, *Spiritual Perspectives and Human Facts*, 68. The original term translated in English by "diagram" is *schema,* which refers to a schematic summary, whether represented graphically or not.

47. "All mysticisms are equally universal in the greater sense in that they all lead to the One Truth. But one feature of the originality of Islam, and therefore of Sufism, is what might be called its secondary universality, which is to be explained above all by the fact that as the last Revelation of this cycle of time it is necessarily something of a summing up." Martin Lings, *What is Sufism?* (Cambridge: Islamic Texts Society, 1993), 22.

48. Ibid., 81.

49. "On the surface of Islam we meet with the features of a Bedouin mentality, which obviously have nothing universal about them." Ibid., 81.

CHAPTER SEVEN. THE QUESTION OF WAR

1. "'Ali ibn Abi Talib's Ethics of Mercy in the Mirror of the Persian Sufi Tradition," Reza Shah-Kazemī and Leonard Lewisohn, *The Sacred Foundation of Justice in Islam,* ed. Ali Lakhani (Bloomington, IN: World Wisdom, 2006), 136.

2. Reza Shah-Kazemi, *Justice and Remembrance: Introducing the Spirituality of Imam Ali* (I.B. Tauris, 2007).

3. "The true warrior of Islam smites the neck of his own anger with the sword of forbearance; the false warrior strikes at the neck of his enemy with the sword of his own unbridled ego. For the first, the spirit of Islam determines Jihad; for the second, bitter anger, masquerading as Jihad, determines Islam." Reza Shah-Kazemi, "Recollecting the Spirit of Jihad," *Sacred Web* 8, 153.

4. Massignon, "Nazareth et nous, Nazaréens, Nasara," in *Opera minora,* vol. 3 (1948), 491.

5. Massignon, "When a State enters into a war, they would call it a just war and ask everyone to be prepared to die for the country." "'Gandhian' Outlook and Techniques," in *Opera minora* III, 367.

6. Massignon, "L'Islam et le témoignage du croyant," in *Opera minora,* vol. 3 (1953), 595.

7. Massignon, "Hindus call them mahatmas, Arabians *abdāl,* and Christians saints, but they are usually ignored during their lifetime. And so, if their posthumous renown gives to their name a special glory, it is not because of their posthumous life, which spiritists and theosophists have not been able to establish with certainty, but to their apotropaian character. That is to say, they are not isolated in time but become part of a homogeneous series, bearing witness to the same certitude about the efficacy of spiritual means in improving corrupted social and political situations with their sense of compassion for the universal." "The Notion of 'Real Elite' in Sociology and History" (1952), in *Opera minora* I, 266–7.

8. Massignon, "La croisade à rebours," in *Opera minora,* vol. 3 (1953), 597.

9. Massignon, "L'expérience musulmane de la compassion ordonnée à l'universel," in *Opera minora,* vol. 3(1955), 650.

10. Ibid., 647.

11. Louis Massignon, *La Guerre Sainte Suprême de l'Islam Arabe* (Paris: Fata Morgana, 1998), 9.

12. Ibid., 10.

13. Ibid., 11.

14. Ibid., 25.

15. Massignon, "La 'futuwwa' ou 'pacte d'honneur artisanal' entre les travailleurs musulmans au Moyen Age," in *Opera minora,* vol. 1 (1952), 396.

16. Corbin, *En islam iranien,* vol. 4, 411.

17. "It is from the paradox of a beauty and a perfection proposed to men, but refused or vituperated by men, that originates the fundamental Shī'ite feeling, which is at the heart of *walāyat* and rules the life of he who is designated, in classical texts, by the Persian word *javānmard,* a word that is best translated by 'spiritual knight', knight of faith." Ibid., 409.

18. Tom Cheetham, *The World Turned Inside Out: Henry Corbin and Islamic Mysticism* (Woodstock, CT: Spring Journal Books, 2003), 9.

19. "The religious 'system' worked out by the Savafids succeeded in putting into place a 'process of substitution': the jurist-theologian took the place of the imam; principles of jurisprudence replaced the teachings of the imams; *walāya,* love/submission/fidelity—that all initiates owe to their initiating Master—was transformed into *taqlīd,* servile imitation of the all-powerful jurist; love for the imams was transformed into a morbid, dolorous cult whose violent group demonstrations were approved and perhaps even encouraged by clerical authority; an official, institutionalized clergy replaced the 'invisible companions' of the Awaited imam. This process took place in

a specific direction: its aim was to drag Imamism into the political arena, apply it on the collective level and crystallize it as an ideology." Amir-Moezzi, *The Divine Guide in Early Shi'ism* (Albany: SUNY Press, 1994), 139.

20. "The Lord appears to each in a form corresponding to the respective capacity of each." Corbin, *Swedenborg and Esoteric Islam*, 51.

21. . "God hath granted a grade higher to those who strive and fight with their goods and persons (*bi-amwalihim wa anfusihim*)." (*Qur'ān* 4: 95)

22. The verb *qa'ada* refers to remaining seated, but also to neglecting one's duties.

23. Sentence attributed to the sixth Imām Ja'far al-Sādiq, cf. Corbin, *En islam iranien,* vol. 4, 414.

24. We implicitly distinguish here a spiritual gnosis that is akin to intuitive, supra-rational "heart-knowledge" by identification between the knower and the known, and a dualistic gnosticist tendency that envisages reality on the level of an irreducible ontological polarity.

25. "The 'horizontal' axis is that of the perpetual Combat: all the way from the pre-existential and cosmic Combat between the Armies of Hiero-Intelligence and those of Ignorance, to the final Battle of the Mahdī against the forces of Evil, passing through the battle that has forever opposed the imams to their enemies." Mohammad Ali Amir-Moezzi, *The Divine Guide in Early Shi'ism: The Sources of Esotericism in Islam* (Albany: SUNY Press, 1994), 128.

26. René Guénon, *The Symbolism of the Cross*, 50.

27. Ibid., 52.

28. René Guénon, *Le Roi du Monde* (Paris, Gallimard), 1958, 47–58.

29. Referring to the attribution of a warlike aspect to Islam, Guénon notes that "short of being blinded by certain prejudices, it is easy to understand that this must be so, for in the social domain, war, as long as it is directed against those who create disorder and aims at bringing them back to order, constitutes a legitimate function, which is fundamentally but one aspect of the function of 'justice' understood in its fullest meaning." René Guénon, *Symbols of Sacred Science* (Hillsdale, NY: Sophia Perennis, 2001), 179.

30. "And I saw heaven opened, and behold a white horse; and he that sat upon him was called Faithful and True, and in righteousness he doth judge and make war. His eyes were as a flame of fire, and on his head were many crowns; and he had a name written, that no man knew, but he himself. And he was clothed with a vesture dipped in blood: and his name is called The Word of God. And the armies which were in heaven followed him upon white horses, clothed in fine linen, white and clean. And out of his mouth goeth a sharp sword, that with it he should smite the nations: and he shall rule them with a rod of iron: and he treadeth the winepress of the fierceness and wrath of Almighty God." (*Revelation* 19:15).

31. "Imperialism can come either from Heaven or merely from the earth, or again from hell; however that may be, what is certain is that humanity cannot remain dissociated into independent tribes like fragments of dust; the bad ones would inevitably fling themselves at the good, and the result would be a humanity oppressed by the bad, and so the worst of all imperialisms. What may be called the imperialism of the good constitutes therefore a sort of inevitable and providential preventive war; without it no great civilization is conceivable." Schuon, *Light on the Ancient Worlds,* 3–4.

32. "Passion dominates him (passional man) and plunges him into the world of appearances; thus his path is first and foremost a penitential one: he either redeems himself through violent asceticism or sacrifices himself in some holy war, or in servitude offered to God." Schuon, *Form and Substance in the Religions*, 217–8.

33. "The idea thus realized by Islam and the Prophet is that of the Divine Unity, the absolutely transcendent aspect of which implies—for the created or manifested world—a corresponding aspect of imperfection. This explains why it has been permissible for Moslems from the very beginning to employ a human means such as war to establish their religious world, whereas in the case of Christianity several centuries had to elapse after the apostolic times before it became possible to use the same means, which is, moreover, indispensable for the propagation of a religion." Frithjof Schuon, *The Transcendent Unity of Religions* (Wheaton-Madras-London: The Theosophical Publishing House, 1984), 114.

34. Schuon, *Understanding Islam*, Bloomington, 20.

35. "(. . .) the Absolute—or consciousness of the Absolute—thus engenders in the soul the qualities of rock and of lightning, the former being represented by the Kaaba, which is the center, and the latter by the sword of the holy war, which marks the periphery." Ibid, 34.

36. "It needs be understood that war is common to all and conflict justice, and that all things come to existence in accordance through conflict and necessity." "War is father and king of all things; and it has manifested some as gods, others as men, he has made some slaves, others free men." Heraclitus, Fragments 82 and 83.

37. "Let us not forget that the 'holy war' is accompanied in Islam by the same mystical justification as in Christian chivalry, notably that of the Templars; it offers a way of sacrifice and of martyrdom which united Christians and Moslems at the time of the crusades in one and the same sacrificial love of God." Schuon, *Light on the Ancient Worlds*, 103–4.

38. Schuon, *Stations of Wisdom,* 148.

39. Schuon, *Roots of the Human Condition*, 84.

40. We follow Joseph Lumbard's use of this term as a spiritual key toward a restoration of traditional knowledge in Islam. Cf. "The Decline of Knowledge and the Rise of Ideology in the Modern Islamic World," in *Islam, Fundamentalism, and the Betrayal of Tradition,* ed.Lumbard, 39–77.

BIBLIOGRAPHY

Corbin, Henry. *Abû Ya'qûb Sejestânî, Le dévoilement des choses cachées—Recherches de philosophie ismaélienne.* Lagrasse: Verdier, 1988.

———. *A History of Islamic Philosophy.* London: Kegan Paul, 1993.

———. *Alone with the Alon—Creative Imagination in the Sufism of Ibn 'Arabî.* Princeton: Princeton University Press, 1990.

———. *Avicenna and the Visionary Recital.* New York: Pantheon Books, 1960.

———. *Avicenne et le récit visionnaire.* Paris: Berg International, 1979.

———. *Avicenne. Le récit de Hayy ibn Yaqzân.* Translation. Tehran-Paris: Société des monuments nationaux de l'Iran, 1953.

———. *Corps spirituel et terre céleste.* Paris: Buchet-Chastel, 1979.

———. *Cyclical Time and Ismaili Gnosis.* London: Kegan Paul, 1983.

———. *En Islam iranien: aspects spirituels et philosophiques.* Vol. 1, *Le shî'isme duodéci-main.* Vol. 2, *Sohrawardî et les Platonicien de Perse.* Paris: Gallimard, 1971.

———. *En Islam iranien: aspects spirituels et philosophiques.* Vol. 3, *Les "Fidèles d'Amour"(Rûzbehân Baqlî Shîrâzî)—Shî'isme et soufisme (Haydar Âmolî, Sa'inoddîn Torkeh Ispahânî, Alâoddawleh Semnânî).* Vol. 4, *L'Ecole d'Ispahan (Mîr Dâmâd, Mollâ Sadrâ, Qâzî Sa'îd Qommî), L'Ecole Shaykhie—Le douzième Imâm et la chevalerie spirituelle, index général.* Paris: Gallimard, 1973.

———. *En islam iranien,* 4 vols. Paris: Gallimard, 1991.

———. *Face de Dieu, face de l'homm—Herméneutique et soufisme.* Paris: Flammarion, 1983.

———. *Hamann, philosophe du luthérianisme.* Paris: Berg International, 1985.

———. *Histoire de la philosophie islamique.* Vol. 1, *Des origines jusqu'à la mort d'Averroës (1198),* in collaboration with S. H. Nasr and O. Yahya. Paris: Gallimard, 1964.

———. *Itinéraire d'un enseignement.* Tehran: Institut Français de Recherche en Iran, 1993.

———. *La philosophie iranienne islamique aux XVIIe et XVIIIe siècles de Mîr Dâmâd à 'Abdorrahîm Damâvandî.* Paris: Buchet-Chastel, 1981.

———. *Le Livre des sept statues.* Paris, L'Herne, 2003.

———. *Le paradoxe du monothéisme.* Paris, L'Herne, 1981.

———. *Les Motifs zoroastriens dans la philosophie de Sohrawardî.* Tehran: Publications de la Société d'Iranologie 3, 1946.

———. *L'Homme de lumière dans le soufisme iranien.* Paris: Librairie de Médicis, 1971.

————. *L'Homme et son ange- Initiation et chevalerie spirituelle.* Paris: Fayard, 1983.

————. *L'Imagination créatrice dans le soufisme d'Ibn 'Arabî.* Paris: Flammarion, 1958.

————. *L'Imâm caché.* Paris: L'Herne, 2003.

————. *L'Iran et la philosophie.* Paris: Fayard, 1990.

————. *Mollâ Sadrâ Shîrâzî, Le Livre des pénétrations métaphysiques (Kitâb al-Mashâ'ir).* Translation from Arabic. Tehran-Paris: Adrien-Maisonneuve, 1964.

————. *Mundus imaginalis, or the Imaginary and the Imaginal.* Ipswich: Golgonooza Press, 1975.

————. *Philosophie iranienne et philosophie comparée.* Tehran-Paris: Buchet-Chastel, 1977.

————. *Rûzbehân Baqlî Shîrâzî : Le Jasmin des fidèles d'amour (Kitâb 'âbhar al-âshiqîn).* Translation, Tehran-Paris: Adrien-Maisonneuve, 1958.

————. *Sayyed Haydar Âmolî (VIIe-XIVe s.). La philosophie shî'ite:* vol. 1 *Somme des doctrines ésoteriques (Jâmi' al-asrâr);* vol. 2 *Traité de la connaissance de l'être (Fî ma'rifat al-wojûd).* Tehran-Paris: Adrien-Maisonneuve, 1969.

————. *Shihâboddîn Yahyâ Sohravardî. L'Archange empourpré.* Translation. Paris: Fayard, 1976.

————. *Shihâboddîn Yahyâ Sohravardî, Le livre de la sagesse orientale, avec les Commentaires de Qotboddîn Shîrâzî et Mollâ Sadrâ Shîrâzî.* Translation. Lagrasse: Verdier, 1986.

————. *Spiritual Body and Celestial Earth: From Mazdean Iran to Shi'ite.* Princeton: Princeton University Press, 1977.

————. *Swedenborg and Esoteric Islam.* West Chester, PA: Swedenborg Foundation, 1995.

————. *Temps cyclique et gnose ismaélienne.* Paris: Berg International, 1982.

————. *Temple et contemplat—Essais sur l'Islam iranien.* Paris: Flammarion, 1981.

————. *The Concept of Comparative Philosophy.* Ipswich: Golgonooza Press, 1981.

————. *The Man of Light in Iranian Sufism.* New York: Shambala, 1978.

————. *The Voyage and the Messenger: Iran and Philosophy.* Berkeley, CA: North Atlantic, 1998.

————. *Trilogie ismaélienne: Abû Ya'qûb Sejestânî: Le livre des sources, Sayyid-nâ al-Hosayn ibn 'Alî: Cosmogonie et eschatologie, Symboles choisis de la Roseraie du Mystère de Mahmoud Shabestarî.* Translation. Tehran-Paris: Adrien-Maisonneuve, 1961.

Guénon, René. *Aperçus sur l'ésotérisme chrétien.* Paris: Éditions Traditionnelles, 1988.

————. *Aperçus sur l'ésotérisme islamique et le taoïsme.* Paris: Gallimard, 1973.

————. *Aperçus sur l'Initiation.* Paris: Éditions Traditionnelles,1946.

————. *Autorité spirituelle et pouvoir temporel.* Paris: Éditions Traditionnelles, 1952.

————. *Comptes rendus,* Paris: Éditions Traditionnelles, 1986.

————. *Études sur la Franc-maçonnerie et le Compagnonnage,* 2 vols. Paris: Éditions Traditionnelles, 1965.

————. *Études sur l'Hindouisme,* Paris: Editions Traditionnelles, 1966.

————. *Formes traditionnelles et cycles cosmiques,* Paris: Gallimard, 1970.

————. *Fundamental Symbols.* Bartlow: Quinta Essentia, 1995.

————. *Initiation and Spiritual Realization.* Hillsdale, NY: Sophia Perennis, 2004.

————. *Initiation et Réalisation spirituelle,* Paris: Éditions Traditionnelles, 1952.

————. *Introduction générale à l'étude des doctrines hindoues.* Paris: Editions Traditionnelles, 1921.

————. *La Crise du monde moderne.* Paris: Gallimard, 1927.

————. *La Grande Triade.* Paris: Gallimard, 1946.

——. *La Métaphysique orientale*. Paris: Éditions Traditionnelles, 1939.

——. *Le Règne de la Quantité et les Signes des Temps*. Paris: Gallimard, 1945.

——. *Le Roi du Monde*. Paris: Gallimard, Paris, 1927.

——. *L'Erreur spirite*. Paris: Éditions Traditionnelles, 1923.

——. *Les Etats multiples de l'Être*. Paris: Editions Traditionnelles, 1932.

——. *L' Ésotérisme de Dante*. Paris: Éditions Traditionnelles, 1925.

——. *Les Principes du Calcul infinitésimal*. Paris: Gallimard, 1946.

——. *Le Symbolisme de la Croix*. Paris: Editions Traditionnelles, 1931.

——. *Le Théosophisme, histoire d'une pseudo-religion*. Paris: Éditions Traditionnelles, 1921.

——. *L'Homme et son devenir selon le Vêdânta*. Paris: Éditions Traditionnelles, 1925.

——. *Man and His Becoming According to the Vedānta*. Hillsdale, NY: Sophia Perennis, 2001.

——. *Mélanges*. Paris: Gallimard, 1990.

——. *Miscellanea*. Hillsdale, NY: Sophia Perennis, 2004.

——. *Orient et Occident*. Paris: Editions Traditionnelles, 1924.

——. *Saint Bernard*. Paris: Éditions Traditionnelles, 1929.

——. *Studies in Freemasonry and the Compagnonnage*. Hillsdale, NY: Sophia Perennis, 2004.

——. *Studies in Hinduism*. New Delhi: Munshiram Manoharlal, 2002.

——. *Symboles Fondamentaux de la Science sacrée*. Paris: Gallimard, 1962.

——. *The Crisis of the Modern World*. London: Luzac & Co., 1975.

——. *The Esoterism of Dante*. Hillsdale, NY: Sophia Perennis, 2004.

——. *The Metaphysical Principles of the Infinitesimal Calculus*. Hillsdale, NY : Sophia Perennis, 2001.

——. *The Multiple States of the Being*. Hillsdale, NY: Sophia Perennis, 2004.

——. *Perspectives on Initiation*. Hillsdale, NY: Sophia Perennis, 2001.

——. *The Reign of Quantity and the Signs of the Times*. Hillsdale, NY: Sophia Perennis, 2004.

——. *The Symbolism of the Cross*. Hillsdale, NY : Sophia Perennis, 1996.

Massignon, Louis. *Akbar Al-Hallaj*. Paris: Librairie Philosophique J.Vrin, 1957.

——. *Essays on the Origins of the Technical Language of Islamic Mysticism*. Translated by Benjamin Clark. Notre Dame, IN: University of Notre Dame Press, 1994.

——. *Hallaj: Mystic and Martyr*. Translated, edited, and abridged by H. Mason. Princeton, NJ: Princeton University Press, 1994.

——. *La guerre sainte suprême de l'islam arabe*. Paris : Fata Morgana, 1998.

——. *La Passion de Hallaj: Martyr Mystique de L'Islam*. Paris : Gallimard, 1975.

——. *Le Dîwân D'Al- Hallâj*. Paris: Librairie Orientaliste Paul Geuthner, 1955.

——. *Les allusions instigatrices—Les méthodes de réalisation artistique des peuples de l'Islam—Introspection et rétrospection—Sur l'origine de la miniature persane*. Paris : Fata Morgana, 2000.

——. *Les Sept Dormants d'Ephèse en Islam et en Chrétienté*. Paris: Librairie Orientaliste Paul Geuthner, 1955.

——. *Les trois prières d'Abraham*. Paris: Le Cerf, 1997.

——. *Opéra Minora*. 4 vols. Collected texts presented by Y. Moubaraq. Beirut: Dar Al-Maaref, 1963.

——. *Parole donnée*. Paris: Le Seuil, 1983.

——. *Sur L'Islam*. Paris: L'Herne, 1995.

————. *The Passion of al-Hallaj: Mystic and Martyr.* Translated by H. Mason. Princeton, NJ: Princeton University Press, 1983.

————. *Testimonies and Reflections: Essays of Louis Massignon.* Selected and Introduced by H. Mason. Notre Dame, IN: University of Notre Dame Press, 1989.

Schuon, Frithjof. *Adastra and Stella Maris. Poems.* Bloomington, IN: World Wisdom, 2003.

————. *Approches du phénonème religieux.* Paris: Courrier du livre, 1984.

————. *Art from the Sacred to the Profane*, edited by Catherine Schuon. Bloomington, IN: World Wisdom, 2007.

————. *Avoir un Centre.* Paris: Maisonneuve & Larose, 1988.

————. *Castes et races.* Lyon: Derain, 1957.

————. *Castes and Races.* London: Perennial Books, 1959.

————. *Christianisme/Islam: Visions d'œcumenisme ésoterique.* Milano: Archè, 1981.

————. *Christianity/Islam: Essays on Esoteric Ecumenism.* Bloomington, IN: World Wisdom Books, 1985.

————. *Comprendre l'Islam.* Paris: Gallimard, 1961.

————. *De l'Unité transcendante des religions.* Paris: Gallimard, 1948.

————. *De quelques aspects de l'Islam.* Paris: Chacornac, 1935.

————. *Dimensions of Islam.* Lahore: Suhail, 1985.

————. *Du Divin à l'humain.* Paris: Courrier du Livre, 1981.

————. *Echoes of Perennial Wisdom.* Bloomington: World Wisdom Books, 1992.

————. *Esoterism as Principle and as Way.* London: Perennial Books, 1981.

————. *Forme et substance dans les religions.* Paris: Dervy-Livres, 1975.

————. *From the Divine to the Human.* Bloomington, IN: World Wisdom Books, 1982.

————. *Gnosis: Divine Wisdom.* London: John Murray, 1959.

————. *Images de l'esprit: Shinto, Buddhisme, Yoga.* Paris: Flammarion, 1961.

————. *Images of Primordial and Mystic Beauty: Paintings by Frithjof Schuon.* Bloomington, IN: Abodes, 1992.

————. *In the Face of the Absolute.* Bloomington, IN: World Wisdom Books, 1989.

————. *In the Tracks of Buddhism.* London: Allen & Unwin, 1968.

————. *Islam and the Perennial Philosophy.* London: World of Islam Festival Publishing Company, 1976.

————. *Language of the Self.* Madras: Ganesh, 1959.

————. *La Transfiguration de l'Homme.* Paris-Lausanne: L'Âge d'Homme, 1995.

————. *Le Jeu des masques.* Paris-Lausanne: L'Âge d'Homme, 1992.

————. *L'Esotérisme comme principe et comme voie.* Paris: Dervy-Livres, 1978.

————. *Le Soufisme: Voile et quintessence.* Paris: Dervy-Livres, 1980.

————. *Les Perles du pèlerin.* Paris: Le Seuil, 1990.

————. *Les stations de la sagesse.* Paris: Buchet, 1958.

————. *Light on the Ancient Worlds.* London: Perennial Books, 1965.

————. *L'oeil du coeur.* Paris: Gallimard, 1950.

————. *Logic and Transcendene.* New York: Harper & Row, 1975.

————. *Logique et transcendance.* Paris: Editions Traditionelles, 1970.

————. *Perspectives spirituels et faits humains.* Paris: Cahiers du Sud, 1953.

————. *Racines de la condition humaine.* Paris: La Table ronde, 1990.

————. *Regards sur les mondes anciens.* Paris: Editions Traditionelles, 1965.

————. *Résumé de métaphysique intégrale.* Paris: Courrier du livre, 1985.

————. *Road to the Heart* [poems]. Bloomington, IN: World Wisdom Books, 1995.

————. *Roots of the Human Condition*. Bloomington, IN: World Wisdom Books, 1991.

————. *Sentiers de gnose*. Paris: La Colombe, 1957.

————. *Songs for a Spiritual Traveler. Selected Poems*. Bloomington, IN: World Wisdom, 2002.

————. *Spiritual Perspectives and Human Facts*. London: Faber, 1954.

————. *Stations of Wisdom*. London: John Murray, 1961.

————. *Sufism: Veil and Quintessence*. Bloomington, IN: World Wisdom, 2007.

————. *Sur les traces de la Religion pérenne*. Paris: Courrier du livre, 1982 .

————. *Survey of Metaphysics and Esoterism*. Bloomington, IN: World Wisdom Books, 1986.

————. *The Eye of the Heart: Metaphysics, Cosmology, Spiritual Life*. Bloomington, IN: World Wisdom, 1997.

————. *The Feathered Sun: Plains Indians in Art and Philosophy*. Bloomington: World Wisdom Books, 1990.

————. *The Play of Masks*. Bloomington, IN: World Wisdom Books, 1992.

————. *The Transcendent Unity of Religions*. London: Faber, 1953.

————. *The Transfiguration of Man*. Bloomington, IN: World Wisdom Books, 1995.

————. *To Have a Center,* Bloomington, IN: World Wisdom Books, 1990.

————. *Treasures of Buddhism*. Bloomington: World Wisdom Books, 1993

————. *Understanding Islam*. London: Allen & Unwin, 1963.

————. *World Wheel: Poems*. 4 vols. Bloomington, IN: World Wisdom, 2007.

INDEX